The Timeless Art
of
Italian Cuisine

Centuries Of Scrumptious Dining

The Essence of Italian Food in more than
170 Traditional Recipes for Today's Cook

Anna Maria Volpi

The Timeless Art of Italian Cuisine by Anna Maria Volpi

Publisher Palatino Inc, - PO Box 27740 - Las Vegas, NV 89126

We made every effort at the time of publication to verify the accuracy of the information and the sources, however readers are responsible for their use of this book. All recommendations are made without any guarantees on the part of the author and the publisher. The author and the publisher disclaim all liabilities in connection with the use of this information.

FIRST EDITION 2003
Publisher Anna Maria Volpi
Design and illustrations by Pietro Mascioni
Editing Netty Kahan
Cover design Keita Yamamura
Cover pictures Marina Inoue

Printed in the USA by Central Plains Book Manufacturing - Winfield, KS

ISBN 0-9729229-0-3

Library of Congress Control Number 2003103177

Publisher's Cataloging-in-Publication Data
(provided by The Donohue Group, Inc.)

Volpi, Anna Maria.
    The timeless art of Italian Cuisine : centuries of
    Scrumptious dining / Anna Maria Volpi ; design and illustrations by
Pietro Mascioni.

    p. : ill. ; cm.

    Includes bibliographical references and index.

    ISBN: 0-9729229-0-3

1. Cookery, Italian. 2. Cookery, Italian--History. 3. Cookery, Italian--Northern style. 4. Cookery, Italian--Southern style. I. Volpi, Anna Maria. II. Title.

TX723 . V65 2003
641.5945-dc21   2003103177

You don't have to cook fancy or complicated masterpieces – just good food from fresh ingredients.

Julia Child

Preface

Someone said that all Italians have an "obsession with food." Begin a conversation with Italians and in a few minutes they will be talking about the wonders of the food of their hometowns. Well, although perhaps not an obsession, food certainly is a national passion—part of a zeal for living well, enjoying life.

I don't remember when it was that I became ardent about food, or at what point in my life I caught my "cooking fever." I always was fascinated by food: mesmerized by the mixes, the manipulation, the infinite tastes, fragrances, and colors; and by the transformation of flour into the innumerable forms and textures once combined with water and shaped by fire.

When I was a child, my mother, sisters, and I went for our summer vacation to a country home in a small town named Subiaco, just north of Rome. A medieval abbey built upon the rocks deep in the valley, a castle, and an old bridge evoked a sense of history and time. The austerity and nobility of the environment contrasted sharply with the simplicity of the lives of our neighbors, the peasants. Their lives appeared to be flowing in slow motion, yet in harmony with nature. They repeated the same gestures year after year, busy in their day-by-day occupations of survival—growing their crops, raising their livestock, and cooking their food. I will never forget the aromas of those times: the perfume from the lime-tree blossoming with white flowers in front of our house; the smoke exuding from the fireplaces into the narrow streets; the scent of the herbs and the tomatoes; and all the foods—the sauces, lamb, and freshly baked breads and cakes.

Baking bread was a big deal. Every other week the wood-burning oven was fired. The hinged top of a large wooden chest was opened and the flour was scooped onto the sieve on top. I stood on tiptoe looking at the flour being sifted to separate the bran. The yeast (nothing other than a piece of the fermented dough from the previous week) was pulled out of a small sack where it was kept and was added to the flour together with water. Kneading by hand was hard work. Yet, soon, a dozen big loaves were set to rise covered with a cloth on a long wooden board in a warm side of the kitchen, close to the fireplace. Then, the trip to the oven: The women walked slowly, carrying the long boards on their heads. Taking advantage of the event, my family prepared more food to be baked—lasagna, tomatoes stuffed with rice, angel food cakes, or some doughnuts. For the peasants it was a life of strife. Those times are now gone, and all those flavors and scents have disappeared forever with them.

Back at home in Rome, when anybody was in the kitchen, I was there too, looking, asking questions, and listening to the never-ending debates between my parents: My Roman father remained unyielding in his persuasion that Rome was the gastronomic *caput mundi* (the capital of the world), and my Sicilian mother tried to convince him that cooking without saffron and fresh fennel was uncivilized. But my greatest mentor was our neighbor Flora. She must have seen in me the granddaughter she never had, because she treated me with unending patience. A clever cook, she knew not only the recipes, but also the tricks to make them succeed.

One wintertime evening visit, when I walked in the door that she normally left ajar so that I didn't even have to knock, she shouted from the kitchen, "Hurry up. Close the door." I saw something on the table, covered with a blanket. She furtively lifted an edge, finally breaking the suspense, and showed me . . . doughnuts! She was protecting them from the cold temperature while waiting for them to rise. In the years that followed, I must have fried her doughnuts a thousand times and I never got tired of seeing peoples' expressions of pleasure and satisfaction while they ate them.

I learned from my father to give careful attention to the basic ingredients, a meticulous precision for the perfect dish of pasta or roast, and, in general, a love for simplicity. My work experiences and travels added to my capabilities with food. As I became more skilled, I also became more ambitious. I wanted to experiment with increasingly sophisticated preparations. I wanted to demonstrate that "I can make it." Later, I realized that the most difficult dishes are not those with a long list of expensive components, but those where very few flavors participate. The greatness of Italian gastronomy is not in strange, unusual combinations: Foreigners often are surprised by the minimalism of Italian cooking, which is based mainly on fresh and tasty ingredients.

I don't even consider myself a "chef," a term that should be reserved for the professionals working in the kitchens of restaurants. Like most of my readers and students, I am basically someone with a love for sharing food, which is an ancient way to communicate: Sitting together at the table unifies a family and draws friends together. Cooking is not merely a matter of processing food; rather it is like a language with thousands of dialects, each dish a word that needs its proper spelling. Like a language, cooking is a product of the territory, and that is why every Italian considers cooking a form of expression, fully integrated in their culture. As is true with language, cooking has deep roots in history. A person's knowledge of how the meals they eat have evolved imbues those dishes with new meaning.

In an age when fast food competes to take away the joy from the kitchen, we think it is important to look back and reflect on the significance of our great cooking traditions. The attentive cook needs to approach traditional cooking with respect for those who, before us, for centuries lit the fire, prepared these dishes, and contributed to their evolution. By understanding these recipes, we can further adapt the old ways to fit our lifestyle.

Similar to a travelogue through time and places, this book follows the Italian peninsula. Every chapter presents the history, the recipes and information about the food from the region.

This book is dedicated to all people who enjoy cooking and are especially fond of Italian cuisine.

I hope you will enjoy this tour together,

Anna Maria

This book was made possible by the help of Pietro Mascioni, my husband, who is co-author and responsible for most of the historic and technical research; Magi who patiently and repeatedly revised all our recipes for accuracy; Keita who designed a great professional-looking cover; Marina who shoots better-than-reality pictures; Netty, who transformed into correct English our "Itanglish"; and Chie, Steve, Tim, Simone, Barbara, Frank, Federica, George, Evelyn, and all our friends and family who helped and encouraged us.

A special thanks to all my students: Over the years I have so much enjoyed cooking together.

Contents

How to Use this Book

- Since Italian meals are rarely made up of only a single dish, the portions may be considered smaller than generally accepted elsewhere. We considered the following quantities per serving to be the general rule:

Pasta	3½ oz	(100 gr)
Rice	3 oz scant	(75 gr)
Meat	4 oz	(120 gr)
Fish	5 oz	(150 gr)

We leave it to the reader to change the quantities of the ingredients if deemed necessary.

- Unless noted otherwise, all the recipes in the book **serve four**, except desserts.

- Not all ingredients available in Italy are easily found outside the region of origin. However, most of the ingredients are readily available at grocery stores or in many Italian specialty shops. For those items difficult to find, we have tried to provide an alternative without compromising the recipe.

- Many of the original recipes call for lard. We have substituted extra-virgin olive oil or butter.

- Oil or butter used to grease pans and flour for dusting are not listed within the ingredients.

- Butter is indicated either in tablespoons or by weight. Refer to page 154 for conversions.

- In Italian cooking, it is very important to start sautéing the garlic and onion while the olive oil is cold. If the oil is too hot, the garlic and onion could burn and give the dish an unpleasant tang. By placing the garlic and/or onion in the pan when the oil is still cold, you can more easily control the amount of cooking, and they will release their flavor a little at a time. You will be able to add other ingredients to the garlic before it begins coloring, and the onion can caramelize nicely on slow heat if indicated for the recipe.

- Following are the descriptions of the most common ingredients used throughout the book:

Bacon is unsmoked. Italian *Pancetta* or *Guanciale,* (pork fat made from the cheeks of pork,) are substituted for unsmoked bacon.

Broth is homemade meat broth as described on page 67, unless noted otherwise. If homemade broth is not available, substitute with canned broth or bouillon cube(s) dissolved in warm water, as indicated in the recipe.

Butter is unsalted butter.

Capers are in salt and not in vinegar or brine.

Cream is heavy whipping cream.

Dry pasta is imported Italian pasta of the best quality, made out of durum semolina. Refer to page 109 for instructions on how to cook pasta perfectly *al dente.*

Eggs are large eggs. The yolks of common eggs found in stores, are generally pale in color. We suggest buying eggs that are specifically indicated as having "golden" yolks.

Flour is all-purpose unbleached.

Frying oil is olive oil other than extra-virgin, or mild vegetable oil such as canola.

Herbs are fresh, unless dried are specifically called for in the recipe.

Italian Sausage is pork sausage of the unflavored type, sold in the United States as "German Bratwurst." Italian sausages sold in stores are generally flavored with herbs, such as fennel or oregano, that are intrusive in most recipes.

Milk is whole milk.

Mozzarella is fresh, soft cheese soaked in its whey, unless indicated otherwise.

Olive oil is Italian extra-virgin olive oil. Extra-virgin olive oil from Liguria or Tuscany is recommended for raw food. Commercial extra-virgin olive oil can be used for general cooking.

Parmigiano cheese is *Parmigiano Reggiano,* preferably aged twenty-four months. Cheese needs to be freshly grated just before serving. As an alternative, aged *Grana Padano* cheese can be used.

Pepper is black pepper, preferably freshly grated from the mill.

Rice is Italian Rice as described on page 38.

Ricotta is fresh sheep- or cow-milk cheese. It is used, drained of its liquid, in many preparations. Place the cheese in a colander for several minutes until all liquid is expelled.

Salt is common table salt. If you use kosher salt, adjust the quantity to compensate for its different intensity of flavor.

Sugar is granulated, unless powdered sugar is specified.

Tomatoes for sauces and other cooked preparations are very ripe fresh peeled tomatoes (see page 120 for indications on how to peel tomatoes). When tomatoes are not in season and the recipe doesn't specifically require fresh tomatoes, substitute with canned peeled whole tomatoes.

What Is Italian Cooking?

Introduction

Many non-Italians identify Italian cooking with a few of its most popular dishes, like pizza and spaghetti. People often express the opinion that Italian cooking is all pretty much alike. However, those who travel through Italy notice differences in eating habits between cities, even those only a few miles apart. Not only does each region have its own style, but each community and each valley has a different way of cooking as well.

1

Every town has a distinctive way of making sausage, special kinds of cheese and wine, and a local type of bread. If you ask people, even in the same area, how to make pasta sauce, they will all have different answers. Variations in the omnipresent pasta are another example of this multiplicity: soft egg noodles in the north, hard-boiled spaghetti in the south, with every conceivable variation in size and shape. Perhaps no other country in the world has a cooking style so finely fragmented into different divisions. So why is Risotto typical of Milan, why did Tortellini originate in Bologna, and why is Pizza so popular in Naples?

This is so for the same reason that Italy has only one unifying Italian language, yet hundreds of different spoken dialects. Italy is a country of great variety, and cooking is just another aspect of the diversity of Italian culture.

This diversity stems largely from peasant heritage and geographical differences. Italy is a peninsula separated from the rest of the continent by the highest chain of mountains in Europe. In addition, a long spine of mountains runs north to south down through this narrow country. These geographic features create a myriad of environments with noticeable variations: fertile valleys, mountains covered with forests, cool foothills, naked rocks, Mediterranean coastlines, and arid plains. A great variety of different climates have also created innumerable unique geographical and historical areas.

Family of peasants going to the market. Engraving by B. Pinelli, circa 1831. "The rich eat what they like, the poor what they can afford." Until a few decades ago peasants in the Italian countryside have always lived through periods of hunger alternating with periods of moderately sufficient food. Peasants' cooking was based on grains and seasonal local vegetable. Bread and pasta were made at home every day; meat and diary came from the few cows, sheep, and chickens.

But geographical fragmentation alone will not explain how the same country produced all of these: the rich, fat, baroque food of Bologna, based on butter, parmigiano, and meat; the light, tasty, spicy cooking of Naples, mainly based on olive oil, mozzarella, and seafood; the cuisine of Rome, rich in produce from the surrounding countryside; and the food of Sicily, full of North African influences.

The explanation is hidden in the past; the multitudes of food styles of Italy mainly result from its history. Divided for a long time into many duchies, princedoms, kingdoms, and states—often hostile to one another—political unification in Italy did not occur until 1861. Many populations in the past three thousand years have occupied Italian territory, and most of them contributed their own traditions. And the original people, the Etruscans and Greeks, left influences still felt today.

Most Italian cookbooks describe the food of the different regions from north to south, following a purely geographical course. We will follow instead the historical path through the events that shaped Italy and its cooking ways. We think that to understand what we eat, we must explore the historical background in which the different ways of cooking developed. Each chapter of this book briefly talks about an aspect of Italy's history, as a way to introduce the recipes. All the recipes throughout the book are authentic and current. Some of them are centuries old, while others are contemporary and modern: evidence of the continuous evolution of Italian cooking.

In **Chapter 1, "All Roads Lead to Rome,"** we will talk about the Romans. They politically controlled the territory about two thousand years ago, integrated Greek civilization, and created an empire that laid the foundations of Western civilization. They imported all kinds of foods from all over the known world. Roman ships carried essential food, such as wheat and wine, as well as a variety of spices from as far away as China, to satisfy the Romans' appetite for exotic ingredients. Roman cooking habits fascinated and influenced generations in the centuries that followed. The fall of the Roman Empire was caused by unstoppable waves of invading people— barbarians who came from as far away as Tibet. They pillaged and

Interior of a Roman Kitchen. Engraving by B. Pinelli, circa 1830. A young woman is removing pasta with a strainer from a cauldron on an open fire, while an older woman is grating cheese. The most common kitchen utensils: terracotta pottery in a niche, a wooden board hanging from the wall, a grille on the fireplace ledge. In the cities, housewives would cook seasonal produces they could afford: flour, vegetables, and meat, imported from the surrounding countryside.

destroyed, but they also took with them new cooking customs. It took centuries before some order was restored and medieval peoples could begin to rebuild something that could be called a cuisine.

In **Chapter 2, "A Land of City States,"** we will talk about northern Italy where, during medieval times, the absence of a powerful central authority allowed the creation of many fiercely independent cities. These *Comuni,* from the Alps to the border of the Kingdom of Naples, progressed faster than the other European towns of that time in wealth, and in artistic and intellectual achievements. The cities of northern Italy developed mostly through the trading of valuable merchandise, such as spices and fabric, with northern Europe and the East. A rich cuisine developed offering great diversity from one town to another. After the decline of the city states, the territory of northern Italy was partially occupied from time to time by France or Austria, which left additional culinary influences in the Northeast.

The richness of the cities of northern Italy is reflected in particular in the creation of a "culture" of fresh pasta. While dry macaroni was an item of mass production, fresh pasta associated with eggs, cheese, sugar, cream, and other expensive items was a luxury item. In **Chapter 3, "The Universal Food,"** we will show how to make fresh pasta and many classic recipes. Even though fresh pasta became diffused throughout the peninsula and outside the borders of Italy, it is in northern Italy that we find the most spectacular recipes. It is no coincidence that many consider Bologna the gastronomic capital of Italy.

In **Chapter 4, "Under the Sign of the Lily,"** we will talk about Tuscany, which represents a phenomenon by itself in Italian history. Starting from the thirteenth century, the city of Florence in particular became rich during the evolution of the banking system. The De Medicis, a family of merchants and bankers, would become patrons of the arts and would accelerate the movement that became known as Renaissance. It was the birth of a new way of seeing human beings as controllers of their own destinies. New social rules were created here and were exported all over Europe, which at that time was on the verge of great transformations due to the discoveries of the age of exploration. The Renaissance initiated a great revolution in the arts, which was also reflected in spectacular and

Cooking meat. Engraving from "Banquets Composition of Food and General Apparatus . . . ." by Cristoforo Messibugo, in Ferrara in 1549. Messibugo wrote a book describing the banquets he had prepared for the Estense court in Ferrara and the most sophisticated recipes he arranged. He showed a high consideration for his profession when he wrote: "I am not going to waste my time to describe some soups of vegetables or beans, or to teach how to fry a fish . . . . that any simple woman can do. But I will talk of the most notable food preparations. . . ."

extravagant new ways of cooking.

While the north would see the creation of many small independent political entities, the south of Italy remained mostly unified for a long time. Separated from the great trading routes with northern Europe, the south suffered greater poverty and isolation. The people of southern Italy made the best of what they had. But it is here, in southern Italy, that spectacular dishes like spaghetti and pizza, originated. In **Chapter 5, "Pizza and Beyond,"** we will talk about

these dishes. Born as the poor people's way of cooking, these dishes were exported by groups of Italian emigrants and disseminated outside their regions of origin, making them extremely popular everywhere.

Dry pasta is the greatest contribution from southern Italy and in **Chapter 6, "Macaroni Addiction,"** we will talk about it. Dry macaroni is suitable for storing, trading, and transporting. The invention of the bronze press industrialized the manufacturing of pasta, making macaroni affordable. Present in Sicily since Arab occupation, macaroni became extremely popular in Naples in the 1700s. It is from there that dry pasta started its journey to conquer the world.

Sicily is the subject of **Chapter 7, "The Island of the Sun."** Sicilian history is fascinating for all the different people that occupied the island during different times. The greatest influence was left by the Muslim occupation that lasted for two centuries. Muslims contributed greatly to Western cuisine with a variety of foods: rice, spinach, alcohol, oranges, lemons, apricots, sugar and more. And in Sicily their influence is still greatly felt today.

The Essence of Italian Cooking

Until a few decades ago, large differences were apparent between cooking in the countryside and in the cities. Peasants had to struggle with periods of hunger alternating with times of modest sufficiency. They had to survive with what they themselves produced: grains, vegetables from their orchards, milk and cheese from a few cows, and meat from chicken and sheep. Pasta and bread were made at home every day.

In the cities, by contrast, it was always possible to get—for a price—food imported from the surrounding countryside. Housewives cooked seasonal produce they could afford, or bought food

prepared in the many shops around town.

In spite of the underprivileged's hardship of having to make the best out of simpler foodstuff, their cooking has turned into some of the most popular Italian recipes. Pizza and pasta are two of the most familiar examples.

At the same time, and on a different level, the cooking of the more affluent and the rich used extraordinary techniques and resources. This is the type of cuisine that is discussed in the cookbooks of the past, because the cooking of the poor was considered inferior and not worth mentioning. Banquets, exotic ingredients, and complex presentations were the work of professional cooks of the time.

Through the centuries, the recipes of the countryside eventually blended with those of the cities, and the simpler preparations of the poor combined with the luxurious cooking of the upper classes. This interaction between different environments and social levels was one of the factors shaping Italian cuisine as we know it today.

Local traditions result from long complex historical developments and strongly influence local habits. Distinctive cultural and social differences remain present throughout Italy, although today mass marketing tends to cause a leveling of long-established values. However, traditional food still is at the core of the cultural identity of each region, and Italians react with attachment to their own identity when they are confronted with the tendency toward flattening their culture.

In a country so diverse, it is impossible to define an "Italian" cooking style, but we can correlate consistency in spite of variety in the Italians' approach toward food.

All Italians eat with gusto. Everywhere their pantries are filled with the same basic products: cheese, sausage, ham, bread, and wine. Vegetables are of high quality and Italians value full natural flavor — everybody is willing to walk the extra distance to buy better and fresher products. The spices added to the dishes mean to enhance the taste of fish or meat. Sauces are the essence and the soul of Italian dishes; usually they are inseparable from the process of dish making.

The Italian menu throughout Italy is usually composed of more than one course: a first course (*primo piatto*) of starchy food like pasta or risotto; a second course (*secondo*) of meat or fish; and a side dish of vegetables (*contorno*). Bread is always present at the table, and fresh fruit is the most common dessert. Wine is generally served at dinner. Espresso coffee is served at the end of the meal. Antipasto (appetizer), sweets, and liquor are only present for more formal occasions.

Italian cooking has evolved for centuries and continues to evolve today; it is informal, it lacks rigid rules, and is adaptive and versatile. Instead of being invented by professional chefs, millions of everyday cooks improvise Italian cuisine daily in their kitchens ❖

Mapping Italian Food

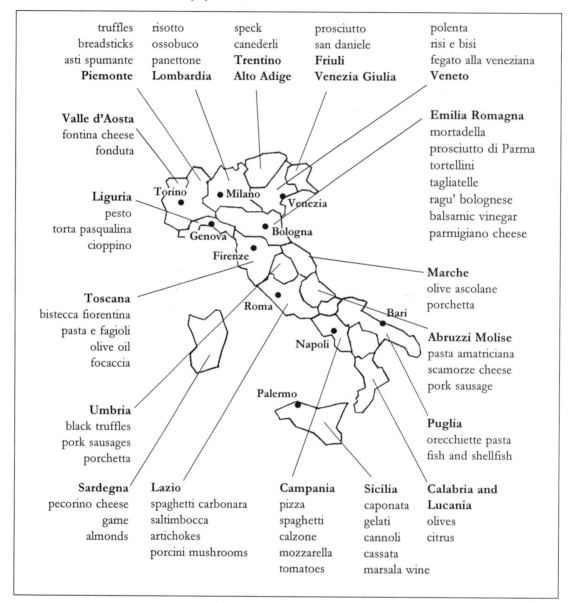

truffles
breadsticks
asti spumante
Piemonte

risotto
ossobuco
panettone
Lombardia

speck
canederli
**Trentino
Alto Adige**

prosciutto
san daniele
**Friuli
Venezia Giulia**

polenta
risi e bisi
fegato alla veneziana
Veneto

Valle d'Aosta
fontina cheese
fonduta

Emilia Romagna
mortadella
prosciutto di Parma
tortellini
tagliatelle
ragu' bolognese
balsamic vinegar
parmigiano cheese

Liguria
pesto
torta pasqualina
cioppino

Torino   Milano   Venezia   Bologna   Genova   Firenze

Marche
olive ascolane
porchetta

Toscana
bistecca fiorentina
pasta e fagioli
olive oil
focaccia

Roma   Bari   Napoli

Abruzzi Molise
pasta amatriciana
scamorze cheese
pork sausage

Umbria
black truffles
pork sausages
porchetta

Palermo

Puglia
orecchiette pasta
fish and shellfish

Sardegna
pecorino cheese
game
almonds

Lazio
spaghetti carbonara
saltimbocca
artichokes
porcini mushrooms

Campania
pizza
spaghetti
calzone
mozzarella
tomatoes

Sicilia
caponata
gelati
cannoli
cassata
marsala wine

**Calabria and
Lucania**
olives
citrus

Piemonte. Closest to France and Switzerland, Torino was the Italian capital before the country's unification. This region is a large producer of rice and has high culinary standards. Specialties: *Grissini* (breadsticks), *Bagna Cauda* (garlic and anchovy dip), *Agnolotti* (the Piemontese version of ravioli), red wine *Risotto*, white truffles, *Gianduiotti* (chocolate and hazelnut cookies), some of the best Italian wines *(Barbera, Barolo, Dolcetto, Barbaresco)*, and Vermouth Martini.

Valle d'Aosta. This corner of Italy exhibits the magnificent mountain scenery of the Alps. A small, steep, bilingual region renowned for its medieval castles, it is full of French influence. Specialties: *Fonduta* (similar to the French fondue but made with *Fontina* cheese), *Blanc Manger* (white cream pudding), and *Tegole d'Aosta* (almond cookies with chocolate glaze).

Lombardia. Industrial in its plains, a tourist attraction with its mountains and astounding lakes, Lombardia is the business heart of Italy. It is home to Leonardo da Vinci's *Last Supper*. Specialties: *Risotto Milanese* with saffron, *Cotoletta Milanese* (fried cutlet similar to the Wiener schnitzel), *Ossobuco* (stewed veal shanks), *Panettone* (Christmas cake), *Bresaola della Valtellina* (cured dry beef), and some of the best Italian cheeses *(Mascarpone, Bel Paese, Gorgonzola,* and *Stracchino).*

Veneto. It is impossible to compress into a few words the richness of this region, with cities like the incomparable Venezia, Vicenza (city of Palladio the architect), Verona (city of Romeo and Juliet), Padova (city of St. Antony), and the lake Garda. Specialties: *Risi e Bisi* (rice and peas soup), *Bigoli* (handmade spaghetti), *Peara'* (sauce based on breadcrumbs and horseradish), *Fegato alla Veneziana* (liver with onions), *Baccala' alla Vicentina* (salt cod with milky sauce), *Polenta* (cornmeal porridge), *Risotto all'onda* (wavy risotto), and magnificent wines (including *Valpolicella, Recioto, Amarone, Soave,* and *Pinot),* and *Grappa* liquor.

Trentino-Alto Adige. Called *Sud-Tyrol* by its German-speaking inhabitants, this is the region of the Dolomiti, breathtaking jagged mountains bathed in an unreal pinkish mauve color. The gastronomic traditions are similar to neighboring Austria. Specialties:

Canederli (dumplings with sausage, breadcrumbs, and eggs), *Strudel* (apple-filled cake), and *Speck* (smoked dry ham).

Friuli-Venezia Giulia. This multiethnic region — with Slavic, Italian, and German influences, — descends from the Alps to the Adriatic Sea and is home to the ancient Roman town of Aquileia. Specialties: *Gulyas* (goulash in the style from Trieste), *Presnitz* (puff pastries with almonds), *Brodetto di Pesce* (fish soup), *Prosciutto San Daniele, Gubana* (cake filled with raisins and almonds), and wines like *Pinot Grigio, Verduzzo,* and *Riesling.*

Liguria. This 200-mile arc-shaped region, called La Riviera, is a narrow strip of coast that drops down from the Alpine side. It is famous for wonderful coastal towns. Genova, its capital city, was home to Christofer Columbus. Specialties: *Pesto Genovese* (famous sauce blend of basil and olive oil), *Torta Pasqualina* (Easter cheese and spinach pie), *Cappon Magro* (Genovese fish salad), *Burrida* or *Cioppino* (a fish soup similar to the French Bouillabaisse), *Minestrone Genovese* (vegetable soup), *Cima di vitello* (stuffed veal), and *Ravioli* stuffed with spinach and cheese.

Emilia-Romagna. Bologna la Grassa (Bologna the Fat One) is this region's capital and also can be considered the gastronomic capital of Italy. The wonderful dishes that originated in this region are all renowned worldwide. Specialties: *Tortellini* (pasta rings filled with meat), *Tagliatelle col Ragu'* (hand made fettuccine with thick meat-tomato sauce), *Lasagne* (layered pasta with white sauce and tomato), *Mortadella* (enormous pork sausage), *Zampone* (pork-leg sausage), *Prosciutto di Parma* (pork ham), *Parmigiano Reggiano* cheese, *Balsamico di Modena* (balsamic vinegar), and wines such as *Lambrusco* and *Trebbiano.*

Toscana. It is impossible not to use superlatives for the region of Dante, Leonardo da Vinci, Michelangelo, Galileo, Machiavelli, Boccaccio, Cimabue, Giotto, Botticelli, Della Robbia, Donatello, Cellini, Brunelleschi, and for cities like Firenze, Pisa, and Siena. Specialties: *Crostini di Fegatini* (chicken liver pate'), *Bistecca Fiorentina* (Florentine steak), *Pasta e Fagioli* (beans soup), *Fagioli all'uccelletto* (stewed beans), *Tortino di Carciofi* (artichokes egg omelette), *Caciucco Livornese* (fish soup Livorno style), *Ribollita* (bread-and-vegetables soup), *Arista di Maiale* (roast pork), *Zuccotto* (ice-cream cake), *Cantucci* (almond cookies), *Panforte di Siena* (honey-and-nuts cake), and wines *(Chianti, Montepulciano, Brunello, Pitigliano, Vin Santo).*

Umbria. Called 'the green heart of Italy', this is a hilly and woody region, with gorgeous miniature cities like Assisi, Gubbio, Orvieto, Spoleto, and Norcia. Specialties: Pork sausages (today pork butchers are still called *norcini,* "natives of Norcia"), black truffles, and *Porchetta* (roast pig with herbs).

Marche. Appennini mountain-range country, this region houses the Republic of San Marino, a minuscule independent sovereign state for the past fourteen centuries. Specialties: *Vincisgrassi* (lasagna with giblets, chicken livers, and white sauce), *Garganelli* (handmade tubular pasta), *Olive Farcite* (stuffed giant olives from Ascoli), and wines (*Sangiovese, Vernaccia,* and *Verdicchio*).

Lazio. This region of Rome is surrounded by beautiful hilly countryside. Specialties: *Fettuccine alla Romana* (paper-thin fettuccine), *Fettuccine all'Alfredo* (dressed with butter and parmigiano reggiano cheese), *Abbacchio alla Cacciatora* (milk-fed lamb hunter's style), *Carciofi alla Giudia* (small young artichokes cooked in olive oil), *Gnocchi alla Romana* (semolina milk-cooked dumplings), *Spaghetti Carbonara* (dressed with eggs and bacon), *Coda alla Vaccinara* (oxtail with tomato and celery), *Saltimbocca* (veal with prosciutto), *Torta di Ricotta* (ricotta cheese cake).

Abruzzi and Molise. This region boasts a mountainous Appennini inland and beautiful sandy beaches. Specialties: Pork sausages, *Maccheroni alla Chitarra* (square spaghetti cut with a special device shaped like a square guitar), *Bucatini all'Amatriciana* (long tubular pasta dressed with tomato, onion and bacon), and wines (*Montepulciano* and *Trebbiano*).

Campania. Napoli and its surroundings are one of the most colorful regions of Italy: full of monuments, art, architecture, wonderful people, and of course one of the best gastronomies of Italy. This is where pasta is at its best, and where pizza was invented. Specialties: *Spaghetti alle Vongole* (spaghetti with clams), *Pizza Napoletana* or *Margherita* (pizza with oregano or basil and mozzarella), *Mozzarella di Bufala* (water buffalo mozzarella), *Calzoni* (folded pizza filled with mozzarella), *Sfogliatelle* (a sort of puff pastries filled with ricotta cheese), *Pastiera* (cake filled with wheat and riccotta cheese).

Calabria and Lucania. The toe of the Italian boot is a poor region, but it has impeccable beaches and untouched mountainsides. Specialties: *Melanzane a Funghetto* (oven baked eggplant), *Morzeddu* (similar to a calzoni filled with giblets), *Sagne Chine* (Calabrian Lasagne), and *Ciro'* wine.

Puglia. This region features flat land by beautiful beaches, and many Norman monuments. Specialties: olive oil, cheeses, mussels, *Orecchiette* (little-ears pasta), *Panzarotti* (mozzarella-filled ravioli), *Carteddate* (honey-covered pastries).

Sicilia. The largest island of the Mediterranean is an ancient mythological land that has been occupied by many civilizations: Greek, Roman, Byzantine, Saracen, Norman, French, and Spaniards — and all are brought together in an apogee of colors, scents, and tastes. Specialties: *Arancini* (fried rice balls), *Caponata* (eggplant stew), *Sugo col Tonno* (fresh tuna fish tomato sauce), *Pasta con le Sarde* (pasta with sardines), *Pasta alla Norma* (eggplant pasta), *Cassata* (Sicilian layer cake), *Cannoli* (fried pasta tubes filled with ricotta cheese), ice cream, candied fruit, almond paste, and wines (*Marsala, Corvo,* and *Moscato*).

Sardegna. A region of ancient and wild land, it possesses one of the most exclusive and astounding seasides. Specialties: *Carasau* (so-called music paper, paper-thin bread), *Aligusta* (sautéed lobster), *Culingiones* (ravioli filled with fresh cheese), *Amaretti* (almond cookies), game, *Pecorino Sardo* (pungent sheep cheese), and wines (*Vernaccia* and *Cannonau*) ❖

CHAPTER 1

All Roads Lead to Rome

The Food of the Capital

Roman eating habits during the empire—the luscious banquets, the magnificence of the food—have fascinated generations. On the opposite hand, what the legionaries and most of people would live on, the "fuel of the empire," was grains: bread and *puls*, sort of a porridge made out of flour. After the fall of the empire, memory of the great Roman cooking traditions was almost completely lost. Nevertheless, Roman culture and eating practices have influenced the many generations that have followed.

*H*ave you ever wondered what it would be like to have a time machine, and to go back in time? Well, imagine yourself in Imperial Rome, let's say around 115 A.D.

Since we are interested in Roman food, the place to be is Trajan's Market, located right behind the forum. Apollodoro, a famous architect from Damascus, has cut away part of the Quirinale Hill that dominated the Forum of Traianus and created the first "mall" of antiquity—one hundred feet tall, with six floors of 150 specialized shops. In this building we can virtually "taste" the heights Roman civilization has reached.

On the first floor, right behind the apse, we see shops of flowers and vegetables. Above it, we find the shops of wine and oil. The third floor opens on one side onto a long balcony overlooking the forum, and on the other side on the street Via Biberatica, (from the word *Pipera*, for "pepper"), where the spices are sold. On the fourth floor, opening on a vast atrium, are shops with the most expensive spices. The fifth floor houses are the government offices in charge of the public distribution of grain and food. And finally, the sixth floor is reserved for the fish shops, with large pools of salt and fresh water.

The Forums are the symbol of Roman power, but these markets show us the opulence of Rome. We can find here local produce and wine, game from neighboring Umbria, and abundant fish from the Mediterranean; but other foods are imported: Salt pickles from Byzan-

The Trajan's Markets were originally considered among the wonders of the world. The present ruins are well preserved, but show only a hint of their original magnificence. The architect Apollodoro built for the emperor Trajan a futuristic complex of 150 shops and offices, practical and monumental at the same time. It was the first equivalent of the modern malls, selling everything from silks and spices to fresh fish, fruit, and flowers.

tium, oysters from Britain, honey from Greece, dates from Syria and Egypt, onions from Wales, dried fruit from Turkestan, and almonds from Anatolia. And look at all the spices. Here we have *garum* from Leptis Magna, *silphium* from Ethiopia, pepper from India, sumac from Syria, coriander from China, sugar from Persia, mace and nutmeg and cloves from Indonesia, and cardamom from Malaysia, as well as Parthian asafetida, and Sinhalese cinnamon.

Roman ships sail from Arsinoe in Egypt to India. Some countries, like Ceylon, accept vases and ceramics in exchange for spices. Indian merchants offering pearls and sapphires, and the Chinese selling precious silk, demand payment in gold.

In 45 A.D., Hippalus, a Roman sailor, found a shortcut to the Orient using the shift in wind direction of the monsoon to go directly from Aden to India, which made the travel much shorter. The journey is extremely dangerous, and only half of the vessels come back, but the high price Romans will pay for spices is worth the risk.

The desire of Romans for spices reached an incredible level. Pliny remarked that the empire was losing "fifty millions sesterces a year" to India. The spice trade is believed, by some historians, to be one of the reasons for the fall of the Roman Empire. The drain of gold created a serious economic crisis that made it more difficult to support the army and stop barbarian incursions.

Roman Banquets

In the Republican times, even the meals of the rich were frugal. Like those of the poor, they were based mostly on bread and *puls* (porridge).

Those times are gone. The rich people of Imperial Rome are not shy about spending their fortunes on exotic foods. The banquets of the Romans have been immortalized in many paintings, mosaics, sculptures, as well as . . . Hollywood movies.

The guests convene at sunset in the *triclinium,* (the formal dining room), decorated with frescoes that depict hunting or fishing scenes, or plants and flowers. The room is furnished with *triclinia,* (beds with three places, hence the name of the room) arranged on three sides of a large table. The guests take their places in the precise order indicated by the host. The closer to the host, the higher the honor. The diners lie on their left sides and use their right hand to take the food from the silver plates. Formal and important dinners could be very elaborate, with many courses of meat, fish, vegetables, and wine.

During the banquet, many types of entertainment amuse the guests: poetry reading, dances, and acrobatics. The food of the rich, maybe for the first time in history, is not only more abundant, but also different from the repast of the poor.

In Imperial Rome, the diet of the poor is still based mainly on cereals. The very poor count on the free distribution of bread to survive. These are the times of "panem et circenses," free bread and free entertainment at the circus to please the populace. Distribution of free grain began in 123 B.C. Today, 320,000 people receive free grain, almost one-third of the population of Rome. The logistic problems of supplies for a city of one million must be enormous, but the Romans are extremely well organized.

For those who can afford it, many types of bread are sold: white, black, rye, oil, egg, and raisin, in addition to focaccia, breadsticks, crackers, and cookies. Vegetables, cheese, eggs, and fish are abundant. In contrast, meat consumption is limited. The average Roman eats about fifty pounds of meat a year, against five hundred pounds of grains. The only meats largely available are game, pork, poultry, and sheep—always bred in large herds in the farms around Rome.

Beef is extremely limited. Cattle are production workers here, used in agriculture and for transportation. Veal is rare, and older cows unable to work give only tough, unpleasant meat.

One prominent figure in this day was Marcus Gavius Apicius, a famous gourmet protagonist in many Roman anecdotes. Seneca gives us an account of his tragic death: After spending most of his fortune to pay for his expensive habits, he discovered that he only had ten million sesterces left. As this was not enough to carry on his costly life, he committed suicide.

Apicius is famous for having written what is considered the first cookbook in human history, *De Re Coquinaria,* (About Culinary Matters). The book we know today is a ninth-century manuscript, probably reproduced from earlier copies from the fourth century, that were integrated with many medieval recipes.

A Roman Banquet in a *Triclinium.* During much of the dinner, each guest leaned on his left elbow, leaving the right arm free. As three men lay on the same couch, the head of one man was near the bosom of the man lying behind him. The rule was that the number of guests should be no less than that of the Graces (3), nor exceed that of the Muses (9).

The book contains about 450 recipes divided in ten volumes by subject. Unfortunately, the recipes are difficult to reproduce: they look more like notes, because there is no indication of the quantities or cooking procedures. And besides, some ingredients are no longer available. The most commonly used sauce in his book is *Garum,* also known as *Liquamen,* a very salty, thick, and tasty fish sauce.

Apicius was an eccentric gourmet. He organized sumptuous banquets and invented lavish dishes like roasted ostrich, flamingo, and nightingales' tongues, all of which he himself cooked. According to Plinius the Elder, Apicius invented a way to force-feed geese to enlarge their liver; that is the French *fois gras* we know today.

Roman Renaissance

Now, returning home in our time machine and looking back, we learn that the fall of the Roman Empire happened gradually between the third through the fifth century A.D. The destruction of the Ostrogoth kingdom by the Huns in eastern Europe generated a chain reaction. The people settled at the eastern boundaries of the Roman Empire saw their only way of escape as westward in the direction of the Roman territories. Rome—in the midst of economic crisis, civil wars,

Horserace during the Roman Carnival. Engraving by B. Pinelli, circa 1830. For centuries, Romans celebrated the carnival. Sponsored by the Pope and the noble Roman families, the festivities acquired political prominence. Thousands of people would travel from all over Europe to assist. The "Palio" was a famous horserace without jockeys, taking place along the Via del Corso; the race became a competition for the best horses. The victory would culminate in a large public banquet and food distribution. The Palio was abolished in 1884 after an accident occurred in front of Queen Margherita.

and headed by weak and inept emperors—was unable to stop the invasions, and before long would succumb to the barbarians. In 410 Rome was sacked by the Goths, and in 456 and in 472 it was plundered by the Vandals. Today the word "vandal" remains synonymous with indiscriminate destruction. Raided by bands of marauders, the Roman Empire no longer existed.

Aqueducts broken, monuments in ruin, Rome was burned and pillaged, and the population fell to 60,000 terrorized, starving survivors. Horrible reports tell of life in the centuries after the fall of Rome.

Famine, plague, and bloody wars raged over the cities and countryside. The barbarian invasions erased communities and cultivated areas, completely annihilating the eating habits of the times.

Medieval people had to start again from scratch, feeding on game, wild grains, and roots—and in some cases anything that was edible— to avoid starvation. The great Roman cooking traditions were completely lost from memory. Trying to date contemporary dishes back to Roman times is merely an exercise, because there was no continuity between then and now.

The barbarians who settled in Italy brought with them new eating habits. Their diet was mainly based on meat, pork fats, and beer, in contrast to the diet of the Mediterranean population, which was based on grain, olive oil, and wine. This contrast is still apparent today between the northern and southern regions of Italy.

In 774 A.D. Charlemagne donated vast territories to the Pope to rule. Rome became the capital of the temporal "State of the Church," which lasted in various forms until 1870.

In the centuries that followed Rome's fall, the city's fortune was erratic until the modern city started to take shape under Pope Giulio II and his successors. They initiated great urban and architectural works, attracting to Rome the best artists of the Renaissance and the Baroque period, such as Michelangelo, Raffaello, Bramante, Bernini, Borromini, and Canova.

Agriculture was reestablished and the countryside around Rome began producing the same sheep, goats, cheeses, and vegetables as in Roman times : *Pecorino*, Roman sheep cheese, has a long history! In the city, large open areas were transformed into gardens planted with vegetables that helped feed the city dwellers. These gardens lasted until Rome became the capital of Italy. Most of these spaces, located in the heart of the city, later were used for new buildings.

For centuries Rome remained a city of a few thousand people: the population was 90,000 at the end of the sixteenth century, and 200,000 when the city became the capital of Italy. The Romans, detached from the political events of the papacy and the nobles, kept on living and cooking in a simple way, utilizing the products of the nearby countryside. The cooking style of Rome and the surrounding country became virtually identical.

On the other hand, the cooking style of the Pope's court and that of the nobles was very similar to that of other courts around Europe — rich and sumptuous.

The *Trionfi della Tavola,* (Triumphs of the Table), is a culinary invention of the Renaissance. Gigantic dishes, they were cooked and assembled like sculptures, to show the artistic ability, more than the cooking skills, of the cook, and to surprise the guests. It might be a peacock, cooked and rebuilt with its plumage and with flames coming out of its beak, or it might be a little gelatin pond with fishes swimming inside or marzipan figures showing classical scenes.

Jewish cooking represents another chapter of Roman history. A city within the city, the Jewish quarter is the oldest community of Rome. Mandated to live in a small suburb, the Jews of Rome developed a kosher cooking that would remain forcibly authentic and separated from any external influence.

The small *trattorie* kept alive the traditions of their ancestors and became prestigious restaurants where today you can taste some of the most celebrated Roman dishes, including the renowned *Carciofi alla Giudia* (artichokes Jewish style). These are large, tender Roman artichokes, deep-fried in olive oil until the outside leaves become brown and crispy.

The historic influence of the rule of the Popes on Rome finally ended on the 20th of September in 1870, when the troops of the Kingdom of Italy entered the city. Rome was annexed and, shortly after, became the capital of Italy. The Pope withdrew into Vatican City, which is still ruled today as an independent state.

And Then Alfredo

In the late 1800s, after becoming the capital city of Italy, and with the massive immigration from the south after World War II, Rome became a true melting pot of different cooking habits.

The first turn in Roman life and cooking came after the royal court and the government moved to Rome in 1871. The military servicemen and bureaucrats mostly came from Piemonte, the businessmen from Lombardia. This was an enormous change for a city that had lived virtually isolated for centuries.

The immigrants brought with them new dishes that eventually entered the Roman culinary tradition: *polenta* (cornmeal), rice and peas, *gnocchi* (potato dumplings), and many others. Gnocchi traditionally is dressed with melted butter or cheese in the north; but in Rome it is dressed with *Amatriciana* sauce (bacon and tomatoes), which is a perfect example of an adaptation that gave this dish a new life.

The population grew steadily, until it reached three million citizens. How did Rome receive the new wave of "invaders"? The tolerant character of the Romans and the charisma of the city made possible everyone's assimilation. Rome became a city full of contrasts, a city chaotic at times, but with a friendly and conciliatory spirit.

New generations of inspired cooks would soon create new exciting dishes, high gourmet cooking, but always in the Roman tradition of simplicity.

In the fifties and sixties, Hollywood discovered Rome, and Paparazzi photographers took photos of actors such as Tyrone Power, Ava Gardner, Richard Burton, Liz Taylor, or Sophia Loren in front of a plate of *Fettuccine all' Alfredo.*

Alfredo was an extravagant cook who used to personally serve his paper-thin fettuccine with golden forks. He invented "triple butter" fettuccine: nothing goes on it other than good parmigiano and a lot of butter.

The *Fettuccine alla Papalina* (in the Pope's style), a tasty variation of

Campo de' Fiori means "Field of Flowers," which is today a cobble-stone-paved plaza in the heart of downtown Rome, where a most colorful farmers market takes place every day. For long time, this plaza was famous as a place for executions. In the center of the plaza is a bronze statue of Giordano Bruno, a Roman philosopher burned alive on February 17, 1600, by the Inquisition for his theories that anticipated elements of modern science. His death became a symbol of the church's intolerance in the face of free thought.

the simple *Carbonara,* was originally a dish served to an unknown cardinal in a restaurant in Rome. The cardinal later became Pope Pius XII, and the fettuccine dish was renamed to commemorate the event.

There are so many Roman dishes that deserve to be mentioned here: from the *Gnocchi alla Romana* (dumplings made of semolina flour boiled in milk), to *Puntarelle* (curly tips of Catalogna chicory dressed with garlic, vinegar, and anchovy sauce); from *Filetti di Baccala'* (salt cod fillet dip in batter and fried) to *Suppli' al Telefono* (rice balls filled with mozzarella cheese, breaded, and fried); from *Pomodori Ripieni,* (large tomatoes stuffed with rice) to *Abbacchio alla Cacciatora* (suckling lamb in the hunter's style, pan-roasted with garlic, rosemary, and vinegar). But the list is endless ❖

Bread

It is no coincidence that bread is the first recipe in this book. Bread, in one form or another, has been a primary form of food for people from the most primitive times. The Greeks picked up the technology for making bread from the Egyptians, and from Greece the practice spread throughout Europe. Bread and wheat were especially important in Rome. The Roman welfare state was based on the distribution of free bread to the people. For a long time, "Panem et Circenses" (bread and entertainment) is what kept Rome running.

Through history, a person's social status could be recognized by the color of bread they consumed. The darker the bread, the lower the social status—this was because white flour was more expensive.

For centuries, bread had spiritual significance. Even the Lord's Prayer asks God to "Give us today our daily bread," implying not only loaves, but also moral nourishment.

Bread remains important to our diet now, and there is a reason for it having such a long history: bread is healthy and nourishing, and fills the stomach as well as the spirit.

Italian households still serve bread with every meal. We think everyone should try to bake a good loaf of country bread: nothing is as satisfying as the taste and smell of fresh-baked bread ❖

PAGNOTTA CASARECCIA
rustic bread loaf

makes 1 loaf
(2 lb or 900 gr)

- 1 cube or 0.6 oz (17 gr) fresh active yeast
- 5½ cups (700 gr) flour
- 2½ tablespoons salt
- 1 tablespoon wheat bran

- Warm 2 cups (450 cc) of water to approximately 100 F (38 C).
- Dissolve the yeast in the warm water. Set it aside for about 5 to 10 minutes until small bubbles form.
- In a large bowl, place 1½ cups (210 gr) of the flour. Pour in the water-yeast mix.
- Stir with a spatula until the dough is well combined and forming strands.
- Add the salt to the remaining flour.
- A little at a time, add the flour to the dough, mixing it with a spatula.
- Transfer the mixture to a lightly floured work surface. First mix with a scraper, then as soon as the dough is workable, knead it with your hands.
- The dough must be kept moist and sticky at all times. Add small amounts of flour while kneading.
- Knead the dough for about 8–10 minutes, folding and pulling, until it still is a little sticky but elastic and smooth.

- Spray a bowl lightly with olive oil. Place the dough in the bowl, cover it with a cloth, and set aside to rise for about 2 hours until it has doubled in size. Make sure the room temperature is at least 70 F (21 C).
- When the dough has risen, push the surface down in the center with the palm of your hand to expel the air.
- Transfer the dough to a lightly floured work surface. Knead the dough for about 5 minutes.

- Shape dough into a round form, tucking the sides under the ball and stretching the surface to make it smooth.
- Line a large oven pan with parchment paper and sprinkle it with half of the wheat bran.
- Transfer the dough on top of the paper, keeping the seam down.
- Sprinkle the top of the dough with the rest of the wheat bran.
- Cover with a cloth, and set it aside to rise again for about 2 hours.
- Preheat oven to 425 F (220 C).
- When the dough is well risen, remove the cover. Optionally, using a very sharp knife or a box cutter, slit across the top of the loaf several times.

- Transfer the loaf to the oven, sliding it very carefully without touching or pushing it. Bake for about 1 hour or until it is deep brown in color.
- When the bread is ready, the surface will crackle, and it will make a hollow sound when tapped. Cool it on a rack at room temperature.

BRUSCHETTA
toasted garlic bread

Italians know the magic of a simple slice of crusty bread dressed with salt and good olive oil. It provides a use for stale bread and makes a good appetizer or snack between meals. *Bruschetta* definitely is the precursor of all "garlic breads" and the French canapé. The main ingredient is the extra-virgin olive oil.

- 4 slices of thick-crusted Italian country bread approximately 3/8 inch (1 cm) thick
- 1 clove of garlic, peeled
- whole small dry red peppers, spicy (optional)
- extra-virgin olive oil
- salt

- Preheat an oven, broiler, or toaster, or light up a charcoal fire.
- Grill the bread on both sides until golden brown.
- Lightly rub the garlic on the surface of the bread.
- If you like, you may also lightly rub the red pepper over the bread.

- Pour a thin stream of olive oil on the bread, and sprinkle with salt. Serve while still warm.

PASTA E CECI
chickpea soup

". . . inde domum me ad porri et ciceris refero laganique catinum," (I was given a bowl of leeks and chickpea lasagna at my house), wrote the Roman poet Orace (Satire). Chickpea soup, flavored with garlic and rosemary, is probably one of the oldest recipes in Roman cooking.

- 11 oz (300 gr) dry chickpeas or 2 cans of chickpeas
- 3 + 2 tablespoons extra-virgin olive oil
- 1 garlic clove, finely chopped
- 1 spring of rosemary
- 2 anchovy fillets, chopped
- 2 tablespoon tomato purée
- salt and pepper
- 6 oz (180 gr) pasta, short *ditali,* or spaghetti, broken in ½-inch (1 cm) pieces

- Soak the dry chickpeas in fresh water overnight or as long as necessary to have them tender.
- Drain the chickpeas when ready to cook. If using canned chickpeas, just drain them from the can water.
- In a large saucepan, put 3 tablespoons of the extra-virgin olive oil, garlic, and the rosemary. Turn heat to medium.

- As soon as the oil becomes hot, add anchovies, and stir to dissolve. This step must be done very quickly to avoid browning the garlic and burning the anchovies.
- Immediately add tomato, chickpeas, and 4 cups (approximately 1 liter water). Bring to a boil.
- Cook for about 20 minutes or until the chickpeas are tender.
- Add freshly grated pepper. Anchovies can be very salty, therefore taste the soup and add salt only if necessary. Remove the rosemary.
- Add the pasta and cook for the time indicated by the manufacturer, checking for readiness from time to time. Pasta is ready when *al dente* (firm but not too soft or overcooked).
- Transfer to individual serving bowls and top with a drizzle of extra-virgin olive oil. Serve warm.

FETTUCCINE ALLA PAPALINA
fettuccine with eggs and bacon

An unknown cardinal of modest habits was served this dish in a small trattoria in Rome. The cardinal became Pope Pius XII, and the dish was then dedicated to commemorate this event.

prepare fresh fettuccine according to the recipe on page 57

- 4 oz (115 gr) butter
- 1 large scallion, finely chopped
- 4 oz (115 gr) prosciutto, diced
- 3 eggs
- 4 oz (120 gr) parmigiano reggiano cheese, freshly grated
- 2 tablespoons heavy cream
- salt and pepper

- Fill a stockpot with water and bring to a boil.
- While waiting for the water to boil, place half of the butter in a frying pan. Turn the heat to medium.
- When the butter starts foaming add the scallion and prosciutto. Sauté until the scallion is soft.
- In a small bowl, beat the eggs, half of the parmigiano cheese, and the cream.
- When the water comes to a boil, add salt and cook the fettuccine, checking for readiness from time to time.
- In a skillet large enough to contain the pasta, put the rest of the butter and turn heat to medium.
- When the butter begins foaming, add the egg mix, toss quickly, and add the sautéed prosciutto, salt and pepper.
- When the pasta is *al dente*, (firm but not too soft or overcooked), drain the pasta and drop it over the egg mix in the skillet, tossing thoroughly.
- Top with the rest of the parmigiano cheese and serve at once.

GNOCCHI DI SEMOLINO AL LATTE
semolina milk dumplings

- 4 cups (approximately 1 liter) milk
- 1 cup (140 gr) semolina flour
- salt
- 3 egg yolks
- 4 tablespoons (55 gr) butter
- 5 oz (140 gr) parmigiano reggiano cheese, freshly grated

- In a saucepan, put the milk and turn heat to medium. When the milk begins boiling, sift in the semolina flour a little at a time, stirring to avoid lumps.
- When all the semolina is added, add salt and cook for about 15–20 minutes, stirring constantly until very thick.
- Turn the heat off and quickly stir in the egg yolks. The eggs need to be stirred in very quickly because they will solidify immediately when in contact with the hot semolina.
- Stir in 2 tablespoons of the butter and half of the cheese.
- Wet a working surface, and spread the semolina uniformly in a thickness of about 3/8 inch (1 cm).
- Cool the semolina at room temperature. Preheat oven to 350 F (175 C). When the semolina is cold, cut in small rounds with a small glass or other tool.

- Butter the bottom of an oven pan and place the gnocchi in rows lightly overlapping.
- Sprinkle with the rest of the cheese, and spread on the rest of the butter in small dice. Place the pan in the oven, and bake for about 15 minutes. Serve hot.

Semolina gnocchi can be prepared a day in advance and baked when ready. Small leftover cuttings that remain after removing the round dumplings can be shaped as small croquettes, covered with breadcrumbs, and fried.

FILETTI DI BACCALA' FRITTI
fried salt cod fillets

Baccala' (salt cod) or *stoccafisso* (air-dried stock fish) was introduced in Venice in the early 1400s. These became extremely popular as a less expensive alternative to fresh fish for meals during the religious fasting days.

Very common all over Italy, salt cod is cooked in Rome in many different ways, including in casserole, baked, or fried as in this wonderful and tasty recipe.

- 1 lb (450 gr) dry salt cod
- 1 tablespoon dry active yeast
- 1¼ cups (300 cc) warm water
- 1 egg
- ½ lb (225 gr) flour
- salt
- frying oil

- Place the salt cod in a container to soak in water overnight, or for as long as necessary to become tender. If possible, change water once in a while.
- In a small bowl, dissolve the yeast in the warm water. Set aside for about 5 minutes. Beat the egg in a separate bowl.
- In a bowl, put the flour, add the water-yeast mixture, egg, and pinch of salt.
- Mix very well together and let it rest for about 1 hour at room temperature.
- Drain the fish, discard the fish skin and the bones if present, and cut the fish in strips.
- In a large skillet, bring oil to frying temperature.
- Dredge the fish fillets in the batter, covering all sides, and fry until gold brown.
- Transfer the fillets on paper towels on a large plate and let the oil drain briefly. Sprinkle with salt. Serve hot.

SUPPLI'
fried rice balls

Suppli' are very popular in Rome where they can be bought in fast food places as hot snacks. When making a risotto it is not unusual to purposely prepare more than necessary to have the leftovers to make *suppli'*. When the mozzarella cheese is added, as in this recipe, they are called *"suppli' al telefono"* (telephone *suppli'*)—because when you bite into them, the melted cheese flows out in a long stripe like the wire that dangles out of the receiver of a telephone.

prepare the meat-tomato sauce according to the recipe on page 62

for the risotto
- 5 cups (1250 cc) broth
- 1½ cup (300 gr) *arborio* rice
- salt
- 4 tablespoons parmigiano reggiano cheese, freshly grated
- 1 tablespoon butter

for the suppli'
- 2 eggs
- salt
- 2 oz (60 gr) flour
- 5 oz (140 gr) approximately bread crumbs
- 2 oz (60 gr) fresh mozzarella cheese, cut in ½ inch (1 cm) dice
- frying oil

preparing the risotto

It is preferable to prepare the risotto one day in advance.

- Warm the broth in a saucepan.
- Place the meat-tomato sauce in a larger saucepan on medium heat and bring to a boil.
- Add the rice to the tomato sauce and turn the heat to medium. Stir with a wooden spoon.
- When the rice begins absorbing the sauce and appears thicker, add ½ cup (120 cc) of the broth and stir frequently.
- When the broth has evaporated, add ½ cup (120 cc) more broth.
- Repeat this step of adding broth and stirring, keeping the rice at the consistency of a dense paste.
- The rice will be ready in about 20 minutes, when *al dente* (firm but not too soft or overcooked).
- When the rice is ready, taste and add salt if necessary. Stir in the parmigiano cheese and butter. Let the risotto cool to room temperature.

preparing the suppli'
- Put the rice in a bowl. Add one egg and mix together.
- In a small bowl, beat the other egg with a pinch of salt.
- On two separate plates, put the flour and the bread crumbs.
- Remove one generous tablespoon of rice and form into an elongated oval ball, placing in the center one dice of the mozzarella cheese.
- Wrap the rice around the cheese and press firmly.
- Continue forming the *suppli'* until all the rice is used.
- One at a time, dredge the *suppli'* first in the flour, then dip in the egg, and finally in the bread crumbs until evenly covered. Press them in the palm of your hands to make the bread crumbs stick to the rice.
- In a large skillet, bring the oil to frying temperature.
- Fry *suppli'* for about 2 minutes, until golden brown.
- Transfer the *suppli'* on paper towels on a large plate and let the oil drain briefly. Serve when still hot.

Artichokes: The King of Vegetables

Artichokes (Cynara Scolymus) are originally from the Mediterranean area. What we eat is the flower bud of this thistle-like plant. The flower, if the plant is allowed to flower, is a large blossom about 6–7 inch (15–18 cm) wide of a deep blue-violet color.

The ancient Romans already knew wild artichokes, (i.e. *Carduos,* their word for thistle). The edible part is the bud bottom, which they called *sfondilos.* The "Globe Artichoke," the refined vegetable we know today, is the result of a selection process that began in the thirteenth century.

In Rome artichokes are deep-fried, boiled, used for *Frittata* (Italian open omelet), for pasta sauce, for risotto, and in a large variety of preparations. The stems of the artichokes are also edible. If those you buy have long stems, just peel them, cut them into pieces, and cook them together with the rest of the artichokes.

Artichokes were introduced in California by Italian farmers in the early 1900s. Today California produces most of the artichokes grown in the United States. These are very flavorful and tender, and they are very large.

American consumers seem to look at size as a sign of quality. Unfortunately, in the case of artichokes, this is not correct. In fact, when too big, artichokes develop in their core those tough, inedible "chokes." In Europe, only small artichoke buds are harvested. Those that eventually have "chokes" don't make it to the market because they are considered of inferior quality, in spite of their size.

Some of the Roman recipes such as *Carciofi alla Giudia* (artichokes Jewish style), and *Carciofi alla Romana* (artichokes Roman style), require the artichokes to be cooked whole. Therefore, if chokes are present, they need to be scooped away, and all the leaves may fall apart while cooking. Look for the small, "baby" artichokes. They shouldn't have chokes and should be fully edible ❖

Cleaning Artichokes

Eliminate outer leaves, bending them and snapping them off, until you reach leaves that are half yellow (toward the base) and half green (toward the tip). Greener, tougher leaves are not edible.

Cut off the end of the stem, leaving it about 1 inch (2.5 cm) long.

Clean the outside of the stem, peeling it with a sharp knife. Uniformly pare the base of the leaves.

Cut off the tip of the central cone, to eliminate the tougher green end of the leaves and obtain a flat surface.

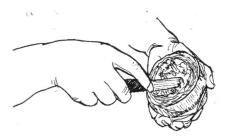

If necessary, scoop away the inside chokes with the tip of the knife until you reach the tender part of the artichoke.

CARCIOFI ALLA ROMANA
artichokes roman style

The artichoke season in Italy begins in December, with the first produce arriving from Sicily, and the season ends in spring with the last artichokes coming from the country around Rome. The artichokes from the area around Rome are large and tender, and one variety in particular, called "cimaroli" (literally "those that grow on the top") are the best ones. Large, globe-like, full of pulp, and with tender leaves, they are picked early, before they develop the unpleasant tough chokes inside.

This dish is good when served warm or lukewarm. If cold, let the artichokes come to room temperature. Avoid warming them for a second time, otherwise their taste will have an unpleasant tang.

Artichokes Roman Style generally are dressed with *Mentuccia (Calamintha Officinalis)*, a type of mint with very small leaves that spontaneously grows in the Rome area. Difficult to find in the United States, the mint can be substituted with parsley instead.

- ◆ 1 large juicy lemon, cut in half
- ◆ 4 artichokes
- ◆ 1 bunch of Italian parsley
- ◆ 2 cloves of garlic
- ◆ salt and pepper
- ◆ 6 tablespoons extra-virgin olive oil
- ◆ ½ glass of water

- Fill a large bowl with fresh water. Squeeze half lemon in the water. Reserve the other half.
- After cleaning each artichoke (see page 19), rub the outside of the artichoke with the rest of the half-lemon and then place the artichoke in the bowl. Placing the artichoke in lemon water will prevent it from discoloring.
- Repeat the step until all the artichokes are clean.
- Chop the parsley and the garlic very finely and mix them together.
- Rinse the artichokes in fresh water to remove the lemon flavor, drain well, shake away the excess water, and pat them with a cloth.
- Rub the outsides and the insides with salt and pepper. Insert the mix of parsley and garlic uniformly among the leaves.
- Place the artichokes in a large saucepan with stems up and

leaves down. Add the extra-virgin olive oil and the water.
- Cover the pan, place paper towels between the pan and the lid, closing it as tightly as possible. Steam will form in the pan while the artichokes are cooking. The paper will prevent the steam from escaping and the artichokes will cook uniformly.
- Turn the heat to medium and cook for about 20–30 minutes. Cooking time may vary, depending on the quality and size of the artichokes. After about 20 minutes test for readiness. When the artichokes are ready, you will be able to easily insert a fork in the thick part of the stem.
- Uncover the pan and turn the heat to high.
- Fry artichokes for a few minutes, turning them carefully on all sides, until the outer and bottom leaves of the artichokes are brown. Serve warm with the cooking oil.

What is Quinto Quarto?

Quinto Quarto translates to "Fifth Quarter." What is it? At the end of last century, one of the most modern slaughterhouses in Europe was built in Rome, in the Testaccio suburb. Hundreds of butchers, called *vaccinari,* (cow workers) worked in the establishment.

Roman butchers were very skilled and famous for their ability to refine any cut of meat. At first the cows were split in half, and then in four quarters. What was left—skin, head, tail, liver, and all the rest of the offal—was called the fifth quarter. Considered meat of poor quality, the *Quinto Quarto* was given to the butchers to round up their meager pay. Apparently, most who received these meats sold them to the restaurants in the area.

Roman cooks have created a culinary universe of first-quality dishes around the "fifth quarter". In about thirty years, the "inferior" cooking of the *vaccinari* became renowned citywide and evolved into dishes for connoisseurs. We present here two of the most famous dishes: oxtail and tripe.

The large use of "weird" meats, such as the *abbacchio* (milk fed lamb), *testina* (lamb's head), *pagliata* (milk-fed lamb bowels), heels, offal, and the like has given Roman cooking a reputation of brutality

Il Macello (Roman butcher shop), engraving by B. Pinelli, 1831. Many shoppers line up to buy meat cut to order on the spot. A sign on the wall reads "veal 7 per pound".

and truculence. Old Roman traditional cooking has never found many fans among new immigrants and tourists. Many culinary guides don't even mention these types of dishes.

Roman meat cooking is not only "fifth quarter." In reality, reflecting the melting pot of races and traditions that Rome is, Roman cooking is very versatile. Its repertory includes side by side delicate gourmet dishes, like the *Saltimbocca,* and robust home dishes like the *Garofolato* ❖

CODA ALLA VACCINARA
stewed oxtail with celery in tomato sauce

Coda alla vaccinara (oxtail in celery sauce) is a wonderful dish. The celery, a vegetable particularly loved by Romans, is added generously to the pan, giving the sauce a distinctive flavor. Sometimes oxtail is difficult to find, even in Rome, where the butcher shops provide it only on order. You can prepare a similar dish, using diced

21

beef, cooking with the same procedure, adjusting the cooking time, and using a large quantity of celery.

- ◆ 3 tablespoons extra-virgin olive oil
- ◆ 2 lb (approximately 1 kg) oxtail
- ◆ 1 medium onion, diced
- ◆ 1 carrot, diced
- ◆ 1 celery stick, chopped
- ◆ salt and pepper
- ◆ ¼ cup (60 cc) dry white wine
- ◆ 1 cup (250 gr) tomato, diced
- ◆ 8 celery sticks, cut longitudinally into strips

- In a saucepan, pour the oil and turn the heat to medium. Add the oxtail and sauté it until the meat is uniformly browned.
- Add the onion, carrot, chopped celery stick, and salt and pepper. Sauté the mixture until the onion is soft.
- Add the wine, turn the heat to high, and let the wine evaporate.
- Add the tomato, and bring the mixture to a boil. When the sauce starts boiling, reduce the heat and add ½ cup (120 cc) water.
- Cover and cook the food until the meat becomes tender and starts coming off of the bone; add some warm water if necessary.
- Add the celery strips, and cook until the celery is tender. Adjust salt and pepper and serve warm.

TRIPPA ALLA ROMANA
stewed tripe with tomato and fresh mint

Trippa alla Romana (tripe Roman style) is a masterpiece by itself. The taste of tripe cooked with tomato blends perfectly with the *pecorino romano* cheese and the fresh mint, giving this dish a unique flavor.

- ◆ 2 lb (approximately 1 kg) tripe
- ◆ salt
- ◆ 2 oz (60 gr) bacon, diced
- ◆ 1 medium onion, diced
- ◆ 2 sticks of celery, diced
- ◆ 1 carrot, diced
- ◆ 3 tablespoons extra-virgin olive oil
- ◆ crushed red pepper
- ◆ ¾ cup (60 cc) dry white wine
- ◆ ½ cup (125 gr) tomatoes, puréed in a blender
- ◆ small bunch of fresh mint
- ◆ 2 oz (60 gr) *pecorino romano* cheese, freshly grated

- Rinse the tripe in fresh water. Fill a stockpot with water, 2 tablespoons of salt, and the tripe.
- Bring to a boil and cook for about 30 minutes to tenderize. Drain and cut the tripe in slices about ¾-inch (2 cm) wide.
- Chop the bacon, onion, celery, and carrot finely together.
- In a saucepan, put the olive oil and turn the heat to medium. Add the chopped vegetables and red pepper.
- Sauté until the onion is soft. Stir in the tripe.

- Add the wine, turn the heat to high, and let the wine evaporate.
- Add the tomatoes, 5–6 mint leaves, and salt, and bring to a boil.
- Turn the heat to low, cover, and cook for about 1 hour or longer, until the tripe is tender.
- During cooking time, stir occasionally and add warm water if necessary to prevent the tripe from sticking to the pan.
- When the tripe is almost ready, remove the lid and let the liquid evaporate to thicken sauce.
- Add about 10 fresh mint leaves, and serve warm, topped with grated *pecorino* romano cheese.

GAROFOLATO
beef stew in tomato sauce with cloves

The extra touch in this dish is in the use of cloves, which gives the sauce its distinctive scent. Cloves (from the Latin word *clavus*, meaning nail), have a scent that can be compared to that of the carnation. In fact, in Italy cloves are called *Chiodi di Garofano*, meaning carnation nails. The Roman name for carnation is *Garofolo*, hence the name for this dish. With *Garofolato* you get a complete meal of two dishes in one: an abundant tomato sauce to dress spaghetti and, thinly sliced, a second course of meat.

serves 6

- 2 lb (approximately 1 kg) meat for roasting
- 2 oz (60 gr) bacon, diced
- salt and pepper
- 3 cloves
- 1 small bunch of Italian parsley, finely chopped
- 2 bay leaves
- ½ medium onion
- 1 celery stick
- 1 medium carrot
- 2 tablespoons butter
- 2–3 tablespoons extra-virgin olive oil
- 1 garlic clove, crushed
- ½ cup (120 cc) red wine
- 1½ cans (800 gr) tomatoes, puréed in a blender

- Pierce the meat in 3 or 4 places, and fill the holes with one dice of bacon, salt and pepper.
- Insert 2 cloves in the ends of the meat. Rub the meat with salt and pepper, and tie it with a kitchen string.
- Tie together the parsley and the bay leaves with kitchen string, to form a little bunch.
- Chop the rest of the bacon, onion, celery, and carrot finely together.
- In a saucepan large enough to contain the meat, put the butter and olive oil and turn the heat to medium.
- As soon as the butter starts foaming, add the chopped vegetables and the garlic clove. Sauté for about one minute, add the meat, and brown uniformly.
- Add the wine, turn the heat to high, and let the wine evaporate.
- Add the tomato, parsley, and the remaining clove.

- Turn the heat to low, cover the pan, and simmer for about 2 hours or until the meat is tender.
- When the meat is ready, uncover and cook for 5 more minutes to thicken the sauce.

SALTIMBOCCA ALLA ROMANA
veal scaloppini with prosciutto and sage

Saltimbocca are veal scaloppini prepared very simply by assembling together slices of tender veal, prosciutto, and fresh sage leaves. "The name means 'jump into the mouth' the idea being that *saltimbocca* is so delicious that [it] prompts you almost by its own volition to pop a piece of it in without hesitating for an instant," as Waverly Root, famous journalist and food writer describes them.

While there are many variations on this dish with the addition of cheese or Marsala wine, we opted for the simplest recipe, as it is cooked in Roman kitchens.

- 2 oz (60 gr) flour
- salt
- 4 veal scaloppini slices, about 1 lb (approximately 450 gr)
- 4 prosciutto slices, approximately 3 oz (80 gr)
- 4 leaves of fresh sage
- 2–3 tablespoons extra-virgin olive oil
- 3 tablespoons (40 gr) butter
- pepper
- ½ cup (120 cc) dry white wine

- Put the flour on a large plate and add a pinch of salt.
- Dredge the veal slices in the flour, so that they are all well covered on both sides. Shake away the excess flour.
- Place a slice of prosciutto and a leaf of sage on each piece of meat. Secure the three together with a toothpick.
- In a large frying pan, put the oil and the butter, and turn the heat to medium.
- When the butter begins foaming, place the meat in the pan, add salt and pepper, and fry gently on both sides until light brown.
- Add the wine, turn the heat to medium high, and let the wine evaporate.
- Place on individual plates, covering the slices with the sauce and serve warm.

Scaloppini are very popular in Italy, but in the United States it is quite difficult to find a butcher who knows how to properly cut them. Scaloppini are thin slices of veal cut from the top round, and the slices should be cut across the vein of the muscles so that the fibers of the meat are short and the meat is tender. If they are cut along the vein, as they usually are in the States, the meat curls and toughens while cooking.

To help prevent the meat from toughening, make the slices very thin and thump them with a meat pounder.

CONIGLIO ALLA CACCIATORA
stewed rabbit with rosemary-vinegar marinade

Alla Cacciatora translates into "Hunter's Style." Hunting is as old as mankind. While Ancient Romans didn't like hunting and despised wild life, the practice of hunting was widely reintroduced by the new populations that occupied Italy after the fall of the Roman Empire. In the Middle Ages and in the Renaissance, when noblemen organized hunting parties and the peasants occasionally poached a hare or a few small birds, cooking wild game was elevated to an art.

More recently, expansion of the human population has tremendously reduced wildlife, and restrictive legislation has made hunting difficult— thus game for cooking is in very limited supply. Yet the way of cooking game in everyday cuisine has translated into some of the most tasteful recipes. *Coniglio alla Cacciatora* is a good example.

Game (such as pheasant, hare, and boar) can have a very strong taste, so the meat is marinated at length in vinegar, wine, and spices. Marinades can tenderize and also enhance or disguise game flavor. The same recipes can be used to cook duck, lamb, or the ubiquitous chicken. "Chicken Cacciatore" is in fact a very popular dish in the United States.

- 2 lb (approximately 1 kg) rabbit, cut into pieces
- 1/3 cup (80 cc) white-wine vinegar
- 1/3 cup (80 cc) dry white wine
- 2 tablespoons rosemary leaves
- 2 whole garlic cloves, crusjed
- salt and pepper (or red pepper)
- 3 tablespoons extra-virgin olive oil
- 1 tablespoon flour or corn starch
- 3–4 anchovy fillets, finely chopped

- The night before the preparation, place the rabbit in a bowl with the vinegar, wine, rosemary leaves, and garlic. Marinate overnight.
- The next day, when you are ready to cook, drain and reserve the marinade. Dry the rabbit with paper towels.
- Place the extra-virgin olive oil in a saucepan and turn the heat to medium.
- When the oil is hot, add the rabbit and brown it lightly on all sides. Add salt and pepper.
- Stir in the flour. Add the marinade, turn the heat to high, and let the liquid evaporate.
- Turn the heat to medium-low, cover, and cook for about 30–35 minutes or until the rabbit is tender.
- Stir occasionally to prevent the rabbit from sticking to the pan.
- When the rabbit is ready, add the anchovies to the pan, stirring vigorously for a few seconds until dissolved. Serve hot.

Crostate

In past times, sweet pastries and confections were an expensive luxury. They were usually associated with celebrations and religious festivities. In those times sugar was a costly item that few could afford. Most often people would content themselves with crumbly cookies, leavened tarts, or breads sweetened with honey and raisins.

When sugar became more affordable, candied fruit, marzipan, and fruit preserved in syrups made their appearance. At the same time, then-exotic spices from the East, long forgotten by the Romans, became popular again. Cinnamon, pepper, and ginger were most frequently used in the bakeries. *Pampepato* and *Panforte* from Tuscany are examples of their use.

In Rome, while the table of the wealthy looked similar to those in other regions of Italy, the lower classes did not make as much progress. Until a few decades ago the most popular sweets were the same you would have found in the provincial Lazio, the country around Rome: *Pangiallo* (honey-and-nuts cake), *Maritozzi* (raisin bread), leavened pound cakes, and cookies.

Today most of the bakeries prepare cakes of foreign extraction such as *Zuppa Inglese,* (layer cake from Tuscany), or *St. Honore* a cake from French tradition. Particularly popular were, and still are, *Crostate,* a type of pie with crusty dough, topped with jam or cheese ❖

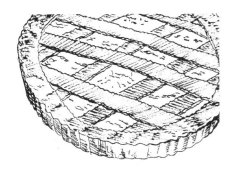

CROSTATA DI RICOTTA

ricotta cheese cake

for the dough
♦ 1 whole egg + 1 yolk
♦ 2½ cups (350 gr) flour
♦ ¾ cup (150 gr) sugar
♦ 6 oz (180 gr) butter, diced (at room temperature)
♦ 1 teaspoon vanilla
♦ pinch of salt

for the filling
♦ 2 eggs
♦ 12 oz (340 gr) ricotta cheese, drained
♦ ½ cup (100 gr) sugar
♦ 4 oz (115 gr) amaretti cookies, crumbled
♦ 2–3 tablespoons rum liquor
♦ 1 cup (150 gr) candied fruit, diced
♦ ½ cup (50 gr) raisins, soaked in warm water and drained

for the egg wash
♦ 1 egg white
♦ 1 teaspoon milk

preparing the dough
• Separate 1 egg yolk from the white, and reserve the white.
• Pour the flour onto a work surface to form a mound shape with a hole in the center.
• In the well, add the sugar, diced butter, 1 egg, 1 egg yolk, vanilla, and a pinch of salt.
• Use a fork to mix the ingredients; then combine the flour and knead the mixture to form smooth dough.
• Cover with plastic wrap and place it in the refrigerator for 1 hour.

preparing the filling
• Separate the yolks from the whites and reserve the whites.
• In a bowl, put the ricotta cheese, sugar, egg yolks; mix them together to obtain a smooth cream.
• Stir in the crumbled amaretti cookies, rum, candied fruit, and raisins.
• Beat the reserved egg whites in a bowl until stiff. With a spatula, combine egg whites with the mixture, stirring gently using a top-to-bottom motion.

assembling the cake
• Preheat oven to 375 F (190 C). Butter a 10-inch (25 cm) shallow tart pan with removable bottom and sprinkle it with a small amount of flour.
• Remove the dough from the refrigerator. Cut out one third of the dough and reserve it.

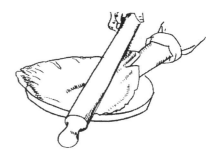

• Reduce the dough to a ¼ inch (0.5 cm) thick disk with a rolling pin.

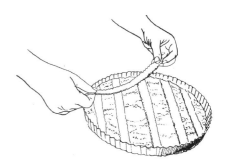

• Cover the bottom and sides of the pan with the dough.
• Fill the pan with the ricotta cheese mixture and level with a spatula.
• Reduce the rest of the dough to ¼ inch (0.5 cm) thick and cut strips ¾ inch (2 cm) wide. Place the strips on the cake, crossing them in a diamond shape.
• Place one last strip as closure all around the border of the pan.
• Prepare the egg wash, lightly beating the egg white and the milk together in a small bowl.
• Brush the egg wash across the dough strips. Bake for about 35–40 minutes, or until golden.
• Let the pie cool at room temperature and then unmould. Serve lukewarm, sprinkled with powdered sugar.

CROSTATA DI VISCIOLE
cherries jam tart

This is the most classic Roman home dessert. Traditionally it is made with *visciole* jam. *Visciole* are a kind of morello, a sour cherry, available in the countryside around Rome. Used in jams and preserves, these cherries have an unmistakable bittersweet taste. You can use any type of jam for this pie. Dark-colored jams, such as strawberry or cherry, look nice in contrast with the light dough.

- 2½ cups (350 gr) flour
- ²/₃ cup (125 gr) sugar
- 6 oz (180 gr) butter, diced (at room temperature)
- 1 whole egg and 2 egg yolks
- pinch of salt
- grated rind of 1 lemon
- ½ lb (225 gr) cherry jam

- Pour the flour onto a work surface, to form a mound shape with a hole in the center.
- In the well, add the sugar, butter, eggs, egg yolks, pinch of salt, and grated lemon rind.
- Using a fork, mix the ingredients together with the flour. Work the paste rapidly with your hands, to form dough—avoid warming the dough too much.
- Sprinkle the work surface with some flour to prevent the dough from sticking to the table.

- When the dough is smooth and consistent, form it into a ball, place it on a plate, cover with plastic wrap, and keep in the refrigerator for about 30 minutes to 1 hour.
- Preheat oven to 350 F (175 C). Remove the dough from the refrigerator.
- Butter a shallow tart pan—11 inches (28 cm) in diameter x ¾-inch (2 cm) deep, with a removable bottom—and sprinkle with a small amount of flour.
- Cut the dough in two parts, one quarter and three quarters large.

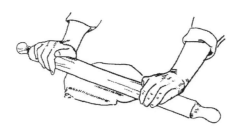

- Using a rolling pin on a floured surface, flatten the larger portion into the shape of a disk.
- Place the disk flat in the pan, and with your fingers push it to uniformly cover the bottom of the pan.

- Prick the surface of the pastry evenly with a fork. This step will prevent the dough from puffing while baking.

- Place the jam in the center of the cake; use a spoon to spread the jam around uniformly.
- Leave the perimeter of the tart free of jam, stopping about ½ inch (1 cm) before reaching the edge.
- Roll small pieces of the remaining dough to form long little sticks approximately ³/₈-inch (1 cm) thick.

- Place the sticks over the jam, creating diamond shapes by overlapping the pieces.
- Place the last stick around the perimeter.
- Flatten the sticks of pastry with the prongs of a fork.
- Bake the cake for about 35 minutes, until the pastry is golden brown.

CIAMBELLE DI PATATE
potato doughnuts

Potato doughnuts are another example of a foreign recipe adopted in Italy. *Krapfen,* which means "fritters" in German, must have been introduced in Italy through the northern regions. They even found their way to Naples, where they are known as *Graf.*

makes about 18

- ½ lb (225 gr) potatoes
- 1 tablespoon dry active yeast
- 3–4 tablespoons milk, warm
- 2½ cups (350 gr) flour
- 2 eggs
- 1 tablespoon (15 gr) butter, at room temperature
- grated rind of 1 lemon
- 1 tablespoon + ½ cup (100 gr) sugar
- pinch of salt
- ¼ teaspoon cinnamon powder
- frying oil

- Boil the potatoes; peel and mash them in a food mill while they are still hot.
- In a small bowl, dissolve the yeast in the warm milk.
- Pour the flour onto a work surface, to form a mound shape with a hole in the center.
- In the well, add the mashed potatoes, eggs, butter, lemon rind, 1 tablespoon of the sugar, the salt, and the milk-yeast mixture.
- Working with your hands, mix the ingredients together to form a very smooth and soft dough, adding some flour to the work surface to prevent the dough from sticking.

- Cut a portion of the dough. On a floured work surface, form little cylinders approximately ½ inch (1.5 cm) thick and approximately 4–5 inches (10–12 cm) long.

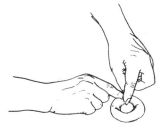

- Close and press the ends together to form small doughnuts.
- Place the doughnuts on a floured surface, cover with a cloth, and let them rest at room temperature for about 1 hour or until they double in volume.
- On a plate, combine ½ cup (100 gr) sugar and the cinnamon powder. Increase the amount of cinnamon powder to taste.
- In a pan, bring the oil to frying temperature. Fry the doughnuts until they are golden brown.
- Transfer the doughnuts on paper towels on a large plate and let the oil drain briefly.

- Dredge the doughnuts in the sugar-cinnamon mixture on all sides, and serve them hot.

MARITOZZI CON LA PANNA
raisin bread with whipped cream

Breakfast has never been an important meal to Italians. Traditionally, it has consisted of just a cappuccino and a croissant. In Rome, people frequently eat this light raisin bread filled with whipped cream.

for the sponge
♦ 1 cube fresh yeast
♦ ¾ cup (180 cc) warm water
♦ ²/₃ cup (100 gr) flour

for the dough
♦ 2½ cups (350 gr) flour
♦ ½ cup (100 gr) sugar
♦ pinch of salt
♦ 2 eggs
♦ 3 tablespoons extra-virgin olive oil
♦ grated rind of 1 orange
♦ 1 teaspoon vanilla
♦ 6 oz (180 gr) raisins, soaked in warm water and drained

for the glaze
♦ 4 tablespoons powdered sugar
♦ ½ cup (120 cc) water

for the filling
♦ 1 cup (230 cc) whipping cream
♦ 1 tablespoon powdered sugar

preparing the sponge
- In a bowl, dissolve the yeast in the warm water. Mix in the flour.
- Cover and set aside in a warm corner of the kitchen for about 1 hour or until it about doubles in volume.

preparing the dough
- In the bowl of a mixer fitted with a dough hook, place the flour, sugar, and a pinch of salt.
- Beat the eggs together with the olive oil.
- Add to the bowl the eggs, orange rind, vanilla, and the sponge. Run the mixer for about 10 minutes.
- Transfer the dough to a bowl lightly sprayed with extra-virgin olive oil.
- Cover with oiled plastic wrap and set it aside in a warm corner to rise for approximately 2 hours or until it about doubles in volume.
- Transfer to a lightly floured work surface. Flatten the dough.
- Spread the raisins on the dough. Fold the dough on itself several times until the raisins are uniformly distributed.
- Line two cookie sheets with parchment paper.
- Cut the dough into 16 small pieces. Shape the pieces into elongated ovals.
- Transfer the dough pieces to the cookie sheets, leaving about 3 inches (7–8 cm) between them.

- Cover loosely with a cloth and set them aside to rise for about 2 hours or until they about double in volume. Rising time will depend on the room temperature.
- Preheat oven to 370 F (190 C).

preparing the glaze
- Prepare syrup by dissolving the powdered sugar in ½ cup (120 cc) of water in a small bowl.
- To glaze the pastry, brush the syrup over the surface of the dough.
- Bake for about 20 minutes or until dark brown.
- Transfer the *maritozzi* onto a rack to cool.

filling the maritozzi
- Whip the cream and powdered sugar.
- Cut the *maritozzi* horizontally, and fill the middle with the whipped cream. Serve lukewarm.

CHAPTER 2

The Land of City States

The Food of Northern Italy

Almost anywhere you travel in Italy north of Rome, in the hill towns and the larger cities of the plains, you can observe fortifications or natural defenses: The walls, battlements, and towers convey the impression of a long history of urban conflicts. The towns, squares, cathedrals, and palaces, however, show a high sophistication in their administration, politics, commerce, and art. It is evident that at a certain point in history these towns acquired a strong sense of pride and independence.

The Comuni

To understand how these cities, known as the *Comuni* evolved, we must go back to Roman times. In those times the law prevented cities from building fortifications because the legions were enough to protect everyone from external violence. With the defeat of the Roman armies, the barbarians were able to swarm through the Italian territory almost without resistance. The cities were sacked, and the survivors took refuge in the most remote areas of the countryside. Inhabitants of northern Italy fleeing the Lombard invasion around 570 A.D. found shelter on the islands along the delta of the Po River. There the city of Venice was founded, protected by the lagoons of the north Adriatic Sea.

The Romans despised the "inferior" barbaric culture, but as the barbarians seized power, they imposed their laws on the land they occupied. These new rulers had different customs and eating habits. The Roman ideology considered uncultivated land insignificant, if not negative. Yet the Germanic populations lived in symbiosis with wild land and forests, where through stock raising, hunting, fishing, and gathering they received most of their food resources. The culture of bread, wine, and olive collided with that of meat, milk, and butter.

The church assimilated those same food symbols of the Romans—bread, wine, and oil—as part of Christian liturgy; and with the barbarians' progressive settling and conversion to Christianity, Roman culture found its way into the

new populations. In addition, the church mandated several fast days during the year when eating meat was forbidden. For this reason, alternate foods were necessary: On fast days, fish, legumes, and cheese were eaten instead of meat, and olive oil was used instead of pork fat. The permanent alternance of these foods was another factor that served to fuse these different civilizations, and in the early medieval times shaped a new European cooking culture.

After 1000 A.D., with the end of the barbaric invasions, the people of Italy began returning to the cities. A widespread increase in population occurred, boosting agricultural production, artisan manufacture, commerce in fairs and markets, and creating important new harbors such as Venice

Piazza delle Erbe ("Square of the Herbs"), in Verona.

This was, and remains today, the most important daily farmers' market in town. Every city in northern Italy has a *Piazza delle Erbe,* in the heart of downtown, close to the main square. Each city also has a palace and a duomo, generally built close by. Their towers and campanili show the juxtaposition of the two main powers of medieval times—the municipality and the church. The Piazzas *"delle Erbe"* of Parma and Mantova are also famous for their beauty.

and Genoa. A new political entity was being created: the Italian *Comuni*. The towns of northern and central Italy organized themselves into autonomous city republics, while the empire and the church had too little power to oppose them. Hostilities were frequent, making fortifications necessary.

We don't know very much about cooking during medieval times other than what has reached us through a few manuscripts. The cooking of the poor has not been documented; but we have many accounts of long periods of famine, and scarcity of food is believed to have been the norm for centuries. The table of the wealthy would not change much in times of famine, while common people would have to resign themselves to a table of food inferior to that normally eaten.

The Banquets of the Signori

In medieval times the large banquets were organized around U-shaped tables—the host would be at the center short end, sometimes on a pedestal. The most important guests would be closest to him. In a famous episode, Dante Alighieri, the celebrated Tuscan poet, was a victim of this protocol.

Invited by the King of Naples, he arrived at the banquet dressed with negligence, as many intellectuals used to do. He was placed at the far end of the table, away from the king. The king later recognized that Dante had not been treated properly, and so he invited Dante again. This time, Dante wore very luxurious dress and was placed close to the king. When the meal was served, Dante began pouring food on his clothes. The king, surprised, asked him the reason for this behavior, and Dante answered, "Holy Crown, I recognize that this great honor that was done, was done to the clothes, and I wanted the clothes to enjoy the food."

The meals were organized in many "services," the most important being the meat (substituted by fish on fasting days). Spices were used generously, as were contrasting tastes of bittersweet and sweet-and-sour, realized by the use of honey, dry fruits, bitter orange, lemon, and *agresto* (unripe grapes). The most conspicuous dishes would be served closer to the host and the important guests. The servings were delivered to the table all at the same time, with no prearranged sequence, and the guests would have to serve themselves from the plates that were close to them.

Guests had individual spoons for soup, but often they would have to share the dishes and knives. Forks became common only centuries later; so food was brought to the mouth with bear hands, while certain hot foods, like pasta, were eaten with the help of a stick. There were no towels. Good education taught to wash hands before dinner, but commonly people cleaned their fingers on the tablecloth.

Later in time, most of the towns coalesced into larger *signorie* (princedoms) that would acquire enormous power and wealth. Italy was divided into five main spheres of influence: Naples in southern Italy, Rome and the States of the Church, Florence with Tuscany, Venice in the northeast, and Milan in the northwest. In the sixteenth and seventeenth centuries, Venice, Verona, Genoa, Florence, Pisa, and Milan all became extremely rich through the commerce with the Islamic world as well as the trade between the Italian territories and northern Europe.

The wealth of the Italian *signori* of the Renaissance is legendary. The Scaligeri in Verona, the Sforza and Visconti in Milan, the Medici in Florence, the Este in Ferrara are still remembered for the splendor of their palaces, their endorsement of the arts, and the magnificence of their banquets. Walking through the streets of Venice today, you would still see the opulence, majesty, and power of this city. Venice, with the largest fleet of the Mediterranean, monopolized the commerce with the East. Venetian merchants would buy in Syria, Egypt, and Turkey the spices and the silks of the Orient, and they would sell them for an immense profit all over Europe.

Many books written during the sixteenth and seventeenth centuries tell about cooking in the courts of the nobility. Among the most famous are *Opera [...]*, by Bartolomeo Scappi (Venice, 1570), who was the cook for Pope Pius V in Rome; *Banchetti [...]*, by Cristoforo Messibugo (Ferrara, 1549), the cook for the Duke of Este. All of them have hundreds of recipes and concentrate on the magnificence of the banquets.

The famous banquet for the marriage of the Duke Alfonso II Este in December 1575 was dedicated to the pagan theme of Neptune, the god of the ocean. Everything was done to recreate the sub-marine world. The scenography was extremely complicated, beginning with frescoes on the ceiling that represented dolphins and sea scenes. The table of the prince was shaped like a reef, the wine cellar designed like a grotto; lace tablecloths reproduced ocean surf; and dishes in maiolica were ordered from Faenza for the occasion. Hundreds of sugar sculptures arrived from Venice. The food was a succession of hundreds of *servizi* of meat, fish, and sweets.

The cooking of the banquets was mostly an exhibition: "A good cook," says Scappi, "like a wise architect, after the design, has to establish good foundations, and then can contribute to the world useful and wonderful constructions . . ." In fact these banquets were rather social and political gatherings than eating experiences—always an exaggerated demonstration of richness and power.

The food, adorned and manipulated after being cooked, was assembled into the famous *trionfi della tavola,* the triumphs of the table. Most of these constructions arrived cold at the table; but that was irrelevant because the taste was less important than the look and most of the dishes were barely tasted. The food of the wealthy was then, more than ever, extremely rich with exotic spices: cinnamon, ginger, cloves, mace, and nutmeg. Sugar, an expensive commodity, was sprinkled everywhere.

Even if America was already discovered in 1492, no mention was made in these later books of the new crops that would revolutionize Western cuisine: Only the turkey, especially roasted, was adopted early for its size and good taste. Side by side with this exaggerated cooking style lived the everyday cooking, the gatherings of the artists and the gourmets, those who cook and dine for the pleasure of taste. During these times, the foundations of many regional, typical dishes were laid down. The *tortelli,* gnocchi, lasagne, and the cheeses, wines, and regional specialties all started to evolve.

Decadence of the City States

The fortune of Italian cities remained unchanged until the fall of Constantinople to the Ottoman Empire and the discovery of America. By then the interest of

73. Vende Formaggio Parmigiano.

world commerce had moved from the Mediterranean to the Atlantic. While in France, England, Germany, and Spain large nations were being created, Italy remained subdivided into many small political and territorial entities. The strategic importance of Italy diminished: The Italian cities could not compete with the larger states and soon became lands of conquest for foreign powers, which would maintain control in different parts of Italy until the unification in 1862. While Piedmont, the States of the Church, and Venice stayed out of these wars, most of the rest of Italy became dominated by Spanish rulers. Later, the Austrians dominated Lombardy and Veneto for about one century.

Even under foreign influence, the Italian cities never lost their identity.

Vende Formaggio Parmigiano (which means "sells parmesan cheese"), an engraving from "Le arti di Bologna" (the arts of Bologna), by Annibale Carracci, Rome 1646. *Parmigiano Reggiano* cheese goes back a long time, from about 1200 A.D. It is a hard cheese that comes in large wheels of about 80 lb (40 kg), 18 inches (45 cm) in diameter. Aging for 24 months gives the cheese a distinctive grainy, crunchy taste. The good Parmigiano cheese is made only in a small controlled area of Italy. Not only does the cheese need to be made in the confines of this district, but also the cows must be raised in the area, fed with grass and hay that grows within that zone.

The mark left by the latest foreign occupations was either limited or fully integrated into the local culinary traditions. At the same time, many unique food ingredients and original cooking techniques were developed and preserved in northern Italy, and they remain very popular all over the world today. A few examples: red radicchio from Treviso, balsamic vinegar from Modena, Parmigiano Reggiano from the Emilia region, prosciutto from Friuli, pesto from Liguria, and tortellini from Bologna.

Every region developed particular qualities depending on the history and geographical location. The lands along the alpine arch all have the characteristic of extending in part over the mountains, and in part in the Po valley.

Two main staples dominate in these areas: in the plain, rice in the form of risotto; and everywhere, maize in the form of polenta.

In spite of the long coastline, the cuisine of the north has fewer fish dishes than one would expect. The Mediterranean Sea is generally not as abundant in fish as the Atlantic. In addition, fish was difficult to deliver and never reached the regions of the interior, where fresh water or lake fishes are moderately present.

In contrast, the cuisine of Venice is rich with mollusks, crustaceans, sardines, and other fishes present in the lagoon. The Liguria region is famous for its cioppino, a fish stew that was transplanted to San Francisco by Genoese fishermen at the beginning of the last century. In this environment, *baccala'* (salt cod) or stockfish (dried cod), which are always available, became two of the main components of the local cuisine, and many sophisticated recipes in the Veneto region include one of them as an ingredient.

A quite different condition is present in the Emilia and Romagna areas, south of the Po River. The fertility of the land, the farming and abundance of wheat, as well as the pork breeding, made Bologna the culinary capital of Italy. Nicknamed *La Grassa* (the fat), this city is celebrated for its many fresh-pasta dishes. These dishes are present with profusion all over northern Italy, but in Bologna they are particularly sophisticated and refined ❖

ZUPPA D'ORZO
barley soup

Popular all over the mountainous Friuli and Trentino regions, barley soup is prepared in many different ways, and sometimes includes potatoes. Our recipe adds a small quantity of olive oil not found in the original preparation.

- 1 cup (150 gr) pearl barley
- 1 stick celery, diced
- 1 carrot, diced
- 1 medium onion, diced
- 3 tablespoons Italian parsley, finely chopped
- 2 cans, approximately 1 lb (450 gr) *borlotti* beans, drained
- 4 cups (approximately 1 liter) broth
- 2 tablespoons extra-virgin olive oil
- 1 oz (30 gr) butter
- 3 oz (85 gr) bacon, finely diced
- salt and pepper

- Soak the pearl barley in a small bowl filled with water for about 1 hour.
- Chop celery, carrot, onion, and half of the parsley finely together.
- Place half of the beans in a food processor and reduce to purée.
- In a saucepan, bring the broth to a boil.
- In a large saucepan, put the extra-virgin olive oil and butter.
- When the butter starts foaming, add the chopped vegetables and

the bacon, and turn the heat to medium.
- Add the puréed beans, the whole beans, the hot broth, salt, and pepper. Stir to combine.
- Drain the pearl barley, and stir into the soup.
- Cook for about 25 minutes, stirring occasionally, to prevent the soup from sticking to the pan. Adjust salt if necessary.
- When the barley is soft, turn heat off, spread the rest of the chopped parsley over the soup, and and let it rest covered in the saucepan for about 5 minutes vefore serving.

If the soup is prepared in advance, the barley will absorb most of the water, and the soup will become very dense. In this case, reserve some of the broth, heat it and stir it into the soup just before serving.

RISI E BISI
rice-and-pea soup

Peas have been cultivated on the hills and fields of Veneto for centuries. This ancient dish from the Serenissima (most serene) Republic of Venice was ritually offered to the doge, the ruler of the city, on the day celebrating Saint Mark. It is popular in all the regions that were in contact with or subject to Venice, including Dalmatia and Greece.

- 2 oz (60 gr) butter
- 2–3 tablespoons extra-virgin olive oil
- 4 oz (115 gr) bacon, finely diced
- 1 medium onion, finely chopped
- 4 oz (115 gr) small peas
- 8 cups (approximately 2 liters) broth
- 11 oz (300 gr) *arborio* or *vialone* rice
- salt and pepper
- 4–5 tablespoons parmigiano reggiano cheese, freshly grated
- 1 tablespoon Italian parsley, finely chopped

- In a saucepan, put the butter, olive oil, bacon, and onion. Turn heat to medium.
- When the onion becomes soft and the bacon is cooked, add peas, 4–5 tablespoons broth, stir, and cover. Cook for about 5–10 minutes.
- Add the rest of the broth, and bring the mixture to a boil.
- Add rice, and cook for about 20 minutes.
- When the rice is *al dente* (firm but not too soft or overcooked), and the soup has a dense consistency, taste and add salt if necessary. Add pepper, parmigiano cheese, and parsley.
- Stir briefly and serve warm.

MINESTRONE
vegetable soup

Minestrone as an expression means "a mixture of all things." In fact, any kind of seasonal vegetables can be used for the preparation of this soup. Every *minestrone* is different from another and is a work of art—with a thousand variations—depending on the season, the region, and the cook. The vegetables are added in different intervals, with the tender ones last, to avoid overcooking them.

serves 6
- 1 lb (450 gr) potatoes
- 4 oz (115 gr) carrots
- ½ lb (225 gr) zucchini
- 1 celery stick
- 4 oz (115 gr) onion
- 4 oz (115 gr) lettuce
- 4 oz (115 gr) fresh tomatoes
- 4 oz (115 gr) beets
- 3 tablespoons extra-virgin olive oil
- 2 tablespoons Italian parsley, finely chopped
- 1 cup (230 cc) homemade broth
- 4 cups water
- salt
- 4 oz (115 gr) short *ditali* pasta, or spaghetti broken in ½ inch (1–2 cm) pieces
- pepper
- 4 tablespoons parmigiano reggiano cheese, freshly grated

- Finely dice the potatoes, carrots, zucchini, celery, onion, lettuce, tomatoes, and beets. Keep each of the vegetables separate
- In a stockpot, put the extra-virgin olive oil, and turn the heat to medium.
- Add the potatoes, carrots, celery, and onion. Sauté the vegetables briefly.
- Add the parsley and tomatoes, and stir all together. Add the broth and water, salt lightly, and bring to a boil.
- After about 10 minutes add the zucchini, lettuce, and beets. Cook for an additional 10 minutes.
- Add the pasta, and let it cook for the time indicated by the manufacturer. Taste for readiness from time to time, until *al dente* (firm but not too soft or overcooked).
- Correct salt if necessary. Add a pinch of pepper and the grated parmigiano.
- Serve warm in soup plates or bowls. Add more freshly grated parmigiano, if desired.

Minestrone doesn't need to have pasta in it. In case the pasta is not included, skip the last step and cook the vegetables a little longer, until ready. To give more taste to the dish, add a little piece of parmigiano or *pecorino romano* cheese (1 oz, 30 gr) to the pot. Let the cheese cook until the end and remove it only before serving.

Gnocchi

The Italian word *gnocco* means "a stupid person." This induced some food writers to declare that the dish *gnocchi* is responsible for the association—but gnocchi is anything but a stupid dish. These small dumplings are one of the oldest preparations in the history of food, recorded as far back as cookbooks of the fourteenth and sixteenth centuries.

They can be made with the most varied ingredients, such as squash, bread, and semolina flour; and they can be flavored with spinach, saffron, and even truffles. They are also one of the most refined dishes, worthy of the most sophisticated menues.

While the ancient *gnocchi* were made with bread or cheese, today they are made with potatoes, which has become traditional in many Italian regions.

To achieve the best results, it is important to choose the right type of potato. The potato needs to be floury, with minimum water content. The best are old Russet potatoes, low in water and high in starch. Round (white or red) or Yukon potatoes would be too waxy, which would make the *gnocchi* either too heavy or too gummy, or would cause them to break apart in the boiling water. The addition of egg to the dough serves the purpose of holding the preparation together better. The choice of the right potato potentially makes the use of the eggs optional. The potatoes can be baked in the oven, but more often are boiled. In this case do not peel them but boil them with the skin on. This will avoid absorption of excess water. For the same reason, don't break or pierce them. Too much water will cause the preparation to absorb too much flour and make the gnocchi too heavy.

In spite of the long description, *gnocchi* are very easy to prepare. Like pasta they can be dressed with many sauces, but are especially good with pesto, *Amatriciana* sauce, *Ragu'*, four cheeses, or butter and fresh tomato sauce, as in our presentation. The taste of this butter-tomato sauce is very delicate and will enhance the taste of the dish ❖

GNOCCHI DI PATATE AL BURRO E POMODORO
potato dumplings with butter-tomato sauce

prepare the butter tomato sauce according to the recipe on page 120

for the gnocchi
- 2 lb (approximately 1 kg) whole old russet potatoes, unpeeled
- 2 cups (approximately 300 gr) flour
- 1 egg (optional)
- 1 tablespoon salt

preparing the gnocchi
- Wash the potatoes, place them in a large stock pot filled with water, and bring to a boil.
- Cook until the potatoes are soft without overcooking to prevent them from breaking. Cooking time may vary depending on the size of the potatoes.
- Peel immediately while potatoes are still hot, and mash them on a work surface using a potato masher or a food mill.
- When the potatoes are cool enough to be handled, add 1 cup (150 gr) of the flour, the egg, and salt. Mix all together to form dough: at this point the dough will be sticky on your hands.
- Sprinkle a little of the remaining flour on the surface, and work the dough with your hands until the potato dough incorporates the flour. Continue adding flour a little at a time until the potato dough is no longer too sticky.
- Cut the dough into four pieces. Sprinkle the work surface with a little flour, and place the first piece on it.

- With your hands, roll the dough into a long stick approximately ¾ inch (2 cm) in diameter.

- Then cut the sticks into pieces ¾ inch (2 cm) long.

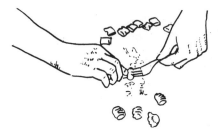

- Roll the pieces along the prongs of a common fork using one finger, in a way that the side of the piece running along the fork will be ruffled and the side you are pressing with your finger will be a little concave.

- A similar result is obtained by rolling the *gnocchi* on the surface of a cheese grater.
- Work constantly on a lightly floured surface. Place the *gnocchi* on a dry and clean cloth. Repeat the step with the rest of the dough.

- Fill a stockpot three quarters full with water, bring to a boil, and add salt. When the water is at a fast boil, drop the *gnocchi* in a few at a time to avoid damaging them. The gnocchi will drop to the bottom of the pan.
- After about 1–2 minutes the gnocchi will come up to the surface, and this will be the sign that they are cooked.

- Don't drain *gnocchi* in a colander as you would do with pasta. *Gnocchi* are very soft and may be damaged. Instead remove them with the help of a large slotted spoon or strainer, draining thoroughly.
- Place in a bowl; add the sauce, the parmigiano cheese, and mix gently together. Serve immediately.

Potatoes

The CIA (Culinary Institute of America) classifies potatoes in three basic varieties:

Idaho and Russet potatoes, also known as "bakers," are high in starch and low in moisture. Therefore, after being cooked they are more granular, floury, and dry. They are preferred for mashed potatoes, gnocchi, croquettes, frying, and baking. Dryness and starch content increase with aging.

All-purpose or "Chef's" potatoes (Yukon Gold are part of this category) have moderate amounts of starch and moisture. They are preferred for salads, scalloped preparations, casseroles, and soups.

New potatoes (Round White, Round Red, Irish) generally are smaller in size and have low starch and high water content. They are good for boiling, steaming, and salads, due to their natural sweet flavor.

Cooking Potatoes

- Remove green spots, sprouts, and eyes from the potatoes, because they can be toxic.
- Cook the potatoes with the skin when possible, to retain their nutrients and flavor.
- When boiled with the skin, the potatoes will absorb a very small amount of water.
- Peel the potatoes while they are still hot.
- When peeling raw potatoes, drop them in cold water after having peeled them to avoid discoloration.

Risotto

How rice arrived in Italy is a controversial issue. It is known that the Arabs took rice to Sicily and Spain. They probably got it from India and extended its use through the territory under their control. Rice was brought into the Po Valley in the fourteenth century—probably from Spain—and found the perfect environment and climate: flat lands, abundance of water, and humidity. Cultivation of rice became intensive in the area for the centuries that followed, so much that rice became a staple in that part of Italy.

The legend of the invention of *Risotto alla Milanese* goes back to the year 1574. The *Duomo di Milano,* the magnificent Gothic cathedral, was being built, and a young apprentice by the name of Valerius was in charge of staining the decorated glass for the windows. Everybody was teasing him because he appeared to have added saffron to the pigments to obtain a more brilliant color. Tired of the teasing, he decided to return the joke and added saffron to the rice to be served at his master's wedding. The rice turned out so good that the idea spread immediately throughout the city and became the popular dish we know today.

The technique for making risotto probably came from trying to cook the rice as a—*puls* (similar to porridge)—boiling it in milk, water, or broth until soft. In fact, a sort of rice porridge cooked in milk and sugar, *rixo in bona manera* ("rice in a good manner"), was documented in Venice since the fourteenth century.

The *Mondine*. In May, every year before mechanization and until the 1960s, thousands of women left their homes in Emilia and Veneto to go to work in the rice fields. They became a legendary sight in northern Italy, inspiring poets, artists, and movie makers. Many women worked for the first time far from home and family ties, in a freedom never dreamed before. For eight hours they worked barefoot in the water, protected from the sun by large straw hats. Dressing in short pants and long sleeves to protect their arms and legs from insects, they slowly walked backward, in a long row, bending toward the ground to pick up the weeds that infested the rice fields. Famous are the melodies they sang—about their tough days, their resentment for the supervisors, but also about love and their home far away.

Risotto is a very simple and nutritious dish, and easy to prepare. There are hundreds of types of Risotto, varying from the flavoring ingredient used; but in all the recipes you will need four basic components: *soffritto* (sautéed vegetables), broth, flavoring ingredients, and Italian rice.

The *soffritto* generally is a combination of vegetables, butter, oil, and finely diced onions, sautéed in a large skillet where rice will be cooked. However, sometimes a special recipe calls for different ingredients.

The broth, depending on the recipe, could be beef, chicken, vegetable, or fish. A good broth—homemade or canned—is the basis of a good risotto. To simplify the recipe, broth can be substituted with one or two bouillon cubes dissolved in warm water.

The flavoring ingredient is what will give the risotto dish its characteristic flavor. Generally it is added to the *soffritto*, and it can be anything from vegetables (such as mushrooms, spinach, or endive), to *ragu'*, seafood, meat, truffles, saffron, or wine, to name some examples.

The Italian rice varieties all have large grains, are rich in starch, and have the capacity of absorbing a considerable amount of cooking liquid while still remaining firm. Three basic types of rice are common in Italy:

Arborio rice is the best-known variety and the Italian housewives' favorite, perhaps because its grain is very large. Arborio Rice is particularly suitable for risotto because it is easy to cook *al dente* without overcooking.

Vialone rice has a smaller grain and is very common in the Veneto area. Generally it is cooked *all'onda* (wavy), that is, consistent but still soft and not too dry.

Carnaroli is first-rate rice, cultivated mainly in the Piemonte area. It cooks uniformly without overcooking, has a very special taste, and mingles very well with condiments. *Carnaroli* will absorb a larger amount of liquid. It is particularly suitable for risotto and rice salad.

At the end, butter and parmigiano cheese generally are added to risotto to complete the dish. The final result is a consistent paste, with the individual rice grains still firm but sticking together due to the high content of starch. Risotto is generally very satisfying and can be served as a first course or as a main course standing on its own ❖

Perfect Risotto

Preparing a good risotto is very easy, but a few guidelines should be followed:

- The rice must not be washed before cooking. Washing would eliminate a large part of the starch that gives the risotto its texture.
- Choose the most appropriate variety of rice for the recipe you will prepare: *Carnaroli* for a consistent risotto, *Vialone* for a *risotto all'onda*, *Arborio* for all the types of risotto.
- Allow about 3–4 oz (75–100 gr) of rice for each serving.
- Use a large double-bottom sauté pan to keep the heat uniform.
- Gently fry the butter and the extra-virgin olive oil (½ tablespoon per person) without browning it.
- Sauté the chopped onion on a low temperature, until translucent.
- Add the rice to the sautéed onion, and toast the mixture on a very low heat for a maximum of 2 minutes, stirring constantly. Do not cook too long or the rice grains could harden. In that case they would no longer cook homogeneously and they could loose their ability to absorb the condiments.

- When the rice is toasted, dry white or red wine can be added if required by the recipe.
- The secret to an excellent risotto is using a good homemade broth (see recipe at page 67). Keep the broth simmering all the time.
- At this point, turn the heat to medium and add half of the indicated amount of broth to the rice.
- Keep the heat at medium until the rice is fully cooked.
- Continue adding the remaining broth, one ladle at a time, stirring often with a wooden spoon to prevent the risotto from sticking to the pan, and until the rice has absorbed all the broth.
- When the rice is close to fully cooked, taste it for readiness—neither too hard nor too soft, but just *al dente*.
- All Italian rices will cook *al dente* in about 18–20 minutes.
- When the risotto is ready, remove the pan from the stove to avoid overcooking.
- Stir into the risotto the butter and the freshly grated Parmigiano Reggiano cheese, as required by the recipe.
- Immediately pour the risotto into a warm serving dish, and wait 2-3 minutes before serving.

RISOTTO ALLA MILANESE
saffron risotto

For many people in Milan, Risotto remains the most important dish. Saffron is the key ingredient of this dish and gives the traditional flavor and color (the word "saffron" comes from the Arabic word for "yellow").

- 5 cups (approximately 1 liter) broth
- ¼ teaspoon saffron powder
- 3 + 2 tablespoons (45 + 30 gr) butter
- 1 medium onion, very finely chopped
- 1½ cups (300 gr) *arborio* rice
- ½ cup (120 cc) dry white wine
- salt and pepper
- 4 oz (115 gr) parmigiano reggiano cheese, freshly grated

- Warm the broth to a simmer.
- In a small bowl, dissolve the saffron in ½ cup (120 c) broth and put this to the side.
- In a large saucepan, put 3 tablespoons (45 gr) of the butter, and turn heat to medium.
- When the butter begins foaming, add the onion. Sauté and stir with a wooden spoon for a few minutes until the onion becomes soft.
- Add the rice; stir for about 2 minutes; add the wine and stir to evaporate it.

- Add ¼ cup (60 cc) broth, and salt and pepper. Stir continuously to prevent the rice from sticking. When the rice begins absorbing the liquid, add more broth.
- Repeat this step of adding the broth and stirring, keeping the rice at the consistency of a dense paste.
- After about 10 minutes, stir in the ½ cup (120 cc) broth that has the dissolved saffron.
- After about 8 more minutes, add 2 tablespoons (30 gr) butter and the grated parmigiano cheese. Continue stirring and adding broth.
- The rice will be ready in about 2 more minutes, when *al dente,* (firm but not too soft or overcooked). Cooking time may vary. Serve warm.

RISOTTO AI QUATTRO FORMAGGI
four cheeses risotto

- 5 cups (approximately 1 liter) broth
- 2 tablespoons extra-virgin olive oil
- 3 tablespoons (45 gr) butter
- 1 medium onion, finely chopped
- 1½ cups (300 gr) *arborio* rice
- ½ cup (120 cc) white dry wine
- salt and pepper
- 2 oz (60 gr) freshly grated parmigiano reggiano cheese

- 2 oz (60 gr) swiss cheese, finely diced
- 2 oz (60 gr) *fontina* cheese, finely diced
- 2 oz (60 gr) gorgonzola cheese, finely diced

- Warm the broth to a simmer. In a saucepan put extra-virgin olive oil and butter, and turn heat to medium.
- When the butter begins foaming, add the onion. Sauté and stir with a wooden spoon for a few minutes until the onion becomes soft.
- Add the rice; stir for about 2 minutes; add wine and stir to evaporate it.
- Add ¼ cup (60 cc) broth, and salt and pepper. Stir continuously to prevent the rice from sticking to the pan. When the rice begins absorbing the liquid, add more broth.
- Repeat this step of adding the broth and stirring, keeping the rice at the consistency of a dense paste.
- After about 18 minutes, stir in the parmigiano reggiano cheese, swiss cheese, *fontina* cheese, and gorgonzola cheese. Continue stirring and adding broth.
- The rice will be ready in about 2 more minutes, when *al dente,* (firm but not too soft or overcooked). Cooking time may vary. Serve warm.

RISOTTO AI FUNGHI PORCINI SECCHI
risotto with dry porcini mushroom

♦ ½ oz (15 gr) dry *porcini* mushrooms
♦ 5 cups (approximately 1 liter) broth
♦ 3 tablespoons extra-virgin olive oil
♦ 3 + 2 tablespoons (45 + 30 gr) butter
♦ 1 medium onion, finely chopped
♦ 1 garlic clove, finely diced
♦ 1 bunch Italian parsley, finely chopped
♦ 1½ cups (300 gr) *arborio* rice
♦ ¼ cup (60 cc) dry white wine
♦ salt and pepper
♦ 4 oz (115 gr) parmigiano reggiano cheese, freshly grated

- In a small bowl, soak the dry mushrooms in warm water for about 1 hour, or until soft.
- Warm the broth to a simmer.
- In a saucepan put the extra-virgin olive oil and 3 tablespoons (45 gr) of the butter. Turn heat to medium.
- When the butter starts foaming, add the onion and garlic, and sauté until the onion becomes soft.
- Add the mushrooms, 3–4 tablespoons of the mushroom water, and half of the parsley, and sauté for few minutes.

- Add the rice; stir for about 2 minutes; add the wine and stir to evaporate it.
- Add ¼ cup (60 cc) broth, and salt and pepper. Stir continuously to prevent the rice from sticking to the pan. When the rice begins absorbing the liquid, add more broth.
- Repeat this step of adding the broth and stirring, keeping the rice at the consistency of a dense paste.
- After about 18 minutes stir in the parmigiano reggiano cheese, and 2 tablespoons (30 gr) butter. Continue stirring and adding broth.
- The rice will be ready in about 2 more minutes, when *al dente* (firm but not too soft or overcooked).
- When the risotto is ready, top with the rest of the chopped parsley. Cooking time may vary. Serve warm.

RISOTTO CON ZUCCA E RADICCHIO
risotto with pumpkin and radicchio

♦ 1½ (500 gr) pumpkin
♦ 5 cups (approximately 1 liter) broth
♦ 3 tablespoons extra-virgin olive oil
♦ 3 + 2 tablespoons (45 + 30 gr) butter
♦ 1 medium onion, finely diced
♦ 1½ cups (300 gr) *arborio* rice
♦ salt and pepper

♦ 4 oz (115 gr) red radicchio, chopped
♦ 4 oz (115 gr) parmigiano reggiano cheese, freshly grated

- Skin the pumpkin, remove seeds, and cut in small dice.
- Warm the broth to a simmer.
- In a saucepan, put olive oil and 3 tablespoons (45 gr) of the butter. Turn heat to medium.
- When the butter starts foaming, add the onion, and sauté until the onion becomes soft.
- Add the pumpkin, and approximately ½ cup (120 cc) broth. Cover and cook for about 5–10 minutes or until soft.
- Add the rice, and stir for about 2 minutes. Add salt, pepper, and ¼ cup (60 cc) broth.
- Stir continuously to prevent the rice from sticking to the pan. When the rice begins absorbing the liquid, add more broth.
- Repeat this step of adding the broth and stirring, keeping the rice at the consistency of a dense paste.
- After about 10 minutes, add the radicchio. Continue adding the broth and stirring as indicated above.
- After about 8 more minutes, add 2 tablespoons (30 gr) butter, the parmigiano reggiano cheese, and continue stirring and adding broth.
- The rice will be ready in about 2 more minutes, when *al dente* (firm but not too soft or overcooked). Cooking time may vary. Serve warm.

RISOTTO CON GLI SPINACI
spinach risotto

- 1 lb (450 gr) spinach
- 5 cups (approximately 1 liter) broth
- 2 tablespoons extra-virgin olive oil
- 3 + 2 tablespoons (45 + 30 gr) butter
- 1 medium onion, finely chopped
- 1 garlic clove, finely chopped
- 1½ cups (300 gr) *arborio* rice
- salt and pepper
- ½ cup (120 cc) dry white wine
- 4 oz (115 gr) parmigiano reggiano cheese, freshly grated

- Clean and boil the spinach. Squeeze it to remove the water as much as possible, and chop finely.
- Warm the broth to a simmer.
- In a saucepan, put extra-virgin olive oil and 3 tablespoons (45 gr) of the butter. Turn heat to medium.
- When the butter starts foaming, add onion and garlic, and sauté until the onion becomes soft.
- Add the rice; stir for about two minutes; add salt, pepper, and wine; and stir to evaporate the wine.
- Add spinach and ¼ cup (60 cc) broth. Stir continuously to prevent the rice from sticking to the pan, and when the rice begins absorbing the liquid, add additional broth

- Repeat this step of adding the broth and stirring, keeping the rice at the consistency of a dense paste.
- After about 18 minutes add the cream, 2 tablespoons (30 gr) butter, and the parmigiano reggiano cheese. Continue stirring and adding broth.
- The rice will be ready in about 2 more minutes, when *al dente* (firm but not too soft or overcooked). Cooking time may vary. Serve warm.

RISOTTO ALLA MARINARA
seafood risotto

- 8 oz (225 gr) small squids
- 4 oz (115 gr) shrimps
- 1½ cup (350 cc) water
- 10 oz (285 gr) clams
- 10 oz (285 gr) mussels
- 5 tablespoons extra-virgin olive oil
- crushed red pepper
- 1 garlic clove, finely chopped
- 2 tablespoons Italian parsley, finely chopped
- 1½ cups (300 gr) *arborio* rice
- ½ cup (120 cc) dry white wine
- 3 cups (approximately 750 cc) fish broth
- salt

- Clean and slice the squid.
- Shell and devein the shrimps.
- In a saucepan on medium heat, put 1½ cups (120 cc) water, and the clams and mussels, and cover.

- Remove the mollusks one at a time as soon as they begin opening.
- Filter the cooking water from impurities and sand, and reserve it.
- Remove clams and mussels from the shells.
- In a large saucepan put olive oil, garlic, red pepper, and 1 tablespoon of the parsley.
- Before the garlic starts coloring, add the rice and sauté for about 2 minutes.
- Add the wine, and turn the heat to medium-high to evaporate it.
- Lower the heat, and add ¼ cup (60 cc) broth.
- Stir continuously to prevent the rice from sticking to the pan. When the rice begins absorbing the liquid, add more broth.
- Repeat this step of adding the broth and stirring, keeping the rice at the consistency of a dense paste. Taste and add salt if necessary.
- After about 15 minutes add the squid and shrimps.
- After about 3 more minutes, right before the risotto is ready, add the clams and mussels.
- The rice will be ready in about 2 more minutes, when *al dente* (firm but not too soft or overcooked). Cooking time may vary. Serve warm topped with the rest of the fresh parsley.

Polenta

The origins of polenta can be traced back to the Etruscans. They prepared a dish called *puls,* a mixture of mashed grains boiled in water, which eventually was enriched with any kind of dressing available at the moment. It was a very practical food—economical and easy to make—and the Romans inherited and diffused it everywhere. Under the name *pulmentum,* it became the food Roman legions ate while conquering the world: The present version of the Roman *pulmentum* is polenta, made today with cornmeal.

Apparently corn was introduced to Italy in 1494 by a Venetian diplomat who received a few seeds as a present, soon after Columbus's return from his travels to the Indies. In Venice, corn was erroneously called *grano turco* (Turkish wheat), a name still used today. Due to its capacity to produce a large yield gradually, corn cultivation was developed all over the Veneto area. Soon, polenta made from corn replaced all other grains (mainly sorghum and millet) used until then. It became the food of all the peasants too poor to afford bread, especially in the mountainous areas and valleys of the Alps. For this reason, for a long time corn was considered a food of inferior quality.

Maize was also a very convenient crop for the owners of large estates to economically feed their workers. Consequently, in large areas of northern Italy, corn polenta became a unique staple—a condition that would soon lead to disastrous consequences: Maize is missing an important vitamin, niacin, indi-

Polenta. From a painting by Pietro Longhi, Venice 1740. The painter left an extensive documentation of everyday life in the city. In this domestic scene, two women pour polenta from the typical copper cauldron. The background shows the fireplace where the polenta was cooked.

spensable for the body; niacin deficiency causes "pellagra," a fatal disease. This illness was unknown to the populations of the Americas who ate corn with other food, therefore integrating the missing element. In northern Italy the phenomenon reached epidemic proportions. After a few decades and thousands of fatalities, the cause was finally understood at the beginning of the 1800s. The addition of a little meat or vegetables to the diet was the easy cure for the disease.

Polenta generally is associated with northern Italy, but it is popular in many regions, and there are many different ways to make it: In northern Italy it would be solid and then cut into slices to accompany other food as a substitute for bread. In central Italy polenta would have the consistency of porridge, and would be dressed with different sauces. Famous is the *Polenta con le Spuntature* (polenta with pork ribs and tomato sauce) of Abruzzi.

Most frequently polenta was made in a large copper cauldron hung over the fire in the wood-burning fireplace, and was stirred continuously with a wooden stick. Then the paste was poured onto a wooden board.

Polenta is an extremely versatile dish that can be fried, grilled, baked, or eaten on its own topped with meat or tomato sauce ❖

BASIC POLENTA

Polenta is generally used in northern Italy as a substitute for bread. It is unmolded from the pot directly onto a wooden board in the shape of a semisphere; then, when cold, it is sliced with a wire. In central Italy it is instead mostly used as a first course by itself. The polenta is poured onto a wooden board and spread in a thin layer, then dressed with different sauces.

Regular polenta cooks in about 45 minutes. The quantity of water will determine the final consistency of the polenta. Stirring polenta can be very hard work, and in Italy electrical devices do the job. Also, precooked polenta, needing only a few minutes of preparation, can be found in the stores. Many Italian manufacturers offer a pre-steamed, good-quality product. If using one of these, follow the manufacturer's directions for time and quantity of water.

♦ 7 cups (1600 cc) water
♦ 2 teaspoons salt
♦ 1 teaspoon extra-virgin olive oil
♦ 17 oz (500 gr) corn flour

• Prepare a saucepan full of water, and bring it to a simmer for eventual use during the preparation.
• In a stockpot, put 7 cups (1600 cc) water, salt, olive oil, and turn heat to medium.
• Just before the water starts boiling, add the corn flour a little at a time, stirring continuously with a whisk, to prevent the polenta from clotting.
• Continue to stir with a wooden spoon, and boil the polenta for about 45 minutes. The absorption of water depends on the quality of the flour. If the polenta becomes too hard, add some warm water to adjust the consistency, until it is like a dense paste.
• While the polenta is still hot, pour it onto a wooden board or transfer it to serving dishes.

POLENTA CON FUNGHI E GORGONZOLA
polenta with mushrooms and gorgonzola

for the dressing
♦ 1 oz (30 gr) dry *porcini* mushrooms
♦ 3 + 1 tablespoons extra-virgin olive oil
♦ 2 cloves of garlic
♦ 4 oz (115 gr) fresh mushrooms, sliced
♦ 1 cup (230 cc) broth
♦ salt and pepper
♦ 6 oz (180 gr) sweet gorgonzola cheese
♦ 1 cup (230 cc) heavy cream
for the polenta
♦ 7 cups (1600 cc) water
♦ 2 teaspoons salt
♦ 1 teaspoon extra-virgin olive oil
♦ 17 oz (500 gr) corn flour

• Soak dry mushrooms in warm water until tender, then drain.
• In a skillet, put 3 tablespoons of the olive oil, and add the garlic. Sauté until the garlic becomes pale gold.
• Remove the garlic from the pan, add the fresh mushrooms and the soaked dry mushrooms.
• Add a small quantity of broth, and salt and pepper; cook for about 20 minutes, adding a little broth when necessary to keep the mixture moist; then turn off the heat.
• Cut the cheese in slices. In a small saucepan put 1 tablespoon olive oil and the cheese on low heat.
• Stir constantly until the cheese is completely melted.
• Add heavy cream, salt and pepper and mix to amalgamate.
• Prepare the polenta as indicated in the previous recipe. Pour into warm, shallow, single-serving dishes.
• Turn heat back on under the skillet that has the mushrooms. Add the cheese-cream mixture, stirring for a little while until it becomes a fluid cream.
• Top the polenta with the mushroom cream and serve immediately.

43

POLENTA TARAGNA
polenta with cheese

Polenta *Taragna* is typical of the northern mountainous area of Veneto, and it is locally prepared using cheeses typical of the area. This dish is often served accompanied by sausage.

- 7 cups (1600 cc) water
- 2 teaspoons salt
- 1 teaspoon extra-virgin olive oil
- 17 oz (500 gr) corn flour
- 5 oz (140 gr) butter
- 10 oz (285 gr) soft cheese such as Italian *fontina*, diced

- Prepare polenta as indicated in basic recipe on page 43.
- Before removing the pot from the stove, add the butter and cheese, and stir to melt them.
- Un-mould the polenta; serve hot.

POLENTA CON LE SPUNTATURE
polenta with pork ribs and tomato sauce

Polenta is always associated with northern Italy, but it is also very common in other regions. This recipe is typical of the Abruzzi and Lazio countryside

for the dressing
- 2½ lb (approximately 1200 gr) pork ribs, (approximately 3 ribs per person)
- 1 medium onion, chopped
- 3–4 tablespoons extra-virgin olive oil
- ½ cup (120 cc) dry white wine
- 2 lbs (900 gr) tomatoes, puréed in a blender
- salt and pepper
- 4 oz (115 gr) *pecorino romano* cheese, freshly grated

for the polenta
- 7 cups (1600 cc) water
- 2 teaspoons salt
- 17 oz (500 gr) corn flour
- 1 teaspoon extra-virgin olive oil

- Separate ribs individually from each other.
- In a large skillet, sauté the onion in the extra-virgin olive oil, until the onion is soft and translucent.
- Add the ribs, and cook them until uniformly brown. Pour wine and let it evaporate.
- Add tomatoes, salt, and pepper. Lower heat to medium-low and cook slowly covered for about 2 hours.
- Prepare polenta as indicated in the basic recipe on page 43. Pour it into warm, shallow, single-serving dishes, in a thin layer approximately ¾ inch (2 cm) thick.
- Top with the ribs, the tomato sauce, and an abundant amount of the grated pecorino cheese

Polenta can also be poured all at the same time onto a wooden board in a single layer approximately ¾ inch (2 cm) thick, topped with the ribs, the sauce, and the cheese. The guests can then serve themselves, cutting out slices of polenta from the serving board.

A Tribe of Meat Eaters

During 566 A.D., the Lombards, led by the young king Alboin, reached the Alps—they were a group of 200,000 including women and children. Alboin had just won a war against the Gepidae, a tribe in constant warfare with them. Having killed Cunimund, the Gepidae king, Alboin fashioned his skull into a cup and took the Cunimund's daughter, Rosamund as his wife.

The Lombards encountered almost no resistance, and soon they conquered most of northern and central Italy. But Alboin wouldn't last long enough to enjoy his victory: In 573 he was murdered—poisoned by a servant on instigation by Rosamund, who never forgave him for having forced her to drink from her father's skull. The occupation of the Lombards lasted for about two hundred years, until they were finally defeated by Charlemagne in 800 A.D.

The Lombards never assimilated with the Italians, who considered them "a disgusting and horrible" race, capable only of plunder and destruction. The cookery of the Lombards was significantly different from that of the Italians and was based on plenty of meat.

The Lombards introduced to Italy the practice of slowly cooking meat for a long time to tenderize it. From those times arose the tradition of *Brasato* and *Stracotto*, slowly cooked meat stews, and the origination of *Bollito Misto* (see recipe next page) ❖

BOLLITO MISTO
mixed boiled meats

Bollito misto is popular all over northern Italy. In the Piemonte region it is prepared using up to fourteen different kinds of meat and served with up to seven sauces. Homemade *bollito* can be a very simple preparation of several types of meats boiled and brought to the table steamy hot.

In Italy, the meats would include beef tongue, veal shanks, *cotechino* (a large pork sausage), *zampone* (pork feet boned and filled with pork meat). In Verona, *Bollito Misto* is served with *Salsa Peara'* (a mild horseradish-pepper sauce). Other sauces include green parsley sauce (see following recipe) or red tomato sauce.

- 1 bunch of parsley
- 2–3 bay leaves
- 1 tablespoon peppercorns
- 1 whole garlic clove, peeled
- 2–3 cloves
- 1 large whole onion, skinned
- salt
- varied choice of meats (depending of availability): beef, beef bone with marrow, hen, turkey, chicken
- 1 whole carrot
- 3–4 sticks of celery

- In a cheesecloth, tie the parsley, bay leaves, peppercorns, and garlic to form a bouquet-garni.
- Stick the cloves on the surface of the onion.
- Fill a large stockpot with water. Calculate approximately ½ gallon (approximately 2 liters) of water and 1 oz (30 gr) salt for every 2 lb of meat.
- When the water is boiling, add the beef, onion, carrot, celery, and bouquet-garni.
- Bring to a boil again; lower the flame; and let the mixture simmer slowly for approximately 1 hour.
- Occasionally, using a strainer, eliminate the foam that forms on the surface of the pot while the mixture is boiling.
- Add the poultry, and continue boiling for 2 more hours, or until the meat is tender.
- When the meat is ready, remove it from the pot, discard the vegetables, place on a warm serving plate, and serve steaming hot, accompanied by the sauce.

The broth can be reserved and used for other recipes. To obtain a good boiled meat, add it to the pot when the water is already boiling. To instead obtain a good broth, place the meat in the pot while the water is still cold.

SALSA VERDE
green sauce

This simple and tasty sauce can be used on either boiled meat or fish. When using green sauce on fish, substitute lemon juice to vinegar.

- ½ lb (225 gr) bread crumbs
- ½ cup (120 cc) meat broth
- 2 eggs, hard-boiled
- 6 anchovy fillets
- 3 tablespoons pine nuts
- ½ lb (225 gr) Italian parsley
- 1 oz (30 gr) capers in salt, rinsed and drained
- 2 garlic cloves
- 1–2 tablespoons (depending on the strength) white wine vinegar
- ½ cup (120 cc) extra-virgin olive oil
- salt and pepper

- Soak the bread crumbs lightly in broth, and squeeze them to remove the excess liquid.
- Chop the eggs, anchovies, pine nuts, parsley, capers, and garlic, by hand or in a food processor finely together.
- Add the lemon juice, and extra-virgin olive oil.
- Combine enough bread crumbs to give the sauce the consistency of a dense paste.
- Add salt and pepper, and stir thoroughly to combine all the ingredients.

BRASATO AL BAROLO
beef pot roast in barolo wine

serves 6

- 2 lb (900 gr) beef for roasting
- 1 oz (30 gr) bacon, diced
- ½ bottle Barolo wine
- 1 carrot, finely diced
- 2 celery sticks, finely diced
- 1 medium onion, finely diced
- 1 bay leaf
- ½ teaspoon cinnamon powder
- 1 tablespoon thyme leaves, finely chopped
- 2 tablespoons butter
- 4 tablespoons extra-virgin olive oil
- 1 tablespoon tomato paste
- 3–4 tablespoons broth
- salt and pepper

- Using a sharp knife, cut a few small incisions on the surface of the meat. Insert the bacon dice into the cavities.
- Place the meat in a saucepan; add the wine, carrot, celery, onion, bay leaf, cinnamon, and thyme. Marinate for about 12 hours.
- Drain the meat and reserve the marinade.
- In a large saucepan, put butter and olive oil; place on medium heat.
- When the butter starts foaming, add the meat and cook it, turning the meat several times until it is brown.
- Add the marinade, and cook on medium-high heat until the gravy reaches the desired density. Occasionally turn the meat to cook it on all sides.
- Dissolve the tomato paste in the broth. Add to the saucepan. Adjust salt and pepper.
- Cook on moderate heat for about 2 hours or until the meat becomes tender, adding a little more broth if necessary.
- Remove the meat from the pan, and filter the gravy through a strainer. Serve the meat lukewarm topped with the gravy.

OSSOBUCO
stewed beef shanks

Beef shanks are a dish typical of northern Italy. The meat is cut transversely from the leg of the animal. The bone that comes with it contains the marrow. Marrow is very flavorful and can be eaten by removing it with a little fork or spoon.

- 2 oz (60 gr) flour
- salt
- 4 slices of beef shanks
- 2 tablespoons extra-virgin olive oil
- 1 tablespoon butter
- 1 medium onion, diced
- pepper
- ¼ cup (60 cc) white dry wine
- 2½ cups (600 cc) broth

- Pour flour onto a plate and add salt, mixing them together. Dredge the shanks in the flour, until covered uniformly on all sides.
- In a saucepan, put oil and butter, and turn heat to medium. When the butter starts foaming, add the shanks and brown them on all sides.
- Add onion, salt, and pepper. When the onion is soft, add the wine and turn the heat to medium-high to evaporate it.
- Add 1½ cups of the broth; turn heat to medium-low; cover and cook very slowly for about 1½ to 2 hours, or until the meat is tender.
- Add a little broth if necessary during cooking time to prevent the food from sticking to the pan.

The meat around the bone is surrounded by a skin. To prevent the meat from curling up while it is cooking, cut the skin with a few vertical incisions. The shanks should not be thicker than approximately ¾ inch (2 cm)—otherwise they may be too tough and would take very long to cook.

CARPACCIO

The Harris Bar in Venice was made famous by Ernest Hemingway in his novel, *Across the River and into the Trees,* where he describes a love scene between an American captain and a young Venetian girl who meet in the restaurant.

Carpaccio was invented by Giuseppe Cipriani, the famous owner of the Harris Bar; he created it for a Venetian countess who couldn't eat cooked meat. He thought of serving her raw meat with a tasty sauce. He named the dish after a famous renaissance painter, and since then the dish has become a classic of international cuisine.

- 12 oz (340 gr) raw fillet mignon
- ½ cup (120 cc) mayonnaise
- 4 tablespoons fresh tomato sauce
- 1 tablespoon mustard
- 2 tablespoons Worchestershire sauce
- 5 tablespoons heavy cream

- Cut the fillet in paper-thin slices, and place in the center of the serving plates.
- Mix thoroughly the mayonnaise, tomato sauce, mustard, Worcestershire sauce, and heavy cream.
- Spread the sauce on the meat slices.
- Optionally garnish with salad leaves.

CAPE SANTE ALLA VENEZIANA
sautéed scallops venetian style

Scallops are found in the sandy bottoms of the Adriatic Sea and constitute one of the typical dishes of the Venetian cuisine, which is rich in mollusks and crustaceans. Also known in France as *Coquilles Saint-Jaques* and in Spain as *Conchas de Peregrino,* scallops have a characteristic fan-shaped shell.

- 12 large scallops
- 3½ oz (100 gr) very fine bread crumbs
- 4–5 tablespoons extra-virgin olive oil
- 1 tablespoon butter
- 1 garlic clove
- 1 small bunch of Italian parsley, finely chopped
- 2 tablespoons dry white wine
- 1 lemon, juiced
- salt and pepper

- Dredge the scallops in the breadcrumbs.
- In a skillet, put olive oil, butter, and garlic on medium heat.
- Sauté briefly, and remove the garlic before it starts coloring.
- Add the scallops, and sauté for about 2 minutes or until uniformly golden.
- Add parsley, wine, and a squeeze of lemon juice, and let the liquid evaporate.
- Adjust salt if necessary, add pepper, and serve warm.

BACCALA' ALLA VICENTINA
baked salt cod vicenza style

- 2 lb (900 gr) salt cod
- salt and pepper
- pinch of cinnamon
- ½ cup (70 gr) flour
- 2 oz (60 gr) parmigiano reggiano cheese, freshly grated
- 1 cup extra-virgin olive oil
- 1 medium onion, finely chopped
- 1 garlic clove, finely chopped
- 8 anchovy fillets, finely chopped
- 2 tablespoons Italian parsley, finely chopped
- ½ cup (120 cc) dry white wine
- 1 quart (approximately 1 liter) milk
- 2 oz (60 gr) butter

- Soak the salt cod in fresh water for about 24 hours, changing the water often, until the cod is soft and the salt has been eliminated. Remove skin if present.
- Preheat oven to 350 F (175 C).
- Cut cod into 3-inch (8–10 cm) squares. Season with salt (only if necessary), pepper, and cinnamon.
- Dredge in the flour, shaking away the excess.
- Place the cod pieces side by side in a pan.
- Spray the parmigiano reggiano cheese on the top.

- In a skillet, put olive oil, onion, and garlic, and sauté them until the onion is soft and translucent.
- Stir in the anchovies and parsley.
- Add the wine, and let it evaporate.
- Combine the milk and butter, stirring them to melt the butter.
- Pour the mixture on the cod. Place on the stove on medium heat, cover and bring to a boil.
- Transfer the food to the oven to simmer and bake for about 1 hour or until the cod becomes soft, and the milk is all absorbed.
- Serve warm, with polenta on the side.

Baccala'

In 1431 a Venetian vessel shipwrecked in one of the most remote islands off the coast of Norway.

Captain Querini brought back home with him dried cod. It was almost immediately a success: stockfish (dried cod) and *baccala'* (salt cod) became very popular all over Italy especially in the north. It was the perfect alternative to fresh fish, which was scarce and went bad quite fast.

There are hundreds of recipes for *baccala'* in Italy. Particularly famous is the preparation from the town of Vicenza, (see recipe on this page).

Not Just Cookies

The variety of northern Italian desserts is striking: elegant and refined cakes from Piedmont (e.g., *Torta Gianduia*); as well as rustic sweets from Veneto (e.g., *Zaleti* and *Torta Sbrisolona*); *Amaretti* cookies and *Chiacchiere* fritters, baked in all regions of Italy; and also original new classics such as *Torta della Nonna* (pine nuts pie); and the world-famous *Panna Cotta* and *Tiramisu'*. The recipes we present here are a very short example—the list would be endless ❖

ZALETI

venetian corn cookies

makes about 2 dozen

- 1½ cups (270 gr) yellow cornmeal
- 1½ cups (210 gr) flour
- ½ cup (100 gr) sugar
- ¼ teaspoon salt
- 1 teaspoon baking powder
- 12 tablespoons (165 gr) butter, diced (cold from the refrigerator)
- ¾ cup dark raisins
- 2 large eggs
- grated rind of 1 lemon
- 2 teaspoons vanilla extract
- powdered sugar, for finishing

- Mix the cornmeal, flour, sugar, salt, and baking powder in a large bowl.
- Combine the butter, leaving the mixture cool and powdery. Stir in the raisins.

- *** *Note:* If using a food processor, place the dry ingredients in the bowl fitted with metal a blade, and pulse. Add the butter, and pulse until mixed finely. Pour into a bowl and stir in the raisins.

- Beat the eggs with the lemon rind and vanilla. Stir into the flour mixture with a fork.
- Preheat oven to 350 F (175 C).
- Flour the dough lightly and divide it into four pieces.
- Roll the pieces into cylinders about 1 inch (2.5 cm) in diameter.
- Flatten the cylinders slightly, and cut them diagonally at intervals of about 1½ inch (4 cm), making diamond shapes.
- Arrange the *zaleti* on a cookie sheet lined with parchment paper, and bake for about 15 minutes, until light golden brown.
- Cool the cookies on racks, and dust them with the powdered sugar.

TORTA SBRISOLONA
almond crumbly cake

- ½ lb (225 gr) almonds, peeled
- ½ lb (225 gr) flour
- ½ lb (225 gr) corn meal
- pinch of salt
- 5 oz (140 gr) sugar
- 8 oz (225 gr) butter, (at room temperature)
- 2 egg yolks
- grated rind of 1 lemon
- 1 teaspoon vanilla

- Preheat oven to 360 F (190 C). Place the almonds in a food processor, and run the blade until the nuts are very fine
- On a work surface, thoroughly mix the flour, the cornmeal, and a pinch of salt.
- Shape the mixture as a mound with a hole in the center
- In the well, add the sugar, butter, almonds, egg yolks, lemon rind, and vanilla.
- Manipulate the ingredients to combine them. It is impossible to make the dough compact, but it is important to amalgamate all the ingredients.
- In a shallow 9-inch (22 cm) oven pan with a removable bottom, place the dough to form a uniform layer, avoiding empty spaces.
- Bake for about 45 minutes, until golden. The final result will be a very crumbly cake that breaks easily when touched.
- Optionally serve it sprinkled with powdered sugar or dipped in *grappa*, a strong spirit from the Veneto region.

AMARETTI
italian almond cookies

- 18 oz (500 gr) whole almonds, blanched
- 11 oz (300 gr) sugar
- 3 egg whites
- grated rind of 1 lemon
- 3–4 drops bitter almond extract

- Preheat oven to 350 F (175 C).
- Place the almonds in a food processor fitted with a metal blade. Run the blade until the almonds are ground.
- Add the sugar and continue to run the blade until the mixture is reduced to a very fine paste. Transfer to a bowl.
- Beat the egg whites until they form peaks.
- Add the egg whites to the almond paste, mixing thoroughly with a spatula.
- Combine the grated lemon rind and the bitter–almond extract.
- Line a cookie sheet or flat oven pan with parchment paper.
- Form small balls the size of a walnut, and place them on the pan approximately 2 inches (5 cm) apart.
- Wet a kitchen towel, and pat lightly the top of the cookies, to make them smooth.
- Bake for about 25 minutes or until a light golden color.

Almonds

Part of the plum family, the almond tree is native to the Mediterranean. Since the almond grows in mild climates, the largest producers are Italy, Spain, Portugal, and California. Spanish missionaries are credited for bringing the almond to California, which is now the world's largest producer.

The bitter almond is a cousin to the sweet almond and contains in its raw state traces of lethal prussic acid. Five unprocessed bitter almonds can be toxic for a child and fifteen can be lethal for an adult. Although the toxicity is destroyed by heat, the sale of unrefined bitter almonds is prohibited in the United States.

Bitter almonds are successfully processed to make almond extract and almond-flavored liqueurs.

Note that bitter almonds can only develop their aroma if water is present.

Almond essence is well suited to flavor cookies, cakes, and marzipan. Because it is very strong, care must be taken not to use too much. If it is not available, kernels of peach or apricot can also be used.

Whole almonds can easily be found in the grocery stores already peeled. If you do not find them, and you need to remove the skins, drop the almonds in boiling water. Blanch the almonds for about 2 minutes, and drain them. You then will easily be able to remove the skins. Spread the almonds on an oven pan and place them in the oven in moderate heat until they are dry.

TORTA GIANDUIA
chocolate-hazelnut layer cake

Gianduia is a very rich cake, originally from the Piemonte region. Its characteristic is a combination of chocolate and hazelnuts.

for the chocolate dough
- 1½ cups (180 gr) hazelnuts
- 7 oz (200 gr) semi-sweet chocolate, finely diced
- 4 + 4 oz (115 + 115 gr) sugar
- 1 + 6 oz (30 + 170 gr) butter, at room temperature
- 8 eggs, separated
- ¾ cup (110 gr) flour

for the chocolate filling
- 1 cup (250 cc) heavy cream
- 12 oz (340 gr) semi–sweet chocolate, diced
- 2 oz (60 gr) butter, at room temperature

for the finishing and the glaze
- ¼ cup (60 cc) rum or brandy
- ¾ cup (180 cc) heavy cream
- 6 oz (180 gr) semi–sweet chocolate, diced

preparing the cake

- Preheat oven to 350 F (175 C).
- Take a 10-inch-diameter (25 cm) oven pan with removable ring, and butter and sprinkle it with flour or line the pan with parchment paper.
- Place the hazelnuts in an oven pan and roast them for 10–15 minutes, until they begin losing their skin. Remove the skins by placing the nuts in a kitchen cloth and rubbing the pieces together.
- Place the chocolate in a small saucepan and melt it at bain-marie on a larger container filled with boiling water, stirring frequently
- Put the hazelnuts in a food processor with 4 oz (115 gr) of the sugar.
- Run the blade until the nuts are reduced to a very fine powder.
- Add 1 oz (30 gr) of the butter, and mix for an additional 1–2 minutes.
- Remove the mixture from the food processor and transfer it to a small bowl.
- Work the remaining 6 oz (170 gr) of butter with your hands for about 2–3 minutes to soften it.
- Combine the hazelnuts, the softened butter, and the melted chocolate, and mix it thoroughly until smooth.
- Combine the egg yolks one at a time with the hazelnut-chocolate mixture, reserving the egg whites.
- Sift in the flour, mixing continuously.
- Beat the egg whites. When they are half beaten, add the remaining 4 oz (115 gr) of sugar, and beat the mixture until peaks are formed.
- Combine half of the egg whites to the hazelnut-chocolate mixture, stirring gently with a top-to–bottom movement.
- When the mixture is soft and homogeneous, stir in the rest of the egg whites.
- Pour the mixture in the oven pan and bake it for approximately 30–40 minutes.
- Remove from the oven and let the cake cool at room temperature

preparing the filling

- Put the cream in a saucepan and turn the heat to medium.
- Remove the pan from the heat immediately before the cream starts boiling.
- Add the diced chocolate, and stir until dissolved.
- Using a fork and a small bowl, beat the butter until so.
- Stir the butter into the cream, and let it cool at room temperature for about 2 hours.
- Place the filling in a food processor, and beat the mixture until very light and soft.

assembling the cake

- Cut the cake into 2 layers. Sprinkle the bottom layer with the rum, and spread half of the filling over it.
- Place the other layer on top, sprinkle it with rum, and spread the rest of the filling on the top and sides of the cake. Place the cake in the refrigerator.

preparing the glaze

- Put the cream in a saucepan and turn the heat to medium.
- Remove from the heat immediately before the cream starts boiling.
- Add the diced chocolate, and stir until dissolved.
- Whisk and beat the glaze until it is very light and soft.
- Remove the cake from the refrigerator, cover it with the glaze, and spread it uniformly with a spatula.
- Put the cake back in the refrigerator for 15–20 minutes to allow the glaze to cool.
- Keep in the refrigerator until serving time.
- Decorate the sides with crushed hazelnuts.

TIRAMISU'
(pick me up)
coffee and cheese cake pudding

Tiramisu' is one of the latest additions to "traditional" Italian cooking. Unknown until about fifteen years ago, when it is believed to have been invented in the town of Treviso in northern Italy, in merely a decade it has become a world-renowned dessert, extremely popular from the United States to Japan. It is considered a *semifreddo* (a dessert served cold, but not frozen). This dessert has many variations, with the only constant ingredient the *mascarpone* cheese.

for the coffee dip
- 1½ cups (360 cc) Italian espresso coffee
- 2 teaspoons sugar

for the zabaglione filling
- 4 egg yolks
- ½ cup (100 gr) sugar
- ½ cup (120 cc) Marsala wine (if not available substitute with other sweet wine like port or Madeira)
- 1 lb (450 gr) *mascarpone* cheese, at room temperature
- 1 cup (230 cc) heavy whipping cream

for the base
- 10 oz (285 gr) *savoiardi* (ladyfinger cookies) (approximately 40)
- 2 tablespoons bitter cocoa powder

preparing coffee dip
- Prepare a strong espresso coffee, about 1½ cups (360 cc).
- Dissolve 2 teaspoons sugar in it, and let the coffee cool at room temperature.

preparing the zabaglione filling

- Beat egg yolks in a heat proof bowl until fluffy. Beat in sugar and Marsala wine.
- Whisk over a pan of simmering water, until the cream thickens.
- Remove from heat and beat in an electric mixer, until cold.
- With a rubber spatula, mash the *mascarpone* cheese in a bowl until creamy.

- Add the mascarpone cheese into the zabaglione, and beat to mix very well
- Whip the cream.
- By hand, fold the whipped cream into the zabaglione–cheese cream, until smooth.

assembling the cake

- Lightly soak the ladyfingers in the coffee, one at a time

- Place them in one layer in a container of about 12 x 8 inches, approximately 2 inches deep, (30 x 20 cm, approximately 4 cm deep).

- Evenly distribute half of the zabaglione cream over the layer.

- Repeat the step with a second layer of ladyfingers, and top with the rest of the cream.

- Sprinkle with the cocoa powder and refrigerate for about 3–4 hours.

Tiramisu' can be prepared in advance and kept in the freezer. Remember to remove it from the freezer enough time in advance to serve it cold at refrigerated temperature, but not frozen. Sprinkle it with more cocoa powder before serving.

Tiramisu' is made in Italy using raw eggs. Today the danger of salmonella is always present, and we prefer to cook the yolks bain-marie and to substitute whipped cream for the egg whites.

TORTA DELLA NONNA
(grandmother pie)
cream and pine-nuts pie

There are probably as many "Grandmother's pies" as there are grandmothers, but this wonderful cake can be found constantly called by this name in many cities of northern Italy

for the dough
- 1½ cups (200 gr) flour
- ¼ cup (35 gr) cornstarch
- ⅓ cup (80 gr) sugar
- 4½ oz (120 gr) butter, diced (at room temperature)
- 2 egg yolks
- 1 teaspoons vanilla
- grated rind of 1 lemon
- pinch of salt

for the custard
- 1¼ cups (300 cc) milk, lukewarm
- 1 slice of lemon peel
- 4 egg yolks
- ⅔ cup (120 gr) sugar
- ⅓ cup (45 gr) flour
- ¾ cup (180 cc) heavy cream
- ½ teaspoon vanilla

for finishing
- 4 oz (115 gr) pine nuts
- powdered sugar for finishing

preparing the dough
- On a work surface, mix the flour and cornstarch. Shape it into a mound with a hole in the center.
- In the well, add the sugar, diced butter, egg yolks, vanilla, grated lemon rind, and a pinch of salt.
- Using a fork, mix the ingredients in the center; then combine with the flour and knead to form a smooth dough.
- Cover the dough with a plastic wrap, and place it in the refrigerator for 1 hour.

preparing the custard
- Warm the milk and the lemon peel.
- In a small saucepan, place egg yolks and sugar, and beat vigorously until they are pale yellow and creamy.
- Incorporate the flour a little at a time.
- Add the warm milk, heavy cream, and vanilla, stirring continuously.
- Place on low heat and continue stirring constantly with a wooden spoon.

- Remove from the stove when the cream starts boiling and becomes denser.
- Remove the lemon peel, transfer the custard to a bowl and cool at room temperature.

assembling the cake
- Preheat oven to 375 F (190 C). Butter a 9 inch (22 cm) pan with removable bottom, and sprinkle it with a small amount of flour.
- Remove the dough from the refrigerator.
- Reduce the dough to a ¼ inch thick (5 mm) disk with the help of a rolling pin.
- Cover the bottom and sides of the pan with the dough.
- Fill the pan with the custard and level with a spatula.
- Spray the pine nuts on the surface of the custard.
- Bake for about 50 minutes. Cool at room temperature, un-mould and serve cold, sprinkled with powdered sugar.

PANNA COTTA
milk and caramel custard

for the caramel
- ½ cup (100 gr) sugar
- ½ teaspoon lemon juice
- 2 tablespoons. water, hot

for the panna
- 1 cup (230 gr) milk
- 1 envelope unflavored gelatin powder
- 2 cups (460 cc) heavy cream
- 1 slice of lemon peel
- 1 piece of cinnamon stick
- ¼ cup (50 gr) sugar

preparing the caramel
- In a small saucepan, put the sugar and lemon juice. Mix very well together with a metal spoon, and place over low heat.
- Stir the sugar-juice once in a while until it becomes dark gold and begins smoking.
- Add hot water, bring it to a boil, and remove the pan from the heat.
- Pour the caramel into a round mould approximately 7 inches in diameter (18 cm) and 2 inches deep (5 cm).
- Swirl the mould in all directions so that the caramel covers bottom and sides.

preparing the panna
- Pour the milk into a small bowl and add the gelatin powder. Let it soak for about 5 minutes.

- In a saucepan, put the cream, lemon rind, cinnamon, and sugar.
- Turn the heat to medium and bring to a simmer. Remove it from the heat and set it aside for about 10 minutes.
- Remove the lemon peel and the cinnamon stick, add the milk-gelatin mix, return it to the stove. Stirring, bring to a boil.
- As soon as the cream starts boiling, remove the pan from heat, pour the mixture into the mould, and let it cool at room temperature.
- Keep it in the refrigerator for at least 6 hours (better if overnight) before serving.
- To unmould it, place the mould for few seconds in very hot water. If necessary, insert a knife all around between the mould and the cream to detach it from the walls. Invert onto a serving plate.

CHIACCHIERE
(gossips)
carnival fritters

These fritters, traditional from the carnival festivities, are familiar all over Italy, where they assume different names—including *Frappe, Frappole, Sfrappole, Flappe* in central Italy, *Cenci* ("tatters") or *Donzelli* ("young ladies") in Tuscany, *Crostoli* ("crusts") or *Galani* in Veneto, *Lattughe* ("lettuce") in Romagna, *Nastri delle Suore* ("ribbons of the nuns") in Emilia, *Bugie* ("lies") in Piemonte, and *Gigi* in Sicily. Is there any other dish with so many names?

- 2 cups (280 gr) flour
- ¹/₃ cup (70 gr) sugar
- 2 oz (60 gr) butter, diced (at room temperature)
- 2 eggs
- pinch of salt
- grated rind of 1 lemon
- ½ cup (120 cc) milk
- 1 teaspoon vanilla
- 1 tablespoon rum
- frying oil
- approximately ¾ cup (150 gr) powdered sugar, for dusting

- In a bowl, place the flour in a mound shape with a hole in the center.
- In the center, add the sugar, butter, eggs, pinch of salt, grated lemon rind, milk, vanilla, and rum.

- Using a fork, mix the ingredients together with the flour. Rapidly work the paste with your hands, to form a dough.
- When the dough becomes consistent, transfer it to a floured work surface.
- Knead the dough for few minutes, but avoid warming it too much.
- Make the dough smooth and very soft. When it is smooth and consistent, form it into a ball, place on a dish, cover, and keep refrigerated for 1 hour.
- Divide the dough into 2 pieces. On a work surface generously sprinkled with flour, use a rolling pin to flatten the dough until it is very thin.
- Cut the dough irregularly into strips 1 x 4 inches (3 x 10 cm) or triangles 4 x 2 inches (10 x 5 cm).
- Flatten and cut the other half of the dough.
- In a large skillet, bring the oil to frying temperature. Fry the strips a few at a time.
- Transfer the strips on paper towels on a large plate and let the oil drain briefly.
- Transfer to a serving plate and sprinkle generously with powdered sugar.

FRAGOLE AL BALSAMICO
strawberries in balsamic vinegar

- 1 lb (450 gr) ripe strawberries
- 1 cup (230 cc) dry white wine
- 1 tablespoon balsamic vinegar *tradizionale*
- 2 tablespoons sugar
- 1 cup (230 cc) whipped cream

- Clean the strawberries removing leaves and stems. Place the strawberries in a bowl. Add wine.
- Rinse the strawberries in the wine to remove impurities. Drain and discard the wine.
- Transfer the strawberries in a serving bowl. Add the vinegar, sugar, and toss to cover the fruit uniformly. Set aside for 15 to 30 minutes.
- Serve topped with the whipped cream.

Balsamic Vinegar

"A little bit of vinegar of Modena, refreshing and balsamic, in a very short time gave me back some of my health and tranquility," wrote Gioacchino Rossini, the famous opera composer. In Italian "balsamic" means therapeutic. In fact since the Middle Ages Balsamic vinegar of Modena was believed to have extraordinary properties. It was said to be able to cure any kind of hillines and even bring the dead back to life. The lengthy secretive method of preparation has contributed to this magic image.

Balsamic vinegar is made from very sweet Trebbiano grapes. They are harvested as late as possible in the season to give them more sugar content. The grapes are crushed, filtered, boiled, and reduced to increase the sugar level. The concentrated juice is then placed in wooden barrels, and added of the vinegar "mother". This is a substance that forms at the surface of the vinegar, and is composed of the bacteria that turn wine into vinegar.

The following year the vinegar, reduced in volume, will be transferred to a smaller barrel of a different wood. The process will be repeated every year, using smaller barrels every time. The different woods used include chestnut, ash tree, cherry, mulberry, juniper and oak. The vinegar is progressively concentrated, and the final product is a dense syrup with a very dark color, and a perfectly balanced sweet and sour taste.

Aceto Balsamico can only be made in the city of Modena. They say "Who produces balsamic vinegar, doesn't do it for himself but for the following generations". There are rare and expensive production lines that date up to 2 centuries. The best *balsamico* for consumption is marked *"tradizionale"* and is aged 12 or 25 years.

CHAPTER 3

The Universal Food

Pasta Fresca

The word *pasta* means "dough" or "pastry" in Italian: Pasta refers to all pastes made of a combination of flour and water. No one knows where pasta was born or who invented it. It was born spontaneously as part of the evolution of mankind. Pasta is a truly universal food, invented when man discovered the first plants of wheat, crushed the seed, and mixed them with some water. Trying to cook this paste was the first step—later this ancestor of pasta was also fried in fat and added to vegetable soups.

Pasta Fresca

Apicius, who wrote a text of cooking in Roman times, described types of fried sweet pasta, similar to the *frappe* still made today in Rome, as well as pies made of strata of pasta similar to the present day lasagne. Another Roman author, Orace, describing his days and his food, wrote that at dinner *lagane* (lasagna) was served—with chickpeas and leeks. In the Renaissance, the lasagna was also eaten sweet and began changing its shape. Cut in strips of different size they became fettuccine and *pappardelle*. At that time gnocchi and filled pasta also made their appearance.

The infinite dishes of pasta can be made either from pasta *fresca* (fresh made) or pasta *secca* (dry pasta). Pasta *fresca* is generally associated with northern and central Italy, where it is made with the addition of eggs. Very often in southern Italy pasta *fresca* is made without the addition of eggs.

Pasta *fresca* falls into two main categories: pasta *liscia* (flat pasta) and pasta *ripiena* (stuffed pasta). Flat pasta is made from flattened dough, cut in long strips. The most common is *tagliatelle,* which receive their name from the Italian word *tagliare* (to cut). In Rome, they took the name *fettuccine* (ribbons) and became very famous in the postwar period, when a cook by the name of Alfredo used a golden fork and spoon to toss them in butter and cream in front of American tour-

Lavorano de Pasta - Passano sapori, (which means "making pasta, preparing flavorings"), engraving from *Opera dell'arte del cucinare,* a book on the art of cooking, by Bartolomeo Scappi, Venice, 1570. Scappi is to cooking what Michelangelo is to fine arts. His book—full of recipes, tips, and illustrations—exemplifies the Renaissance practicality, elegance, and scientific method that greatly influenced Europe through the seventeenth century.

ists and movie stars at his restaurant. This method of dressing fettuccine today carries his name, *All' Alfredo.* Pasta *liscia* is also served in the form of lasagne—large squares of pasta layered with cheese, white sauce, and *ragu',* and baked in the oven.

The other type of pasta *fresca* (*ripiena,* stuffed pasta) can be made in the largest variety of shapes and filled with meat, fish, vegetables, cheeses. These types of pasta are common in northern and central Italy and less in the south. Those areas were historically poorer, and people's pantries lacked the abundance of eggs and ingredients necessary to make the dough and the stuffing.

Many stories surround the appearance of stuffed pasta. Raviolis apparently were invented in the city of Genova, a city of sailors, and their name comes from a word in the Ligurian dialect that means "rubbish" or "leftovers." Apparently, on Genovese ships leftover foods were chopped up together, stuffed into envelopes of pasta, and served at a later time. During long sails, making use of the leftovers was important so that no food was wasted.

Tortellini, the "Number One" dish in Bologna was present in the kitchens of the region since at least the thirteenth century. Tradition has it being invented by a cook who, inspired by the navel of a beautiful woman, then molded the pasta in that shape.

Stuffed pasta takes many names: *agnolotti* (in the Piemonte region) with ruffled edges; *cappelletti* (in the Emilia region) with a half-moon shape; tortellini (in the city of Bologna) by the characteristic ring shape; ravioli, folded squares filled with ricotta cheese and spinach; cannelloni or *manicotti*, large rolled squares of pasta, filled and baked. Pasta can also make simple and delicious desserts, such as sweet ravioli.

To have a good dish of fresh pasta in Italy you don't necessarily have to make it by yourself at home. Many small artisan shops make daily, or even on order, any kind of fresh flat or filled pasta.

In the past, making fresh pasta and bread was a daily activity. Every house had a large wooden chest with a flat-hinged top for the flour and yeast. The flour was scooped onto the top, and either bread or fresh pasta was kneaded on the wood several times a week. Tender, moist, and very tasteful, no industrial product can compare with fresh pasta.

From north to south all Italians eat a lot of pasta, and in all families one or more recipes are handed down from mother to daughter. Cooking is constantly evolving with innovation and experimentation in homes and in professional kitchens, but in every region the traditional recipes are practiced and respected ❖

PASTA FRESCA A MANO
fresh pasta by hand

ingredients

- **3 cups flour** (15 oz, approximately 400 gr). Use normal unbleached all-purpose flour. Other flours can eventually be used in place of, or in addition to the base flour. Semolina or bran would add more texture to the dough, but make it harder.
- **4 eggs.** Use only very fresh, large eggs. Most of the industrially produced eggs are very light in color and have light taste. Buy eggs that are specifically indicated as having "golden" yolk, from farm-bred chicken.
- **1 tablespoon extra-virgin olive oil.** This gives more smoothness to the dough and makes it easier to knead.

optional ingredients

Salt. It is optional, and most pasta makers add salt only to the condiments.

Flavoring ingredients. Additional taste can be given by adding to the dough parmigiano cheese, wine, or spices.

Coloring ingredients. For different coloring use only natural ingredients, such as the **saffron** for intense yellow, **red beet** for violet, **tomato paste** for red, **spinach** for green, **bitter chocolate** for dark brown, and **squid ink** for black. Quantity of egg should be reduced proportionally when adding coloring ingredients.

equipment

Cutting board. Use a wooden board that should be approximately 2 feet wide x 3 feet long (60 x 90 cm), made out of compact hardwood that doesn't chip when hit by the knife. The long edge should have on the bottom an additional wooden trim. This prevents the board from sliding while you knead the dough.

Rolling pin. This should be one solid perfect wooden cylinder with rounded edges, about 3 feet long (90 cm) x 2 inches in diameter (5 cm).

Knife. Use a sharp cook's knife.

Spatula. You need a large square spatula to clean the board from pasta residues.

Sift the flour. Pour it on the wooden board. Shape it into a mound, and hollow the center.

Break the eggs and pour them in the hollow.

Add 1 tablespoon of extra-virgin olive oil, and a pinch of salt (optional).

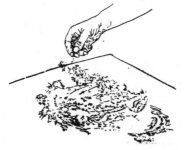

After cleaning the pasta residues off the work surface, pour a thin layer of flour to prevent the fresh pasta from sticking on it.

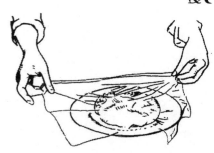

Cover with a moistened cloth or a plastic wrap, and let the dough rest for 30 minutes to 1 hour.

Using a fork, beat the eggs together. Gently bring some of the flour into the egg mix.

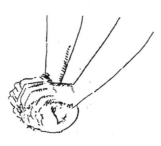

Return the dough to the work surface, and knead the pasta, pushing with the palm of your hands.

Cut the ball in 4 pieces. Lightly sprinkle the board with flour. Place one ball on the board, and flatten it slightly.

Continue drawing flour into the eggs a little at a the time until all the flour is absorbed.

Alternatively push and fold the dough. Repeat this step for 8 to 10 minutes, or until the dough feels smooth and firm.

Spin the rolling pin forward and backward over the dough several times. Turn the dough one quarter and repeat the steps in order to make the dough circular.

Use your hands and a spatula to obtain a uniform mixture.

Make a round, smooth ball and place it on a plate.

When the dough is thin enough, curl it around the pin.

Roll again forward and backward several times. While rolling the pin, move your hands laterally to flatten the pasta.

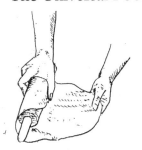

When the pasta sheet is about $1/32$-inch to $1/16$-inch (1–2 mm) thin, place it flat on a lightly floured cloth to dry for about 15–20 minutes.

Using the Hand Pasta Machine

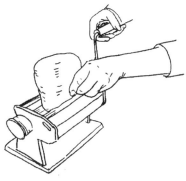

Flatten the dough to about ½-inch (1 cm) thick. Pass it through the rollers of the machine set to the widest setting.

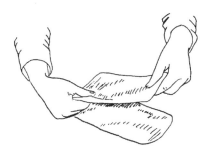

Fold the dough on itself and press to remove the air. Pass it through the machine again. Repeat this step 6–7 times.

Set the machine one notch lower and pass the dough through the rollers once. Move the dial to the next notch and pass the dough through the machine again. Repeat this step until the desired thickness is reached.

Tips for a Perfect Pasta

Make a firm dough
Sometimes the flour may absorb more liquid than expected or the eggs may be too small. In this case add an extra egg yolk, or a small quantity of water.

Keep everything clean
Keep the board and your hands always well floured, to prevent the dough from sticking. Also keep hands and board clean from pasta residues that could pierce the flattened pasta sheets.

Wood must be kept dry
Never wash the board or the rolling pin. First, keep them clean of pasta residues by scraping with a spatula or brush; then, clean them with a moistened cloth.

Be comfortable
Work comfortably, with hands free of rings or bracelets. Dress in an apron, short sleeves, a hat, or maybe a scarf across the forehead.

Room conditions are important
Avoid working in an area too ventilated, too hot, or too humid. Your dough could dry too much. In this eventuality add a little bit of water to the board. If the dough is too soft add a little bit of flour.

No machine, if possible
The dough should be made by hand. The heat of the hands, while working, heats the fats and proteins of the eggs, increasing the flavor of the pasta. Working by hand will help you understand when the dough is ready and has the right consistency. Using a machine makes pasta smoother and harder; while pasta by hand will be less smooth, it will be soft and moist, and will be excellent in retaining the sauce. A little more work, but how rewarding!

How to Cut Pasta

Pasta cut varies from region to region, and even from one town to the next. *Capellini* (angel hair) are generally boiled in a good meat stock, *Quadrucci* (small squares) are used for soups, *Maltagliati* (randomly cut pasta) for rustic beans or chickpea soup. *Garganelli* and *Farfalle* are dressed with light buttery sauce. *Fettuccine* and *Pappardelle* are used with any kind of tomato or "light" sauce, but prevalently with tomato-meat sauce or *ragù*.

Fettuccine, *Tagliatelle*

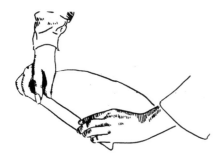

Flour the surface lightly. Pick up one edge of the pasta sheet, and fold it about 3 inches. Then fold it again and again and again, until the whole sheet is folded in a long flat roll, about 3 inches wide.

Cut the roll across in slices about ¼-inch wide. Open the rolls and spread the fettuccine out on a clean cloth for the last drying stage.

Capellini (Angel Hair)

Proceed as you would for fettuccine, but cut the roll across in very thin slices no more than ¹/₁₆-inch

Pappardelle

Cut the pasta sheet in strips about ¾-inch to 1½-inch (2–4 cm) wide using a fluted pastry wheel. In absence of a pastry wheel, proceed as you would for fettuccine, cutting ¾-inch to 1½-inch (2–4 cm) wide slices.

Maltagliati (Badly Cut)

Proceed as you would for fettuccine. Cut the rolls across about ¾-inch (2 cm) wide. Turn them sideways and cut diagonally in an irregular way, to obtain triangular or trapezoidal shapes.

Quadrucci (Squares)

Proceed as you would for fettuccine. Cut the rolls across ¼-inch (6 mm) wide. Turn them sideways and cut again ¼- inch (6 mm) long, to obtain small squares.

Fresh Pasta Cuts

Capellini	Angel hair
Tagliatelle, Fettuccine	Little ribbons ¼-inch (6 mm) wide
Pappardelle	Wider cut about ¾ inch (2 cm)
Lasagna	Wider cut for layered pasta
Maltagliati	("Badly cut") Irregular cut for soup
Quadrucci	Little squares for soups
Farfalle	("Butterflies") Squares pinched in the middle to form a butterfly shape
Garganelli	Small ruffled tube shapes
Orecchiette	("Little ears") Little concave dumplings
Pasta alla chitarra	("Guitar pasta") Pasta cut with a special guitar-like device

FETTUCCINE ALL' ALFREDO
fettuccine alfredo

The original *Fettuccine Alfredo* is a very simple recipe—only paper-thin egg fettuccine, in the style of Rome, and a lot of butter and good *Parmigiano Reggiano* cheese. It was created in 1914 by Alfredo, a brilliant Roman cook, to help his pregnant wife recover her lost appetite.

prepare very thin fresh fettuccine according to the recipe on page 57

- ½ lb (225 gr) butter, diced (at room temperature)
- salt
- ½ lb (225 gr) parmigiano reggiano cheese, freshly grated

- Place half of the butter in a serving bowl. Keep the bowl warm.
- Cook the fettuccine in abundant salted water.
- When the pasta is perfectly *al dente,* (firm but not too soft or overcooked), reserve a few tablespoons of the cooking water.
- Drain without shaking the colander too much, so that the pasta doesn't become too dry.
- Drop the pasta in the bowl, top with the rest of the butter and the parmigiano reggiano cheese. Add a small quantity of the reserved cooking water if the pasta appears too dry.
- Toss vigorously, and serve immediately, accompanied by a small bowl with more grated parmigiano reggiano cheese, for the guests to add if they would like.

TAGLIATELLE AL RAGU' BOLOGNESE
fettuccine with ragu' bologna style

Ragu' is a meat sauce typical of the city of Bologna, where it is served mainly to top *tagliatelle*, the local version of fettuccine. It is a very thick sauce that needs to simmer slowly for several hours.

prepare the fresh fettuccine according to the recipe on page 57

- 2 oz (60 gr) bacon
- 1 celery stick
- 1 medium carrot
- 1 medium onion
- 2 + 2 oz (60 + 60 gr) butter
- 3–4 tablespoons extra-virgin olive oil
- salt and pepper
- ¾ lb (340 gr) ground beef
- ¾ lb (340 gr) ground lean pork meat
- 3–4 oz (approximately 100 gr) prosciutto, finely ground
- ½ lb (225 gr) unflavored Italian sausage, skin removed
- 1 cup (230 cc) dry red wine
- ¾ lb (340 gr) tomatoes, puréed in a blender
- 1 cup (230 cc) broth (if necessary)
- 2 tablespoons milk or heavy cream
- 5 oz (140 gr) parmigiano reggiano cheese, freshly grated

- Chop the bacon, celery, carrot, and onion finely together.
- Place 2 oz (60 gr) of the butter and olive oil in a medium size saucepan. When the butter starts foaming add the chopped vegetables, salt, and pepper.
- Sauté until the onion becomes soft and translucent.
- Add the ground beef, ground pork, ground prosciutto, and sausage.
- Turn the heat to medium and cook until meat is browned. Stir and break the meat in small bits with a wooden spoon.
- Add the wine. Turn the heat to medium-high and let the wine evaporate.
- Add the tomato and lower the flame to a very slow simmer. Let the sauce cook very slowly for at least 3 hours. Add a small quantity of broth if the sauce thickens too much.
- Stir in the milk (or cream) and 2 oz (60 gr) butter just before removing the saucepan from the heat. Adjust salt and pepper.
- Cook fettuccine in abundant salted water until perfectly *al dente* (firm but not too soft or overcooked).
- Drain the pasta, top with the *ragu',* the parmigiano reggiano cheese, and toss.
- Serve accompanied by a small bowl with more grated parmigiano reggiano cheese.

61

Lasagna

Almost every region in Italy has its own type of lasagna. Sometimes the name "lasagna" indicates simply a dish of flat large egg noodles dressed with tomato sauce.

The multilayered lasagna is also called *Pasta al Forno* (baked pasta). The many regional types of lasagna include *Lasagne di Carnevale* (carnival lasagna) from Naples, made with meatballs, sausage, ricotta, mozzarella cheese, and hard-boiled eggs; *Lasagne al Pesto* (pesto lasagna) from Liguria, filled with pesto; *Lasagne Verdi* (green lasagna) from Bologna, made with green fresh pasta; *Vincisgrassi* from the Marche Region, a type of layered lasagna with giblets, chicken livers, and white sauce; *Lasagne all'Albese* (lasagna in the style of Alba, a town in the Piemonte Region), with white sauce, parmigiano cheese, and truffles; and *Lasagne Ricotta e Spinaci* (lasagna with ricotta cheese and spinach), from Roma. The variations are innumerable and include all combinations of meats, vegetables, eggs, hams, and more.

The most popular type, the one we propose here, originated in Bologna. It is made with layers of pasta filled with white sauce and tomato sauce, topped with Parmigiano cheese.

To prepare *lasagna al forno* (baked lasagna) in the style of Bologna, three components are needed:

♦ *Sugo di carne* (meat–tomato sauce)
♦ *Balsamella* (white sauce)
♦ fresh pasta

SUGO DI CARNE
meat–tomato sauce

In many regions meat sauce is represented by the traditional *ragu'*. It is a very thick, rich, and tasty sauce that requires about 3–4 hours of preparation. The meat sauce of this recipe is full in taste, but takes less time to prepare, which makes it practical for everyday, faster cooking.

To add taste to the sauce, a mixture of different ground meats can be used, such as half beef and half pork. The addition of milk helps reduce the acidity of the tomatoes if they are not ripe enough. This sauce, besides being the perfect complement for lasagna, is also excellent as a dressing for pasta (e.g., spaghetti or fettuccine). Add the sauce to the freshly drained pasta, top with grated parmigiano cheese, toss, and serve at once.

♦ 3 tablespoons extra-virgin olive oil
♦ 3 tablespoons (45 gr) butter
♦ 1 medium onion, finely diced
♦ 1 carrot, finely diced
♦ ½ stick celery, finely diced
♦ 1 garlic clove, diced
♦ ½ lb (225 gr) ground meat
♦ ¼ cup (60 cc) dry white wine
♦ salt and pepper
♦ 2½ cups (550 gr) tomatoes, puréed in a blender
♦ pinch of nutmeg
♦ 2 tablespoons milk or heavy cream

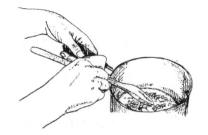

- Place oil and butter in a saucepan, and turn the heat to medium.
- When the butter starts foaming, add the onion, carrot, celery, and garlic.
- Sauté and stir until the onion is soft and translucent.

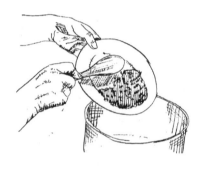

- Add the ground meat. Stir with a wooden spoon, and break the meat into small bits. Cook until the meat is fully browned. Add the wine, salt, and pepper. Turn the heat to high, and let the wine evaporate.
- Add the tomato, nutmeg, and milk. When the sauce starts boiling, turn the heat to low.
- Cover the saucepan and simmer slowly for about 1 hour, stirring occasionally.

BALSAMELLA
white sauce

- 4 tablespoons (55 gr) butter
- 2 oz (60 gr) flour
- 2¼ cups (500 cc) milk
- salt
- 1 oz (30 gr) parmigiano reggiano, freshly grated
- pinch of nutmeg

Balsamella

White Sauce is known as *Béchamel* in France, where it is thought to have been invented by Louis de Bechameil (steward of the royal household under Louis XIV in the mid-1600s), a nobleman with a passion for cooking. It is hard to believe that such a simple sauce—made of ingredients widely used and available—was suddenly discovered by a French nobleman.

In fact, white sauce has been around for long time. Caterina de' Medici's cooks brought to France a recipe for a white sauce named *Colletta*.

In the northern Italian region of Emilia people claim to have used *Balsamella*—a sauce made of flour, butter, and milk—since medieval times. Italian *Balsamella* has added Parmigiano Reggiano cheese and nutmeg.

- Place butter in a saucepan and turn the heat to low. When the butter is melted, remove the saucepan from the stove.

- Sift the flour into the butter a little at a time, stirring continuously to combine them.
- Add the milk a little at a time.
- Put the saucepan back on the stove and slowly stir with a wooden spoon, until the sauce starts boiling and becomes thicker.
- Remove from the stove. Add salt, and stir in the grated parmigiano cheese and pinch of nutmeg.

LASAGNA AL FORNO
baked lasagna

serves 6

prepare the sugo di carne (meat–tomato sauce) according to the recipe on page 62

prepare the balsamella (white sauce) according to the recipe on this page

prepare the fresh pasta according to the recipe on page 57

for the lasagna
- salt
- 1 teaspoon extra-virgin olive oil
- 6 oz (approximately 180 gr) parmigiano reggiano, freshly grated

cutting fresh pasta

- When the pasta sheets are dry enough, roll them around the pin and transfer them to a slightly floured cutting board one at a time.

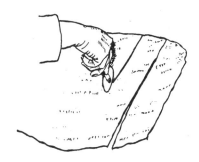

- Cut the pasta sheets across in strips. Make the strips 4 ½ inch (11 cm) wide or a width that fits your pan in even multiples. Spread them out on a clean cloth.
- Cut the strips in sections about 6 inch (15 cm) long.

assembling and baking

- Bring water to a boil in a stock-pot. Add salt and 1 teaspoon of olive oil. Prepare a separate container of cold water.
- Cook the fresh pasta strips until *al dente* (firm but not too soft or overcooked). Cooking time will be less than 5 minutes.

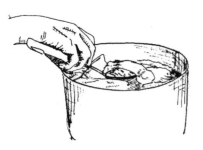

- Remove the pasta strips with a slotted spoon, drop them briefly in the cold water to stop the cooking process, and place in a colander to drain.
- After the strips are drained, place them flat on a kitchen cloth and tap them gently with the cloth to dry.

- Preheat oven to 350 F (175 C). Butter a flat oven pan approximately 9 x 12 inch (22 x 30 cm) and spread over it 2–3 tablespoons of tomato sauce.

- Place one layer of pasta strips, spread with the tomato sauce, the *balsamella* sauce and grated parmigiano.

- Repeat the layers until all ingredients are used.
- Bake for about 25–30 minutes. Serve hot.

Lasagna can be conveniently prepared in advance, refrigerated or frozen, to cook at a later time.

The quantity of fresh pasta indicated in the recipe on page 57 could be excessive for this dish. Leftovers of the flattened dough can be cut into a different shape (such as fettuccine) and used for a different preparation.

LASAGNA VEGETARIANA
vegetarian lasagna

serves 6

prepare the fresh pasta according to the recipe on page 57

cut lasagna strip as indicated at page 63

prepare the balsamella (white sauce) according to the recipe on page 63

for the vegetable filling

- 2 eggplants, approximately ½ lb (225 gr)
- 1 bell pepper
- 2 oz (60 gr) frozen peas
- 2 tablespoons extra-virgin olive oil
- 1 garlic clove, peeled and crushed whole
- 2 small carrots, diced
- 2 scallions, diced
- 3 small zucchini, diced
- salt and pepper

preparing the vegetable filling

- Dice the eggplants. Roast the bell pepper, peel, and dice.
- Boil the peas for 5 minutes and drain.
- In a skillet, sauté the garlic in the olive oil over medium heat.
- Remove the garlic before it starts coloring.
- Add all the vegetables. Sauté for about 10 minutes on medium heat. Add salt and pepper.

assembling the lasagna

- Bring the water to a boil in a stockpot. Add salt and 1 teaspoon of olive oil. Fill a separate container with cold water.
- Cook the fresh pasta strips until *al dente* (firm but not too soft or overcooked). Cooking time should be less than 5 minutes.
- Remove the pasta strips with a slotted spoon. Drop them briefly in the cold water to stop the cooking process, and place in a colander to drain.
- After the strips are drained, place flat on kitchen cloth and tap them gently with the cloth to dry.
- Preheat oven to 350 F (175 C).
- Butter a 9 x 12 inch (22 x 33 cm) baking pan.
- Line the pan with one layer of pasta strips. Spread one fourth of the *balsamella* sauce, one-third of the vegetables, and one fourth of the grated parmigiano on top of the strips. Repeat the layers until all ingredients are used.
- Top with the remaining *balsamella* sauce and parmigiano cheese.
- Bake for about 25–30 minutes or until golden. Let stand 5–10 minutes before serving.

Fresh Stuffed Pasta

Stuffing pasta is a very old practice that in time has reached a degree of perfection. The shapes are innumerable and change from town to town.

The stuffing can be vegetables or a variety of meats, and even sweets. The names are sometimes confusing, but the combinations they represent are elegant and luscious.

Some examples:

Tortellini (Bologna) ring-shaped dumplings stuffed with a variety of meats

Offelle (Friuli-Venezia Giulia) ravioli made of potato pasta, filled with spinach and sausage

Ravioli, Pansoti (Liguria) large square shapes filled with ricotta and spinach, mushrooms, pumpkin.

Agnolotti (Piemonte) square shaped pasta pockets stuffed with pork meat

Cappelletti (Emilia) small half-moon shapes stuffed with meat

Casonsei (Veneto) ruffled half moons stuffed with pork meat

Cannelloni, Manicotti (Lazio and Campania) large rolls stuffed with meat

Cialzones (Friuli) half-moon shapes, stuffed with cheese

Culingiones (Sardinia) square-shaped pasta pockets, stuffed with fresh cheese

RAVIOLI CON RICOTTA E SPINACI
ravioli filled with ricotta and spinach

Ravioli are popular all over Italy. They are prepared with many different fillings: cheese, mushrooms, pumpkin, and fish are used. People also serve sweet ravioli filled with jam or cream. In Rome, ravioli are very large in size and are filled with ricotta cheese and spinach.

serves 6
for the filling
- 1 lb (450 gr) fresh spinach
- 1 lb (450 gr) ricotta cheese, thoroughly drained
- 1 egg
- 4 oz (115 gr) parmigiano reggiano cheese, freshly grated
- salt and pepper
- pinch of nutmeg

for the dough
- 3 cups (400 gr) flour
- 4 eggs
- 1 tablespoon extra-virgin olive oil

preparing the filling
- Boil the spinach in lightly salted water. Place the boiled spinach in a cheese cloth and form a small sack. Squeeze the sack to expel as much water as possible. Chop the spinach finely.
- Place the spinach in a bowl. Combine the drained ricotta, egg, parmigiano cheese, salt, pepper, and a generous pinch of nutmeg. Taste and adjust the salt, pepper, and nutmeg if necessary.

- Prepare the pasta dough using the recipe on page 57. Make the dough very soft and moist. Use the minimum flour necessary, just enough to prevent the dough from sticking to your hands while working.

- Cut the dough in two parts. Place one of the pieces on the work surface, and flatten it with a rolling pin until it is very thin.

- Repeat the same steps with the other half of the dough, making a pasta sheet of the same size. Set it aside, covered with a moist towel if necessary to prevent the pasta from drying too much.

- Place about 1 teaspoon of the filling on the dough, spaced 2 inches (5 cm) apart.

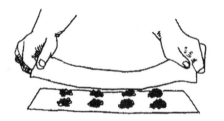

- Cover with the second dough and press the pasta around the fillings so that the 2 layers touch each other. Press firmly to bond the 2 pasta sheets together.

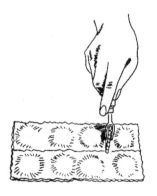

- Separate the ravioli by cutting with a pastry wheel.

- Bring water to a boil in a stockpot. Gently drop the ravioli in the boiling water a few at a time, and cook until the pasta is *al dente* (firm but not too soft or overcooked).

- Drain ravioli, picking them from the boiling water with a slotted spoon. Place in a serving dish and top with the dressing.

Ravioli can be dressed in many different ways: with *ragu'*, tomato sauce, or simply with melted butter and sage.

Drain the filling ingredients very well to prevent the ravioli from breaking while boiling.

If you like the stuffing to be aromatic, add more freshly grated nutmeg.

Sometimes the dough will dry too much while you are working, which prevents the pasta sheets from being "gluey" enough to stick to each other. If this happens, brush the surface of the bottom pasta sheet with egg white

CANNELLONI
baked stuffed pasta rolls

Cannelloni are rolls of pasta filled with ground meat. They are filled in many different ways, such as with ricotta and spinach, or with vegetables.

serves 6
prepare the sugo di carne (meat–tomato sauce) according to the recipe on page 62

prepare balsamella (white sauce) according to the recipe on page 63

prepare the fresh pasta according to the recipe on page 57

for the filling
- 3 tablespoons (45 gr) butter
- 2 tablespoons extra-virgin olive oil
- 1½ lb (675 gr) ground meat
- salt and pepper
- pinch of nutmeg
- 2 + 2 oz (60 + 60 gr) parmigiano reggiano cheese, freshly grated
- 1 teaspoon extra-virgin olive oil

preparing the filling
- Place the butter and olive oil in a frying pan over medium heat.
- As soon as the butter starts foaming, add the ground meat, salt and pepper.
- Cook, stirring and breaking the meat into small bits, until fully browned.
- Place the meat in a food processor, and run the blade until the meat is reduced to a very fine paste.
- Place the meat in a bowl, and stir in nutmeg and 2 oz (60 gr) of the parmigiano cheese. Add 3–4 tablespoons of *balsamella* sauce to obtain a soft consistency.

assembling the cannelloni
- Cut the fresh pasta sheets in squares approximately 4 x 4 inch (10 x 10 cm).
- In a stockpot, bring the water to a boil. Add salt and 1 teaspoon of olive oil. Prepare a separate container with cold water.
- Cook the pasta squares, until perfectly *al dente* (firm but not too soft or overcooked).

- Remove the pasta from the boiling water with a slotted spoon.
- Drop the squares briefly in the cold water to stop the cooking process, and place in a colander to drain.
- After the pasta squares are drained, place them flat on a kitchen cloth and tap them gently with the cloth to dry.
- Preheat the oven to 350 F (175 C). Butter a flat oven pan, approximately 9 x 12 inches (22 x 30 cm).
- Spread the bottom of the pan with 3–4 tablespoons of tomato sauce.

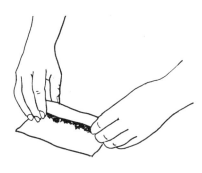

- Place 1 pasta square on a work surface, cover it with approximately 1 tablespoon of the meat filling, and roll the pasta to form a cylinder. Place the first *cannellone* in the pan.
- Repeat this step with the rest of the ingredients, placing the *cannelloni* side by side in the pan until it is full.
- On the top, uniformly spread the tomato sauce, *balsamella* sauce, and 2 oz (60 gr) of parmigiano cheese.
- Bake for approximately 20 minutes, or until the parmigiano cheese begins melting.

BRODO DI CARNE
basic italian broth

- 2 lb (approximately 1 kg) meat for broth, cut in large chunks
- 2–3 cloves
- 1 whole large onion
- 1 whole large carrot
- 2 celery sticks
- 1 little bunch of Italian parsley
- 1 tomato, whole
- 4–5 black pepper corns
- pinch of nutmeg
- 1 tablespoon salt

- In a large stockpot, pour approximately 1 gallon (4 liters) of water. Place the meat in the pot.
- Stick the cloves on the surface of the onion.
- Add into the pot the onion, carrot, celery sticks, parsley, whole tomato, and peppercorns.
- Season with a pinch of nutmeg and add salt.
- Bring the water to a boil, and cook until the meat is tender.
- Let the broth cool at room temperature. With a slotted spoon, remove most of the fat from the surface of the broth.
- Remove the meat from the pot, and filter the broth using a very fine strainer.

TORTELLINI IN BRODO
tortellini in broth

There are many version of the recipe for Tortellini in Emilia. The controversy over the best recipe became so harsh that a group of gourmets from Bologna, in order to placate the argument, decided to notarize and file with the Chamber of Commerce the "true" Tortellini recipe.

**makes about 200
serves 8**
prepare the broth according to the previous recipe

for the filling
- 3½ oz (100 gr) chicken breast
- 3½ oz (100 gr) veal
- 3½ oz (100 gr) pork meat
- 1 tablespoon butter
- 2 tablespoons extra-virgin olive oil
- 1/3 cup (80 cc) dry white wine
- 3½ oz (100 gr) prosciutto
- 3½ oz (100 gr) *mortadella*
- 3½ oz (100 gr) parmigiano reggiano cheese, freshly grated
- 1 egg
- ½ tablespoon butter, lukewarm
- pinch of nutmeg
- salt and pepper

for the dough
- 3 cups (400 gr) flour
- 4 eggs
- 1 tablespoon extra-virgin olive oil

preparing the filling
- Cut the chicken breasts, veal, and pork into small dice.
- In a saucepan, place butter and olive oil, and turn the heat to medium.

- When the butter starts foaming, place all the meats in the pan. Cook them until they are uniformly brown.
- Add the wine, turn heat to high, and let the wine evaporate.
- Place the meat in a food processor. Add the prosciutto and *mortadella*. Run the blade until all the meats are reduced to a very fine paste.
- Place the meat paste into a bowl. Add the parmigiano reggiano cheese, egg, butter, nutmeg, salt, and pepper. Combine thoroughly all the ingredients.

preparing the pasta dough

- Prepare fresh pasta using the recipe for fettuccine on page 57, making the dough very soft and moist. Use just enough flour to prevent the dough from sticking to your hands while working.
- Cut the dough in two parts. Place one of the dough pieces on the work surface, and flatten it with a rolling pin, until it is very thin. Repeat with the other piece of dough.
- Cut the pasta sheet in 1½-inch (4 cm) squares. Place a pinch of the filling in each square.

- Close the square to form triangles and press the edges to seal.

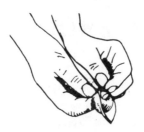

- Fold the edges around your index finger and press the extremities together to form a cuff.
- Pinch the edges firmly while closing the ring shape. Fold down the top corner of the triangle.
- Bring to a boil approximately 1½ quarts (1500 cc) of broth in a stockpot.
- Place the tortellini in the boiling broth and cook until *al dente* (firm but not too soft or overcooked). Cooking time may vary depending on the freshness of the tortellini. Dried tortellini can take a little longer than freshly made tortellini.
- Place tortellini in serving bowls, top with freshly grated parmigiano cheese and, optionally, with freshly grated nutmeg.

Traditionally, tortellini are prepared in homemade broth. Tortellini has a very delicate taste, which the broth enhances.

Because Tortellini take long time to prepare, generally they are handmade for special occasions. They make an elegant dinner for Christmas and other festivities. In Italy many pasta shops sell excellent freshly made tortellini.

You can prepare tortellini several weeks in advance and freeze them. Just drop the frozen tortellini in the boiling broth when needed.

TORTELLINI CON PANNA E PISELLI
tortellini with cream-and-pea sauce

Gourmet cooks from Bologna will say that there is no other way to enjoy tortellini than in a good broth. We still like to try other less traditional ways, such as with this delicious dressing.

- 2 tablespoons (25 gr) butter
- 2 tablespoons extra-virgin olive oil
- 1 unflavored Italian sausage, skin removed
- ¼ cup (60 cc) dry white wine
- 1 cup shelled fresh or frozen peas
- salt and pepper
- 1 cup (230 cc) cream
- 1 lb (450 gr) tortellini
- 4 oz (115 gr) parmigiano reggiano cheese, freshly grated

- In a large skillet, place the butter and olive oil, and turn the heat to medium.
- When the butter starts foaming, add the sausage and break it with a fork into small pieces. Sauté until fully browned.
- Add the wine; turn the heat to high, and let the wine evaporate.
- Add the peas, salt, and pepper. Turn heat to low and cook the mixture for approximately 10 minutes, until the peas are tender.
- Add the cream and stir for about 1 minute. Remove from heat.

- Cook the tortellini in salt water, tasting for readiness from time to time. Remove 2 minutes earlier than necessary.
- Drain tortellini very well, pour it into the skillet over the sauce. Turn heat to medium-high, and sauté for about 1 minute. Remove from the heat before the sauce becomes too dense on the pasta.
- Pour into a large salad bowl, top with the parmigiano cheese, and serve immediately.

Pasta & Pastarelle

Today *pasta* means a savory dish and *pastarelle* is the Italian word for sweet pastry. But the dividing line between savory and sweet pastry has always been thin. It was especially uncertain in the past, when there was much indifference in the distinction between salty and sugary, and any dish could hold both.

Sweet things could be served indiscriminately at the beginning or end of the meal, because before the Renaissance, the succession of dishes was not established the way it is today. Before sugar became affordable, it was common practice to add nuts, plums, dates, figs, or raisins to pastes and breads to give them a sweet-sour taste—a practice that is still alive in many Italian preparations. Following here are two very old recipes for sweet "paste" that seem to jump out of an ancient cookbook, for their simplicity and similarity with their savory equivalents ❖

RAVIOLI DOLCI
sweet ravioli

for the custard
- 1 cup (230 cc) milk
- 1 teaspoon vanilla
- 3 eggs
- ½ cup (100 gr) sugar
- 1 oz (30 gr) flour

for the filling
- 2 oz (60 gr) candied orange, diced
- 2 oz (60 gr) raisins
- 2–3 tablespoons Cointreau or other sweet liqueur
- 3½ oz (100 gr) ricotta cheese, thoroughly drained

for the dough
- 2 cups (280 gr) flour
- 1 oz (30 gr) sugar
- 4 oz (115 gr) butter, diced (at room temperature)
- 2 eggs for the dough + 1 egg for the egg wash
- 2–3 tablespoons milk
- grated rind of 1 lemon
- pinch of salt
- ¹/₃ cup (75 gr) powdered sugar (for finishing)

preparing the custard
- Pour the milk and vanilla in a saucepan on medium heat. Remove from the stove as soon as the milk starts boiling.
- Separate the egg yolks from the whites. Reserve the whites to be used later in the recipe.
- In a saucepan, beat the yolks with the sugar, until they are swollen and about double in volume.
- Sift in the flour, mixing slowly with a wooden spoon.
- Slowly add the vanilla-milk, constantly stirring.
- Place the saucepan over medium heat, stirring slowly, and remove from the stove as soon as the custard starts boiling.
- Pour the custard into a bowl and cool it at room temperature. Stir occasionally to prevent a patina from forming on the surface.

preparing the filling
- Soak candied fruit and raisins in the Cointreau for about 10–15 minutes.
- Add the ricotta cheese to the custard, stirring to form a smooth cream.
- Remove raisins and candied fruit from the liqueur and drain them thoroughly. Discard liqueur.
- Add the candied fruit and raisins to the cream mixture.
- Place the cream in the refrigerator while preparing the dough.

preparing the dough
- Butter 2 flat oven pans and spread a little flour over them.
- Pour the remaining flour onto a work surface to form a mound shape with a hole in the center.
- In the well, add the sugar, butter, 2 eggs, milk, grated lemon rind, and pinch of salt.
- Using a fork, mix the ingredients together with the flour.
- Knead for 2–3 minutes until a smooth dough is obtained.

69

assembling the ravioli

- Preheat oven to 350 F (175 C).
- Prepare the egg wash, beating the remaining egg in a small bowl.
- Take out the filling from the refrigerator.
- Cut the dough in half. With a rolling pin, reduce one half of the dough to a thin layer, and cut it into circles 2½ inches (6–7 cm) in diameter.
- In the center of each circle place approximately 1 teaspoon of the filler; brush the edge with the reserved egg whites; and close it by folding it in two.
- Press the edges together with the prongs of a fork.
- Repeat the step with the rest of the dough.
- Brush the top surface of the ravioli with egg wash, and place them on the oven pans.
- Place the pans in the oven for about 20–25 minutes or until the ravioli are golden.
- Cool at room temperature and sprinkle with powdered sugar.

Sweet ravioli can also be fried and filled with a variety of sweet ingredients such as jam, custard, and chestnuts.

FETTUCCINE CARAMELLATE
caramelized fettuccine

This is a little-known recipe for an unusual dessert and one of my childhood favorites. Although it is elaborate to make, the final result is worth it. This recipe uses a technique similar to the one for regular fresh fettuccine (see recipe for fresh pasta on page 57). To make crunchy and crisp fritters, form very thin dough.

- 2 cups (approximately 300 gr) flour
- 3 eggs
- 1 teaspoon vanilla
- pinch of salt
- grated rind of 1 lemon
- 1 tablespoon sugar (for the dough)
- 1½ cups (300 gr) sugar (for the filling)
- frying oil

- Pour the flour onto a work surface, to form a mound shape with a hole in the center.
- In the well, add the eggs, vanilla, pinch of salt, grated lemon rind, and 1 tablespoon of the sugar.
- Using a fork, mix the ingredients together with the flour. Use your hands to combine the ingredients and work the paste to form a uniform, smooth dough. Work the dough as when making fresh pasta (see page 58).
- Shape the dough like a ball, and place it in a bowl. Cover it with a cloth, and let it rest for about 30 minutes.
- Cut the dough in two, and place one half on the work surface.

- Using a rolling pin, make a thin, flat sheet as though making fresh pasta.
- Uniformly cover the surface of the dough with half of the sugar for the filling.
- Fold the extremity, and roll the dough on itself to make a flat roll about 2 inches (5–6 cm) wide. Cut the roll into ribbons about ¼-inch (5 mm) wide, as though you were making fettuccine (see page 60).
- You will now have many spiral ribbons about ¼-inch (5 mm) wide, 2 inches (5–6 cm) long and about ½-inch (1.5 cm) thick, filled with sugar in the spaces formed by the spiral shape.
- Gently place the ribbons on a plate, taking care not to break them.
- Repeat the steps with the second piece of dough.
- Bring the oil to frying temperature in a large frying pan. The oil must be very hot for this preparation. To test the oil temperature, drop a little crumb of pasta in the oil. If the oil is hot, the crumb will fry very quickly.
- Place the ribbons gently in the pan, side by side in one layer.
- The hot oil will melt the sugar forming a caramel.
- When the ribbons are ready, they will curl up, slightly open, and form irregular shapes.
- When they are dark brown, remove them from the pan.
- Place them on a plate on paper towels, and let the oil drain briefly.

The fried sweet pasta ribbons can be served hot or lukewarm.

CHAPTER 4

Under the Sign of the Lily

The Food of Tuscany

With its enchanted landscapes and rolling hills covered with bright yellow fields of sunflowers, olive groves, and grapevines, Tuscany is the Italian region in every foreigner's dreams. During the Renaissance, this magic land gave birth to some of the most influential characters in Western civilization: artists and architects, saints and philosophers, navigators and scientists. These include Amerigo Vespucci, the merchant and navigator who gave America its name; Giovanni da Verrazzano; Leonardo; Michelangelo; Lorenzo de' Medici "The Magnificent"; Brunelleschi; Della Casa; Galileo; Giotto; Donatello; Botticelli; Dante; Machiavelli; and Boccaccio, to mention only a few.

The Renaissance

The Etruscans, who inhabited Tuscany before the Romans, had a reputation for being great eaters and wine drinkers. Their habits were considered by many to be degenerate and to be the cause of their decline.

In Roman times, until the fall of the Roman Empire, Tuscany cooking coincided with that of Rome itself. After the year 1000, and after the Crusades opened the way to the East, with the fear of barbarian incursions diminishing, the northern Italian cities became the center of production and commercial power.

At the end of the twelfth century, in spite of the permanent hostility between the factions loyal to the Pope *(Guelfi)*, and those devoted to the emperor *(Ghibellini)*, Florence grew to be independent and the most powerful city of Tuscany. The lily became the symbol of Florence and its supremacy.

The food of the time was simple and meager; dishes were based on grains or chestnuts, and were merely flavored with herbs: breads such as *focaccia*, and *castagnaccio* come from those times. Towards the middle of the 1300s, economic recovery set the basis for the supremacy that the gastronomy of Tuscany and Florence would hold for the first few centuries that followed.

Improved agricultural techniques made more widely available the products of the Tuscan countryside that we so much appreciate today: wine, olive oil, vegetables, pork, and all sorts of game. Shops

Map of Italy during the Renaissance at the end of fifteenth century. The boundaries of the small states that divided Italy remained almost unchanged until 1860. The country as we know it today was finally unified under the rule of the Savoia, the Piemontese royal family.

offered *porchetta* (roasted piglet flavored with Tuscan herbs), cow meat, chicken, lamb, vegetables, and fish from the Arno River. Many of the recipes of the time remain alive in Tuscan cooking today.

In 1434, the town of Florence became a *signoria* and Cosimo de' Medici, powerful merchant and banker, became the lord. He governed with such wisdom that he was declared "Father of the Homeland" at his death. In 1439, the council of the Roman and Greek churches was held in Florence, as guests of the Medici.

One story says that, on this occasion, two important terms of Tuscan cooking were born. While in a banquet, Greek Cardinal Bessarione tasted some roasted piglet, and he exclaimed, "Aristos!" meaning "the best" in Greek. The Florentines present at the table thought he called that meat dish by that name, and since then *Arista* became the name of the whole loin of pork.

Again, Cardinal Bessarione, when tasting a sweet wine exclaimed, "This is Xantos!" alluding to a similar wine produced in Greece. Those who were listening thought that he wanted to say the wine was so good as to judge it *santo* (holy). From that day, this special wine has been called *Vin Santo* (holy wine), offered in all of Tuscany as a dessert wine to be drunk with the famous *Cantucci* "*biscotti.*"

Lorenzo "The Magnificent," son of Cosimo de' Medici, succeeded his father at age twenty. He ruled Florence with great determination and liberalism. That same year, he married a lady of Roman nobility. The event was celebrated with great feasts and banquets. One aspect of these events was the distribution to the population of a profusion of food, including hundreds of chickens, ducks, fish, game, calves, and barrels of wine.

Wrote Lorenzo, a poet himself:

"Quant'e' bella giovinezza
che si fugge tuttavia
chi vuol essere lieto sia
del doman non v'e' certezza"

(How beautiful is youth, that runs away so fast, who wishes to be happy so, there is no certainty in tomorrow.)

In harmony with this thought, Lorenzo surrounded himself with a large court of painters, artists, architects, writers, and poets, and made Florence the liveliest center of the time. He was also an enthusiast of good food, and a good cook himself.

Piazza dei Miracoli (Miracle's Square), Pisa. Arranged like jewels on an immense green lawn, the white marble buildings embraced by the fine-lace look of colonnades, statues, and arches are in a magical balance between the earth and the sky. The square is an eloquent demonstration of the cultural heights reached by this Tuscan *Comune*. For centuries, Pisa was in a perpetual power struggle with Florence, for political and military control over Tuscany.

Lorenzo's death in 1492 ended an era—on the same year as the discovery of America, which would bring so many changes to the history of the world and would also forever change the gastronomy of the West.

Since Florence was one of the greatest commercial nexus of the time, Tuscan cooking was enriched earlier by the produce of the new world than the fare of many other countries. New beans, potatoes, maize, and chocolate were tasted here, even while they were still considered ornamental plants in other parts of Europe.

Caterina de' Medici

A lesser-known figure of the Renaissance, Caterina de' Medici (niece of Lorenzo), unwillingly became one of the most influential people in culinary history. In 1533, at age fourteen, she was married to Henry of Orlèans, the future king of France.

Her life was difficult because, from the beginning, Caterina was not what Henry expected: She was chubby, with a big nose and the round eyes typical of all the Medici.

73

Henry married her only because he was forced by political reasons. In a short while, he betrayed her with a beautiful and older milady, Diana de Poitiers—a humiliating relationship Caterina couldn't ignore.

Unpopular with the French people, Caterina was called the Italian "grocer" because she was from a rich family of bankers but not of noble blood progeny. In addition, she was expected to give an heir to the crown of France: For years the couple tried in vain. With her marriage in jeopardy, she feared being repudiated and sent back to Italy.

The superstition of that time induced Caterina to try to become pregnant by any expedient from special dishes believed to help: artichokes, *cibreo* (chicken gizzards), and disgusting potions of all kinds. Finally, after ten years, a renowned physician of the Louvre diagnosed the two partners with congenital anomalies. Simple remedies finally allowed her to give birth to nine children in the next eleven years, four of them future kings and queens.

Only after the death of Henry was she able to get rid of the intruding presence of Diana, as well as to affirm her abilities as a strong ruler and wise politician—even in the midst of the turbulent and bloody events that took place in the years that followed.

When she moved to France, a crowd of friends, servants, and waiters accompanied her. The Florentine cooks who went with her brought the secrets of Italian cooking to France, including peas and beans, artichokes, duck in orange *(canard a l'orange)*, and *carabaccia* (onion soup). But especially the

Apparato di convito (Apparatus for a Banquet), Francesco Ratta, 1639. Parading the great food preparations at the banquets in the form of *Trionfi della Tavola* (Triumphs of the Table) is the most striking manifestation of Renaissance cooking. These gigantic gastronomic creations are mounted, mostly for show: a peacock with all his feathers, and flames coming out of the beak; or live birds coming out of a paste sculpture; or large decorations of sugar depicting deities, fountains, or other forms. The cooks, like architects, would prepare sumptuous dishes to impress the guests.

pastry makers, as Jean Orieux (a biographer of Caterina) wrote, demonstrated their innovative genius with sorbets and ice creams, marmalades, fruits in syrup, pastry making, and pasta. A certain Sir Frangipani gave his name to the custard and the tart known in France as *Frangipane*.

Caterina also brought with her to the French table new protocol, such as the separation of salty and sweet dishes, at a time when all over Europe sweets were still consumed together with meat and fish in the style of the medieval times. Everyone in France was amazed by the Florentine elegance Caterina introduced: gracious table setting and dining, embroidery and hand-

kerchiefs, light perfumes and fine lingerie, as well as luxurious silverware and glasses.

The French were also introduced to the new etiquette: Published in 1588 by Giovanni della Casa, the book *"Il Galateo"* sets the rules for good conduct, one area in which Florence far surpassed the rest of Europe. Caterina introduced to France the use of the fork. Meanwhile Giovanni Della Casa was advising, "When you are eating, do not masticate noisily or crouch over the food, without raising your face, as if you were blowing a trumpet" and "avoid rubbing your teeth with your napkin, or worse, with your fingers. Do not scratch yourself, or spit, or at least only do it reservedly."

At that time, French cooking already was a rich, evolving discipline, and the presence of the new style profoundly influenced French cuisine for the next centuries. Jean Orieux wrote: "It was exactly a Florentine who reformed the antique French cooking of medieval tradition; and was reborn as the modern French cooking." The French cooks improved and magnified the Florentine contribution, and while in Italy many dishes and techniques were being forgotten, the French made them into an international cuisine.

French Cooking Returns

With the decadence of the Medici family, the Grand Duchy of Tuscany slowly faded away. After the death of the last of the Medici, the Grand Duchy was given to the Lorraine, a French-Austrian dynasty, followed by Napoleon, by the return of the Lorraine again after the fall of Napoleon's empire, and finally by the annexation to the Kingdom of Italy in 1860.

From 1865 to 1871, Florence was the capital of Italy. Florentine cuisine in those years seems to have forgotten the Tuscan way of cook-

Chianti originates its name from "clante," the name of the Etruscan families inhabiting the area two thousand years ago. Not only is it the name of the most celebrated Tuscan wine, but it also defines one of the most beautiful areas of the Tuscan countryside. Enchanted landscapes and rolling hills are covered with bright yellow fields of sunflowers, olive groves, and grapevines, as well as the typical farmhouses surrounded by cypress trees.

ing; the official dinners only proposed French dishes and wines. The presence of the royal Italian court, originally from Piemonte and influenced deeply by the French style, had caused the Florentines to value only what came from across the Alps.

French cuisine dominated in Italy and added a lot to the language of cooking. Many French words remained in everyday use, such as *menù, dessert,* and *buffet,* just to mention a few. The French also brought back to Italy many dishes of the grand cuisine that originated in Italy, were taken to France by Caterina de' Medici, but had fallen into disuse—for example, the *bèchamel (balsamella)* and *crepes (crespelle).* French cooking certainly added the use of butter to Florentine cooking.

But while French cooking dominated official cuisine, the taste for genuine Tuscan cooking was kept alive in more modest environments. The strong traditions of Tuscan

cooking soon made a great comeback, thanks to many gourmets who used the antique flavors, followed the old recipes, and treasured the genuine, gastronomic dishes of Tuscany.

Tuscan cooking today is characterized by simple food, not covered in heavy sauces. Cooking is done with olive oil—used as salad dressing, poured over bread, and in soups and stews. Beans are a staple. Sage, rosemary, thyme, and marjoram are popular herbs. The farmland produces olive oil and wine, wheat, and fruits. Chickens, ducks, rabbits, cows, and pigs are raised in small estates. The vegetables grown here include artichokes, asparagus, spinach, beans, and peas; and, a great number of wild mushrooms, including *porcini* and morels, is found ❖

CROSTINI CON I FUNGHI
mushroom toasts

- 1½ lb (675 gr) fresh *porcini* mushrooms (use chanterelle mushrooms if *porcini* are unavailable)
- 1½ tablespoons (25 gr) butter
- 4 tablespoons extra-virgin olive oil
- ½ medium onion, finely chopped
- 1 garlic clove, finely chopped
- 1 tablespoon Italian parsley, finely chopped
- salt and pepper
- ½ cup (120 cc) broth
- 1 white bread baguette, cut in ½ -inch-thick (1 cm) slices

- Clean the mushrooms and separate the stalks from the caps. Chop the mushrooms coarsely.
- In a skillet, place butter and oil over medium heat. When the butter starts foaming, add the onion, garlic, and parsley.
- Sauté until the onion becomes soft and translucent. Add the mushrooms, salt, and pepper.
- Cook for about 5 minutes stirring continuously.
- Gradually stir in some of the broth to keep the mushrooms moist and tender. Cook for about 8–10 more minutes.
- Toast the bread slices in the oven. Spread each slice with a generous tablespoon of the mushrooms and serve.

CARABACCIA
onion soup

Carabaccia is onion soup Florentine style. A similar dish named *carabazada* appears in the recipe book of Cristoforo Messisbugo published in 1549. Without a doubt, it is a precursor of the French *soup d'oignons*.

- 5 + 2 tablespoons extra-virgin olive oil
- 2 lb (approximately 1 kg) onion, finely sliced
- 3 celery sticks, finely diced
- 2 carrots, finely diced
- 4 cups (approximately 1 liter) broth
- salt and pepper
- ¾ lb (340 gr) stale bread
- 4 tablespoons parmigiano reggiano cheese, freshly grated

- In a medium saucepan, put 5 tablespoons of the olive oil, and turn heat to medium. Add the onion, celery, and carrots.
- Sauté on moderate heat until the onion becomes soft and translucent. Add a small quantity of broth if necessary to prevent the onion from sticking to the pan.
- Add the broth, salt, and pepper. Cook for about 10 minutes.
- In a frying pan pour 2 tablespoons extra-virgin olive oil. Bring the oil to frying temperature.
- Cut the bread in thin slices, and fry them until brown.
- Place the bread in serving bowls, cover with the hot soup, and spread with the grated parmigiano cheese.

PASTA E FAGIOLI
bean soup

Bean soup is traditionally slowly cooked in terracotta pots, often with the addition of prosciutto or pork meat to enhance its flavor.

- 11 oz (315 gr) dry *borlotti* beans
- 1 quart (approximately 1 liter) water
- 3 tablespoons extra-virgin olive oil
- 2 oz (60 gr) bacon, finely chopped
- 1 medium onion, finely diced
- 1 stick celery, finely diced
- 1 carrot, finely chopped
- 2 tablespoons fresh ripe tomato, finely diced
- 2 cups (460 cc) broth
- salt and pepper
- 5 oz (140 gr) short *ditali* pasta, or spaghetti broken in ½ inch (1–2 cm) pieces
- 4 tablespoons extra-virgin olive oil, for topping

- Clean and wash the beans the night before. Place them in a container, and cover with fresh water. Let the beans soak in the water overnight.
- The next day, when ready to cook, drain the beans.
- In a stockpot, pour 1 quart (1 liter) water and add the beans. Boil for about 20 minutes or until the beans are tender.
- In a stockpot, pour the extra-virgin olive oil, and turn the heat to medium.

- Add the bacon, onion, celery, and carrot. Sauté for 2–3 minutes, or until the onion becomes soft. Stir in the tomato.
- Transfer about one third of the beans to a plate. Using a potato masher, reduce the beans to a paste.
- Add to the stockpot the beans (with their cooking water), the puréed beans, and the broth. Bring to a boil. Add salt and pepper.
- Cook for about 15 minutes, until the ingredients are well blended.
- Add the pasta and cook for the time indicated by the manufacturer, checking for readiness from time to time. Pasta is ready when al dente (firm but not too soft or overcooked). Adjust the salt if necessary.
- Place the soup in a large bowl or single serving dishes. Top with the extra-virgin olive oil and serve warm.

PASTA CON LE NOCI
pasta with walnut sauce

This ancient recipe from Tuscany resembles the traditional pesto, but adds the milder taste of the walnuts and omits the strong taste of garlic.

prepare the fresh fettuccine according to the recipe on page 57

- ½ lb (225 gr) walnuts, shelled
- 4 oz (115 gr) pine nuts
- 2 oz (60 gr) parmigiano reggiano cheese, freshly grated
- 2 oz (60 gr) *pecorino* (romano) cheese, freshly grated
- 2 oz (60 gr) basil leaves (approximately 40 leaves)
- ½ cup (120 cc) extra-virgin olive oil
- 2 tablespoons heavy cream
- salt and pepper

- Place the walnuts, pine nuts, parmigiano cheese, pecorino cheese, and basil leaves in a mortar. Using a pestle, reduce to a dense, creamy paste.
- Combine olive oil and heavy cream to the paste. Add salt and pepper.
- Cook the pasta until al dente (firm but not too soft or overcooked).

Beans

Common beans (*phaseolus vulgaris*) were imported in Europe after the discovery of the American continent. It was one of the few edible vegetables to have almost immediate diffusion. The reason is probably that beans, (the black-eyed variety originally from North Africa) were already known for centuries.

Beans are legumes, which are the richest source of vegetable protein. They are a very high source of soluble fiber. Rich in complex carbohydrates, they are an excellent source of energy.

The combination of beans and grains can be an ideal low-fat, cholesterol-free alternative to meat. By consuming other complementary proteins, such as rice or bread, at any time during meals, you can meet your body's complete protein requirements.

Beans can play an important role in gluten-free, diabetic, low-salt, and low-calorie, low-cholesterol, high-iron and high-fiber diets.

Beans also act as an appetite suppressant. Because they digest slowly and cause a low, sustained increase in blood sugar, researchers have found that beans can delay the reappearance of hunger for several hours, enhancing weight-loss programs.

To prepare the dry beans rinse them under cold running water.

When soaking dry beans add $1/8$ teaspoon of baking soda to soaking water to reduce indigestible sugars that cause flatulence.

After soaking, rinse beans again before cooking in fresh water. Rinse beans after cooking if recipe allows.

When using canned beans in water, discard canning liquid and rinse beans under cold running water.

- Before draining, reserve a few tablespoons of the cooking water.
- Drain the pasta and pour into a serving bowl. Top the pasta with the walnut pesto. Add a small quantity of the reserved water if the pasta is too dry. Toss and serve immediately.

The sauce can also be obtained by running all the ingredients through a food processor, until reduced to a fine paste. Dry spaghetti can be used if fresh pasta is unavailable.

PAPPARDELLE AL SUGO DI LEPRE
pappardelle with hare sauce

Pappardelle are a type of fresh handmade egg pasta cut in large strips, a minimum of one to two inches wide. The pasta needs to be very thin and soft. The *pappardelle* with hare sauce is a specialty of Tuscany, where hunting is still broadly practiced and hare is frequent. However, because this meat commonly is unavailable elsewhere, it can be substituted with rabbit, or the recipe can be enjoyed even using the ever-present chicken.

- 3–4 tablespoons extra-virgin olive oil
- 1 medium onion, finely chopped
- 1 carrot, finely chopped
- 1 celery stick, finely chopped
- 1 hare or rabbit, cleaned and cut in large pieces, including the liver
- 1 cup (230 cc) Chianti wine

- 1 lb (450 gr) tomato, puréed in a blender
- 1 carrot, diced
- ½ onion, diced
- 1 celery stick, diced
- 1 oz (30 gr) butter
- 2 oz (60 gr) *pecorino* (romano) cheese or parmigiano cheese, freshly grated
- salt and pepper

prepare the fresh pasta according to the recipe on page 57

cut the pappardelle in strips a minimum of 1 inch (2–3 cm) wide as shown on page 60

- In a skillet, pour the olive oil, and add the chopped onion, chopped carrot, chopped celery, salt, and pepper. Sauté until onion is soft and translucent.
- Add the meat and cook until browned on all sides. Add the diced livers, and brown briefly.
- Add the wine and let it evaporate.
- Add the tomato, lower the heat to a simmer, and cook for about 30 minutes or until the meat is tender. Add salt and pepper if necessary.
- Stir occasionally, adding some water or broth if the sauce is too thick.
- Prepare a bouquet garni using the diced carrot, diced onion, and diced celery. Place in a large pot full of salted water, and bring to a boil.
- Cook the pasta in the pot with the bouquet garni until *al dente* (firm but not too soft or over-cooked).
- Discard the bouquet garni, drain the pasta, and place it in a serving bowl.

- Top with the meat sauce and toss. Serve hot, topped with the butter and the cheese.

Game

In many areas of Italy, most of the small farms that could not be run productively have been abandoned. The deserted fields have again become the dominion of wildlife that in the past was threatened by human presence.

Hare, quails, pheasants, birds of all kinds, and especially boars are back. The limits that were placed on hunting have been lightly eased to reduce the increasing wild animal population. Boar sausage and seasoned hams are easily found today in many specialty stores, and are appreciated by gastronomes.

Tuscany cooking has many dishes for wild game, and many are based on excellent marinades to soften their strong taste.

Boar often requires a rich and long marinade, and makes very rich dishes—tasty and highly valued. It can be stewed or cooked with sour apples (the classic and exquisite *dolce-forte* recipe that dates back to the Renaissance) or simply cooked in a saucepan with herbs, lemon juice, and wine.

PASTA CON IL SUGO DI FEGATINI

pasta with chicken liver sauce

- 3 tablespoons extra-virgin olive oil
- 3 tablespoons butter
- 2 oz (60 gr) bacon, diced
- 4 oz (115 gr) onion, diced
- 2 oz (60 gr) carrot, finely diced
- ½ stick of celery
- ½ lb (225 gr) ground meat
- 2 oz (60 gr) chicken livers, diced
- salt and pepper
- ¼ cup (60 cc) dry white wine
- 1½ cups (400 gr) tomatoes, puréed in a blender
- pinch of nutmeg
- 2 tablespoons milk
- 2 oz (60 gr) parmigiano reggiano cheese, freshly grated

prepare the fresh fettuccine according to the recipe on page 57

Dry spaghetti can be used if fresh pasta is unavailable.

- In a saucepan, pour the oil and add the butter and bacon, and turn the heat to medium.
- When the bacon becomes lightly browned, add the onion, carrot, and celery. Sauté until the onion is soft and translucent.
- Add the ground meat. Cook while stirring and breaking the meat into small bits, until fully browned.
- Add the chicken livers, salt, and pepper. Stir to combine.
- Add the wine, turn heat to high, and let the wine evaporate.
- Add the tomato, nutmeg, and milk. Turn heat to low as soon as the sauce starts boiling.
- Cover, and cook slowly for about 1 hour. Add some water if the sauce appears to be too thick. Stir occasionally.
- Cook pasta until *al dente* (firm but not too soft or overcooked).
- Drain the pasta and pour it into a serving bowl. Top with the sauce and grated parmigiano cheese. Serve at once.

GNOCCHI GNUDI

spinach gnocchi

Gnocchi are generally associated with potato dumplings, traditional in many regions of Italy. Before the potato was introduced they were made using different ingredients such as bread crumbs or cheese.

- 1½ lb (675 gr) spinach leaves
- 8 oz (225 gr) ricotta cheese, thoroughly drained
- 1 egg + 1 egg yolk
- 3½ oz (100 gr) parmigiano reggiano cheese, freshly grated
- pinch of nutmeg
- salt and pepper
- 1 cup (125 gr) flour
- ½ cup (110 gr) butter
- 4 fresh sage leaves
- 1 tablespoon extra-virgin olive oil

- In a large saucepan, bring salted water to a boil. Add the spinach and boil it for about 10 minutes.
- Drain the spinach, place it in a cheese cloth, and form a small sack. Squeeze the sack to expel as much water as possible. Chop the spinach very fine.
- Place the spinach in a large mixing bowl. Add the ricotta cheese, egg, egg yolk, half of the grated parmigiano cheese, the pinch of nutmeg, and salt and pepper.
- With a fork, combine all the ingredients thoroughly until a smooth paste is obtained.
- Dust your hands with flour. Pick up a spoonful of the mixture. Roll it into small balls in your floured palms, flatten slightly, and shape into little oval dumplings. Coat lightly with flour.
- Place the butter and sage leaves in a small saucepan. Turn heat to low and warm gently to melt the butter. Turn off the heat and leave it to stand.
- Bring to a gentle boil a very large saucepan full of salted water.
- Add 1 teaspoon of olive oil to prevent the dumplings from sticking to one another. Gently drop the dumplings into the boiling water, a few at a time.
- The dumplings will fall to the bottom of the pan. They are ready as soon as they rise to the surface, after simmering for very short time.
- Remove the dumplings with a slotted spoon. Drain very well and place in warm serving dishes.
- Top with the sage-flavored butter and the remaining parmigiano cheese. Serve at once.

79

FOCACCIA AL ROSMARINO
rosemary flatbread

Focaccia and *schiacciata* (flat bread) are common in many parts of central and southern Italy. In Tuscany they are dressed with herbs, tomatoes, or grapes, as in the recipes that follow.

- 2½ teaspoons active dry yeast
- 1¹/₃ cups (310 cc) water, lukewarm
- 6 tablespoons extra-virgin olive oil
- 2 teaspoons salt
- 3¼ cups (450 gr) flour
- 1 tablespoon coarse salt
- 2½ tablespoons fresh rosemary leaves

- Dissolve the yeast in the lukewarm water. Set aside for a few minutes. Add 3 tablespoons of the extra-virgin olive oil to the water-yeast mix.
- In a large mixing bowl, add the 2 teaspoons salt to the flour.
- With a spatula or wooden spoon, vigorously stir the yeast-water mixture into the flour, until soft dough is obtained.
- Transfer the dough to a bowl that has been lightly spread with extra-virgin olive oil.
- Cover with plastic wrap, and place in a warm corner of the kitchen. Let the dough rise for about 1 hour, or until about doubled in size.
- Spread extra-virgin olive oil lightly on a 12 x 16-inch (30 x 40 cm) baking pan.

Invert the dough from the bowl into the pan.
- At this point the dough is very light and soft. Avoid pressing or stretching it too much. Flatten the dough with the point of the fingers until it reaches the edges, and the pan is fully covered.
- Cover the dough with oiled plastic wrap, and place the pan in a warm corner of the kitchen to rise for 1 more hour.
- Preheat oven to 450 F (230 C).
- Dimple the *focaccia* with your fingertips to create small depressions.
- Spread the remaining olive oil, the coarse salt, and the rosemary leaves uniformly on the surface of the *focaccia*.
- Bake the *focaccia* on the lower shelf of the oven for about 25 minutes, until the surface is golden and the bottom is light brown.
- Lift a corner of the *focaccia* to check readiness before removing it from the oven.

SCHIACCIATA CON L'UVA
flatbread with grapes

for the dough
- 2 teaspoons active dry yeast
- 1¹/₃ cups (310 cc) water, lukewarm
- ¼ cup sugar
- 3½ cups (500 gr) flour
- pinch of salt
- ½ cup (110 gr) butter, lukewarm
for the topping
- 1 lb (450 gr) black grapes
- 3 tablespoons sugar

- Dissolve the yeast in the lukewarm water. Set aside for a few minutes. Add sugar to the water-yeast mix.
- Sift the flour and salt in a large bowl.
- Add the butter to the flour mixing with your hands. Add the water-yeast mixture to the flour.
- Transfer the mixture to a work surface and knead until the dough is smooth.
- Transfer the dough to a bowl lightly spread with extra-virgin olive oil.
- Cover with oiled plastic wrap, and place in a warm corner of the kitchen. Let the dough rise for about 1½–2 hours, or until doubled in size.
- Spread extra-virgin olive oil lightly on a 12 x 16-inch (30 x 40 cm) baking pan. Invert the dough from the bowl into the pan.
- At this point the dough is very light and soft. Avoid pressing or stretching it too much. Flatten the dough with the points of the fingers until it reaches the edges, and the pan is fully covered.
- Dimple the *focaccia* with your fingertips to create small depressions. Spread the grapes and the sugar on the surface of the *focaccia*.
- Place the pan in a warm corner of the kitchen to rise for 1 more hour.
- Preheat oven to 425 F (220 C).
- Bake the *focaccia* on the lower shelf of the oven for about 15 minutes.
- Lower the heat to 375 F (190 C) and bake for 15 more minutes, until the surface is golden and the bottom is light brown. Lift a corner of the *focaccia* to check for readiness.

ARISTA ALLA FIORENTINA
pork roast with rosemary

serves 6

- 3 lb (approximately 1500 gr) pork ribs
- 1 garlic clove, finely diced
- 2 tablespoons fresh rosemary leaves
- salt and pepper
- 2 lb (approximately 1 kg) potatoes, in large wedges
- 6 tablespoons extra-virgin olive oil

- Preheat oven to 380 F (190 C). Cut incisions on top of the pork meat, to partially separate the ribs.
- Detach the meat from the ribs and fold the top of the meat so that the rib bones are clean.
- Mix the garlic, rosemary leaves, salt, and pepper.
- Using a sharp knife, make some incisions on the meat, and fill them with the herb mixture.
- Rub the surface of the meat with the rest of the rosemary-garlic mixture.
- Tie the meat piece with a kitchen rope. Place in an oven pan of adequate size.
- Dress potatoes with salt and pepper, and place them in the pan around the pork ribs.
- Spread the extra-virgin olive oil over the meat and the potatoes.

- Place in the oven for 1–1½ hours.
- Test for readiness with a thermometer. If no thermometer is available insert in the meat the blade of a small, sharp knife. The meat is ready when the knife comes out quite dry.
- Decorate with a fresh rosemary branch. Serve immediately, while still hot, with the potatoes on the side.

PAPARO ALLA MELARANCIA
duck in orange

Duck in orange was a common dish at the court of the Medici, and it is believed Caterina, daughter of Lorenzo II, introduced the dish to France when she moved there.

- 4 oz (115 gr) prosciutto, finely chopped
- rind of 1 orange, finely chopped
- 2 + 1 oz (60 + 30 gr) butter
- pinch of nutmeg
- salt and black pepper
- 1 duck, cleaned and flamed
- ½ cup (120 cc) dry white wine
- 2 oranges, juiced, the rind very finely diced
- 1 lemon, juiced, the rind very finely diced
- 2 tablespoon Grand Marnier, or other orange brandy
- 1 orange, sliced (for decoration)

- Combine the prosciutto, rind of the 1 orange, 2 oz (60 gm) butter, nutmeg, salt, and pepper.
- Spread the mixture inside the duck. Close the opening of the duck with kitchen rope.
- Put the 1 oz (30 gr) butter in a large skillet over low heat. As soon as the butter starts foaming, add the duck and brown on all sides.
- Add the wine, orange juice, rind of the 2 oranges, lemon juice, lemon rind, salt, and pepper.
- Cover and cook on low heat for about 90 minutes, or until the duck is tender. Add a small quantity of broth if necessary to prevent the duck from sticking to the pan.
- Remove the duck from the skillet, transfer to a serving plate, and keep it warm.
- Lower the heat, and add the Grand Marnier to the skillet.
- Stir with a wooden spoon, scraping the cooking residues from the walls and bottom of the skillet.
- Filter the sauce through a fine strainer.
- Decorate the duck with the orange slices, cover with the sauce, and serve warm.

CIBREO DELLA REGINA
sautéed chicken livers

The *cibreo* was among the dishes that Caterina de' Medici took with her when she moved to France. She was so crazy about this preparation (not exactly easily digestible) that she had dangerous indigestions from having eaten too much. The original recipe includes chicken crests and wattles, as well as "chicken beans," that is, the undeveloped chicken eggs. We have no doubts about the good taste of these ingredients, but we prefer to propose a simpler recipe, easily achievable in a modern kitchen.

- 2 oz (60 gr) flour
- salt
- 1 lb (450 gr) chicken livers, in large pieces
- 2 oz (60 gr) butter
- 1 small onion, finely diced
- 1 cup (230 cc) broth
- 2 egg yolks
- ½ lemon, juiced
- pepper
- 4 slices country bread, toasted

- Place the flour with a pinch of salt in a shallow dish. Dredge the chicken livers in the flour.
- In a skillet, place the butter over medium heat.
- When the butter starts foaming, add the onion.
- Sauté until onion is soft and translucent.
- Shake away the excess flour from the chicken livers and add them to the skillet.

- Add a few tablespoons of the broth. Cook until the livers are tender, stirring and occasionally adding more broth if the livers become too dry.
- While the livers are cooking, lightly beat the egg yolks, lemon juice, salt, and pepper together.
- When the chicken livers are ready, turn off the heat. Add the egg mixture, stirring thoroughly.
- Adjust salt and pepper. Serve warm accompanied by slices of toasted country bread.

FUNGHI TRIFOLATI
sautéed mushrooms

- ¾ lb (675 gr) fresh mushrooms
- 2 tablespoons extra-virgin olive oil
- 1 garlic clove, sliced
- pinch of crushed red pepper
- salt
- 1 tablespoon Italian parsley, chopped

- Clean the mushroom, and cut them in slices.
- In a frying pan, pour the olive oil and add the garlic and red pepper.
- Turn the heat to medium. Sauté briefly. Add the mushrooms before the garlic starts coloring. Add salt.
- Cook over medium heat until the mushrooms are tender.
- Top with the fresh parsley and serve warm.

Extra-Virgin Olive Oil

Olive oil has been known in the Mediterranean area since the Iron Age. In Egypt, ancient Greece, and Rome it was also used in the preparation of perfumes and medicines. The healthiest of the cooking fats, olive oil contributes to the production of "good cholesterol."

Olive oils not indicated as extra-virgin often are extracted using chemicals, and they are not recommended even if labeled as "light." Extra-virgin olive oil is obtained exclusively by cold pressing.

Unfortunately, this classification is far from enough to define the quality of the product: It only establishes a minimum of purity, but allows the producers to use blends of oils of unknown origin. The discriminating consumer should look on the label for the region of production and make sure that the oil was bottled by the producer at his factory.

Italian olive oils are considered the best in the world. The country is geographically varied and produces olives as varied as the climate of the different regions. Oils from the south are generally stronger in taste, while those from the North are milder. The best premium olive oils (and the most expensive) come from Liguria and Tuscany.

FAGIOLI ALL' UCCELLETTO
sautéed beans with sage

"Beans in the style of little birds" is the meaning of the name of this recipe, which derives its title from a preparation for game using similar ingredients.

- 1 lb (450 gr) dry *cannellini* beans
- 4–5 tablespoons extra-virgin olive oil
- 2 garlic cloves, crushed whole
- 5–6 sage leaves
- salt and pepper
- 4 oz (115 gr) fresh ripe tomatoes, peeled and diced

- Clean and wash the beans the night before, place them in a container, and cover with fresh water. Leave the beans to soak in the water overnight.
- Drain the beans the next day, when you are ready to cook.
- Put the beans in a stockpot full of water, and boil for about 20 minutes, or until the beans are tender.
- In a skillet, pour the extra-virgin olive oil, and turn the heat to medium.
- Add garlic and sage, and sauté until the garlic starts coloring to a very pale brown.
- Add the beans, salt, and pepper. Sauté over low heat for about 2–3 minutes.

- Add the tomatoes. Cook uncovered over low heat for about 20 minutes or until the beans are tender and the sauce thicker.
- Stir occasionally, adding a small quantity of water if the beans become too dry.

FAGIOLI AL FIASCO
beans in the flask

In past times, the white *cannellini* beans were cooked in a flask peeled of its straw wrapper. The flask was placed on hot ashes of the fire of a wood-burning oven after bread was baked. The flask rested on the pile of ashes, and the beans cooked very slowly for a number of hours at a very low temperature.

- 1 lb (450 gr) dry *cannellini* beans
- 3 garlic cloves, whole
- 4–5 tablespoons extra-virgin olive oil
- 5–6 sage leaves
- salt and pepper

- Clean and wash the beans the night before; place them in a container; and cover them with fresh water. Leave the beans to soak in the water overnight.
- Drain the beans the next day, when you are ready to cook.
- Preheat oven to 220 F (110 C).
- Slip the beans into a flask peeled of its straw wrapper, or other heavy bottle.

- Add the garlic cloves, olive oil, sage, and 6–7 tablespoons of water, enough to prevent the beans from drying while they cook.
- Place in the oven for about 3–4 hours, or until the beans are tender. Taste for readiness.
- Cool at room temperature Add salt and freshly ground black pepper. Serve the beans topped with a drizzle of fresh extra-virgin olive oil.

FIORI DI ZUCCHINA FRITTI
fried zucchini flowers

- 1 teaspoon active dry yeast
- 1 cup (230 cc) warm water
- 1 cup (150 gr) flour
- salt
- 8 zucchini flowers
- 4 anchovy fillets, cut in half
- 2 oz (60 gr) mozzarella cheese, diced
- frying oil

- Dissolve the yeast in the warm water. Set aside for about 2–3 minutes.
- In a bowl, pour the flour and a pinch of salt. Stir in the yeast mixture.
- Mix well to obtain a semi-liquid batter. Cover and set aside for about 30 minutes.
- Very carefully clean the zucchini flowers, removing the in-

side stems. Avoid breaking the flowers.

- Fill each flower with a half anchovy and a few mozzarella pieces.
- In a skillet bring the oil to frying temperature.
- Dip each flower in the batter, and fry until golden color.
- Place the zucchini flowers on paper towels on a large plate and let the oil drain shortly. Serve hot.

CASTAGNACCIO
chestnut cake

In the past, chestnuts were considered an important staple in parts of Tuscany where the chestnut tree grows abundantly. This cake was a way for Tuscan people to enjoy this delicious nut, using the simple ingredients from their pantries.

- 1 lb (450 gr) chestnut flour
- salt
- ½ cup (120 cc) + 1 tablespoon extra-virgin olive oil
- ½ cup (50 gr) + 1 tablespoon pine nuts
- ½ cup (50 gr) + 1 tablespoon raisins, soaked in water and drained
- 2 tablespoons fresh rosemary leaves

- Preheat oven to 350 F (175 C).
- Place the chestnut flour in a bowl. Slowly add some water

until it forms a dense cream. Stir carefully to avoid lumps.

- Add a pinch of salt, and the ½ cup of the olive oil. Stir thoroughly until it forms a thick emulsion.
- Add ½ cup of the pine nuts and ½ cup of the raisins to the chestnut paste.
- Spread a 9-inch-diameter (22 cm) oven pan with 1 tablespoon of olive oil. Transfer the chestnut paste to the pan.
- Decorate with the remaining pine nuts, raisins, and the rosemary leaves.
- Bake for about 1 hour or until the surface is brown. Serve warm from the pan.

CANTUCCI
tuscan almond biscotti

Biscotti in Italian means cooked twice, just the way these cookies are prepared. The word was later extended as a generic word for any kind of cookie.

- 2 cup (280 gr) flour
- ⅔ cup (130 gr) sugar
- pinch of salt
- 1 teaspoon baking powder
- 3 eggs + 1 for egg wash
- 1 teaspoon vanilla
- ¾ cup (75 gr) whole almonds

- Combine the flour, sugar, salt, and baking powder in a bowl. Form a hole in the center.

- Beat 3 eggs with the vanilla, and add them to the flour.
- Mix with a spoon or spatula, until they form a smooth dough.
- Set aside the dough for about 2 minutes.
- Preheat oven to 350 F (175 C).
- Flatten the dough approximately ⅜ inch (1 cm) thick.
- Transfer the dough to a lightly floured work surface.
- Spread the almonds uniformly on top of the dough.
- Fold the dough on itself several times, until the almonds are uniformly distributed within the dough.
- Divide the dough into 3 pieces and form 3 cylinders approximately 12 inches (30 cm) long, slightly flattened.
- Place the cylinders on a cookie pan covered with parchment paper.
- Prepare the egg wash by beating the egg with a pinch of salt.
- Brush the egg wash on the dough.
- Bake for approximately 30 minutes, until the surface is golden but the dough is still soft.
- Remove from the oven; cut in slices diagonally, approximately ⅜-inch (1 cm) thick.
- Place the slices back on the pan, and bake for approximately 15 more minutes.

The cookies should be served with sweet Tuscan Vinsanto wine for dipping.

FRITTELLE DI RISO
rice fritters

- 2 cups (460 cc) milk
- ½ cup (100 gr) *arborio* rice
- 2 tablespoons butter
- ¼ teaspoon salt
- ¼ cup (50 gr) sugar
- 1/3 cup (45 gr) flour
- grated rind of 1 orange
- 3 egg yolks, separated from whites
- ½ cup (50 gr) candied orange, diced
- 2 tablespoons Grand Marnier, or other orange brandy
- frying oil

- In a saucepan, bring the milk to a boil. Add the rice. Cook at a full boil for about 10 minutes.
- Stir in the butter, salt, 2 tablespoons of the sugar, the flour, and the grated orange rind. Remove from the heat and cool to room temperature.
- In a small bowl, combine the yolks, candied orange, and Grand Marnier.
- Stir the egg yolk mixture into the rice until fully combined.
- In a separate bowl, beat the egg whites until they form peaks. Fold the egg whites into the rice, with a gentle top-to-bottom movement.
- In a skillet, bring the oil to frying temperature. Drop the rice mixture into the hot oil, one tablespoon at a time, and fry until golden on all sides.
- Remove the fritters from the skillet with a slotted spoon, and transfer on paper towels on a large plate and let the oil drain briefly.
- Spread the remaining sugar on the fritters and serve hot.

TORTA FRANGIPANE
frangipane almond cake

This almond tart receives its name from a Florentine nobleman. He is credited in France as being the inventor of a delicious almond cream.

for the dough
- 1¾ cups (250 gr) flour
- 5½ oz (150 gr) butter, lukewarm
- ½ cup (100 gr) sugar
- 2 egg yolks
- ½ teaspoon vanilla powder
- pinch of salt

for the filling
- 4½ oz (125 gr) butter, lukewarm
- 2/3 cup (125 gr) sugar
- 2 eggs
- 4½ oz (125 gr) almonds, peeled and finely ground
- 1/3 cup (45 gr) flour
- ½ teaspoon almond extract

for finishing
- 1 egg white, for brushing
- powdered sugar, for dusting

preparing the dough
- Pour the flour onto a work surface, to form a mound shape with a hole in the center.
- In the well add the butter, sugar, egg yolks, vanilla powder, and pinch of salt.
- Using a fork, mix the ingredients together with the flour.
- Knead the paste rapidly with your hands to form dough—avoid warming the dough too much.
- Sprinkle the work surface with just enough flour to prevent the dough from sticking to the surface.
- When the dough is smooth and consistent, form it into a ball, place in a plate, cover with plastic wrap, and keep in the refrigerator for about 30 minutes.

preparing the filling
- Whip the butter and the sugar together, by hand or with an electric mixer, until fluffy.
- Gently add the eggs, almond, flour, and almond extract.

assembling the cake
- Preheat oven to 375 F (190 C). Remove the dough from the refrigerator.
- Butter a shallow 8-inch (20 cm) tart pan with removable bottom—and sprinkle with a small amount of flour.
- Cut the dough into two parts, one quarter and three quarters large.
- Briefly knead the larger dough. Using a rolling pin on a floured surface, flatten the larger portion into the shape of a disk.
- Wrap the dough around the floured rolling pin. Place the dough flat in the pan; and with your fingers, push it to uniformly cover the bottom of the pan.

- Prick the surface of the pastry evenly with a fork to prevent the dough from puffing while baking.
- Pour the almond batter in the pan. Spread uniformly.
- Flatten the reserved dough and cut it into strips. Place the strips over the cake, creating a lattice shape. Brush with the egg white.
- Bake for about 40 minutes, until the pastry is golden brown. Sprinkle with powdered sugar before serving.

ZUCCOTTO
whipped cream trifle

This dessert, filled with ice cream or whipped cream, is the modern version of a layer cake from Florence, not conventionally arranged, but shaped in the form of a dome. *Zuccotto* it is said to have been inspired to the shape of the cupola of the Duomo of Florence.

for the sponge cake
- 5 eggs
- 1 teaspoon vanilla powder
- ¾ cup (150 gr) sugar
- ¾ cup (110 gr) flour
- ¹/₃ cup (50 gr) corn starch
- pinch of salt

for the filling
- ¾ cup (approximately 180 cc) Cointreau liquor or rum
- 3 cups (750 cc) whipping cream
- ¾ cup (90 gr) powdered sugar
- 1 teaspoon vanilla powder
- 2 squares (60 gr) unsweetened dark chocolate, grated

- 3 tablespoons (30 gr) peeled almonds, very finely chopped
- ½ cup (60 gr) candied orange and citron, diced
- 2½ squares (75 gr) semi–sweet chocolate, coarsely chopped

preparing the sponge cake
- Preheat oven to 350 F (175 C).
- Butter a round cake pan of about 9 inches (22 cm) in diameter x 2 inches (5 cm) deep.
- Line the pan with a disk of parchment paper.
- In a bowl, mix the eggs, vanilla, and sugar.
- Beat vigorously with an electric mixer for about 10–15 minutes, or until the mixture is very soft and doubled in volume.
- On a plate, sift the flour, cornstarch, and a pinch of salt together.
- Sift the flour into the beaten eggs. Fold the mixture thoroughly with a rubber spatula, 3–4 times, mixing gently with a round, top to bottom, movement.
- Pour the mixture in the pan, and smooth the top with a spatula.
- Bake for about 30–45 minutes, or until golden.
- Transfer to a rack to cool to room temperature.

filling and assembling the cake
- Cut the sponge cake in slices about ³/₈-inch (1 cm) thick.
- Line a round bowl, approximately 7½ inches (18 cm) in diameter and approximately 4½ inches (11 cm) deep, with plastic wrap.

- Line the inside of the bowl with the cake slices.
- Cut the slices in wedges, if necessary, to uniformly cover the surface of the bowl in a shaped design.
- Brush the cake slices with Coitreau.
- Whip the cream, sugar, and vanilla until firm.
- Fold the dark chocolate, almonds, and candied fruit into the whipped cream.
- Transfer half of the cream mixture to a separate bowl.
- Melt the semisweet chocolate in a double boiler, or in a small saucepan over boiling water.
- Gently fold the melted chocolate into one half of the cream.
- Spread the white cream inside the bowl over the sponge cake.
- Fill the rest of the bowl with the chocolate cream until completely full.
- Cover with foil, and freeze for at least 3–4 hours.
- The cake needs to be served cold but not frozen. To test whether the cake is ready for serving, insert a skewer in it to test its softness.
- Remove the cake from the freezer, and place in the refrigerator to soften before serving, about 6–7 hours.
- If the cake is removed from the freezer and kept at room temperature, it will take about 3 hours to be ready for serving.

CHAPTER 5

Pizza and Beyond

The Food of Southern Italy

Southern Italy is very different from the regions of the north and the center. The predominant presence of the sea makes it a truly Mediterranean territory, with a cuisine rich in piquant food, tomatoes, eggplant, lamb, and fish. Naples was the capital of southern Italy for centuries, and it is famous for its pizza, pasta, and tomatoes. The Calabria and Lucania regions, mountainous areas where life remains simple and frugal, contrast with the Apulia region, a flat agricultural land where produce and pasta prevail.

The Warriors from the Cold

After the barbaric invasions, the political situation in southern Italy was stabilized for a few centuries. A Lombard kingdom was established south of Rome; the Byzantine Empire controlled some regions; and Sicily was under Saracen control. Amalfi, a small town north of Naples, won independence in the seventh century and became a maritime power long before Venice did. The city grew into a republic of 80,000 and was one of the main trading ports of the Mediterranean.

Then, in 1016, the destiny of southern Italy dramatically changed: a local baron brought into the area a group of Norman mercenaries. During the next few decades the Normans seized most of the southern regions from the Byzantines and threw the Saracens out of Sicily. The Normans established their capital city in Palermo and created a multicultural kingdom that lasted for more than a century, where Christians, Greek Orthodox, Jews, and Muslims could live together.

In 1220, Frederick II—one of the most extraordinary figures of the Middle Ages—was crowned king. He was a munificent monarch, a diplomat and a warrior, as well as an architect and poet. In those times of violence and intolerance, he reigned in harmony with the people. For his astonishing qualities he was called *stupor mundi* ("wonder of the world").

'O pazzariello (the town crier, the herald). The town crier, together with writing on walls, are the oldest forms of advertising.

Dressed in a colored uniform, and accompanied by a small band playing drums, cymbals, and other, unusual instruments, the crier went through the *vicoli* (the small streets) of Naples, dancing and singing in rhyme, and followed by a crowd of kids and spectators.

He was advertising a new wine merchant or a new pasta seller. In one hand he had a stick, or a big cowbell; in the other perhaps a flask to pour the wine directly in the mouths of the public, or a basket with pasta samples.

After his death, the intrigues of the church and the greed of foreign powers started a series of events that would bring southern Italy under the dominion of the Spanish crown. For a long time, the country was treated as a colony, exploited for its products. In addition, the barons of the *latifundiums,* the large agricultural estates into which the south was divided, remained the most influential authority, able to bargain power for themselves with any succeeding government.

During this period, a different mentality established its roots in southern Italy—it was a perspective that gave more importance to clan loyalty than to the rule of law. Banditry and revolts by an often-anarchic population were frequent. Subsequent repressions and the In-quisition used as political instruments, became a way of life in this land for a long time. These events later caused the formation of mafia-like secret societies.

After a short occupation by the French during Napoleon's empire, the "Reign of the Two Sicilies," became an independent state under the Bourbons, creating a time of fairly grandiose rule. The seventeenth and eighteenth centuries saw vast palaces built, the economy revived, and intellectual life improved. After the discovery and excavation of the Roman city of Pompeii, which had been destroyed by the Vesuvius volcano in Roman times, Naples became one of the most important centers to visit in Italy; it attracted many intellectuals from all over Europe.

Southern Italy during the past centuries had a complex history. Although the rich conducted a life similar to that of the upper classes of other parts of Italy, the poor were really poor. In Naples and in the Campania region, the cooking style reflects this, where the dishes of evident Spanish or French influence come together with those of the common people.

Naples is particularly rich in inventive dishes, the fruit of the resourcefulness of the people. Complicated dishes like the *sartu'* (rice timbale filled with peas and meat balls), *ragu'* (thick tomato sauce), and *gatto'* (potato casserole), all of French origin, live side by side with an extensive cuisine of seafood. Two dishes of the poor, pizza and pasta, became extraordinarily successful. Both dishes have traveled successfully with Italian emigrants, establishing roots all over the world, and pasta in particular has become a dominant phenomenon in Italian cooking culture.

Lampare (boats for fishing with lamplights) are common all over the Mediterranean. At sunset, the boats leave the harbor to venture into the bay. In the dark of the night, they look like small flames rocking in the deep blue sea. The fish, attracted by the brightness, are captured in large nets. In the morning, the fish will be sold to the markets and restaurants of Naples. Freshly captured fish does not need complex cooking. Southern Italian cuisine is rightly famous for countless simple and delicious fresh fish recipes

Tomato Revolution

At the basis of Neapolitan cooking is an ingredient that would deserve a separate chapter: the tomato. We cannot think today of cooking Italian without it. The tomato arrived in Europe from South America, but people began using it a couple of centuries later. The spread of the tomato as a cooking ingredient began only in the eighteenth century. Then it quickly took the kitchen by storm and entered into most of the preparations. Fresh tomatoes go on the pizza and on hundreds of pasta and fish dishes. In the Campania region, the quality is excellent and a large industry flourishes producing tomatoes—canned, whole, or concentrated.

The Calabria region has the shape of a long peninsula with a mountainous spine, where nature is violent and "the rivers are torrents." The region flourished during the early times when the Greeks established colonies there. Later the coast was infested by Saracen incursions, and most of the population took refuge on the mountains to escape the threat. Difficulties in communication and living conditions changed the people into an isolated, patriarchal society. As a result, the cooking is represented by archaic dishes: cabbage-and-bread soup, *lagane,* sausages, game, fish, olives, figs, and almonds—all dating back to ancient history—while lamb meat and cheese, widely common, bring to mind a disappearing pastoral way of living.

Lucania got its name from the Lucanians, the initial inhabitants of the land. The other name of the region, Basilicata, dates back to the Byzantine domination. *Basileus* is the Greek word for king, therefore meaning that it was a province of the Byzantine Empire. The kitchen still reflects the traditions of the original people, who were shepherds and hunters. Some dishes are ancient recipes typical of a primitive society: the simple lamb cooked with garlic and herbs, pork baked in the oven, sausage, *pecorino* cheese, the aroma of rosemary, olives, and the vegetables such as chickpeas and lentils. All these ancient foods contrast with other dishes flavored with cinnamon and saffron, of decadent Bizantine influence.

Apulian cuisine is quite different from that of its neighbors. Apulia is a flat land rich in production of wheat and vegetables. The abundance of vegetables and fish make these ingredients predominant in the diet of the region, even more than meat. The region is renowned for its dishes of mussels and oysters, as well as crustaceans and mollusks in general. Pasta dough is very common, showing up in many shapes made simply with flour and water and without eggs. Above all are the famous *orecchiette*, little handmade ear-shaped pasta, which are dressed with all kinds of vegetables or sauce.

The diffusion—if not the "invention"—of dry pasta is still one of the greatest accomplishments of southern cooking. The technique for drying was perfected in the town of Gragnano, a few miles from Naples, allowing industrial production of this most Italian of the foods ❖❖

INSALATA DI FRUTTI DI MARE
seafood salad

serves 6

- 2 lb (approximately 1 kg) clams
- 2 lb (approximately 1 kg) mussels
- 1 lb (450 gr) scallops
- 1 lb (450 gr) rawshrimps
- 1 lb (450 gr) small squid
- 2 lemons, juiced
- 2 cloves of garlic, finely minced
- 2 tablespoons Italian parsley, finely chopped
- 2 sticks celery, finely sliced
- ½ cup (120 cc) extra-virgin olive oil
- salt and pepper

- Wash the clams and mussels to eliminate sand and impurities.
- Wash the scallops and the shrimps in fresh water.
- Wash the squid and eliminate the skin and the interior. Separate and chop the legs, and cut the bodies in little rings.
- In a large skillet, pour approximately 1 cup (250 cc) water, and add the clams and mussels. Place the lid on the skillet and cook until the shells open.
- Remove the clams and mussels from the shell, and place them in a bowl. Filter away the sand and residues, and keep the cooking water.
- In a medium-size pan, pour 2 cups (approximately 500 cc) of water, and bring to a boil. Place the scallops in the pan, and cook for about 2 minutes until they

begin coloring. Drain the scallops with a slotted spoon.

- Again bring to a boil the cooking water used for the scallops. Place the shrimps in the boiling water, and cook them until they become red, in about 2–3 minutes. Drain with a slotted spoon. Let the shrimps cool, and eliminate the shells.
- Bring the water to a boil again, and blanch the squid for about 30 seconds. Drain the squid in a colander; place them for few seconds in cold water to stop the cooking process. Drain and dry, patting them with tissue.
- Drain all the seafood thoroughly. Combine the clams, mussels, scallops, shrimps, and squid in a large bowl.
- In a small bowl, combine the lemon juice, garlic, parsley, celery, olive oil, salt, pepper, and ½ cup (120 cc) of the reserved clam cooking water. Stir into the bowl with the fish.
- Place the bowl in the refrigerator for about 30 minutes before serving.

COZZE GRATINATE
mussels gratin

- 2 lb (approximately 1 kg) mussels
- 1 garlic clove, finely chopped
- 2 tablespoons Italian parsley, finely chopped
- 3 tablespoons extra-virgin olive oil
- 2 oz (60 gr) bread crumbs
- salt and pepper
- 2 lemons, wedged
- ½ lb (225 gr) fresh, ripe tomatoes

- Clean the mussels under fresh water. Cut off the "beard."
- Place the mussels in a large saucepan full of water.
- Turn the heat to medium. As soon as the mussels open, lift them from the pan one by one.
- Remove the mussels from the shells.
- Set the half shells aside. Discard the mussels that do not open.
- Preheat oven to 450 F (230 C).
- In a bowl, combine the garlic, parsley, olive oil, and bread crumbs.
- Add the mussels, salt, and pepper, and mix them until all the mussels are well covered. Set aside for about 30 minutes.
- Using a vegetable peeler, remove the skin from the tomatoes.
- Cut the tomatoes in half, and remove the seeds and liquid.
- Cut the tomatoes in thin slices.
- In a large flat oven pan, place the half empty shells.
- Place one mussel in each shell; and spread the bread crumb mixture leftover from the bowl, evenly over the mussels.
- Put one slice of tomato atop each mussel.
- Place the pan in the oven just long enough to form a thin crust. Serve hot, along with lemon wedges.

SPAGHETTI ALLA TRAPANESE
pasta with fresh tomato and basil

- ½ lb (225 gr) fresh ripe tomatoes, peeled, seeded and finely diced
- 1 garlic clove, finely chopped
- 6–8 basil leaves
- 2 oz (60 gr) almonds, finely sliced
- 3–4 tablespoons extra-virgin olive oil
- 1 teaspoon capers in salt, rinsed and drained, finely chopped
- 1 teaspoon lemon juice
- salt and crushed red pepper
- 1 lb (450 gr) spaghetti

- Put tomatoes in a small bowl. Add the garlic, almonds, extra-virgin olive oil, capers, lemon juice, salt, and red pepper.
- Combine all ingredients thoroughly with a fork, smashing the tomatoes. Set aside for about 1 hour.
- Cook pasta in abundant salted water. Follow manufacturers instructions, checking for readiness from time to time. Pasta is ready when *al dente* (tender but not too soft or overcooked).
- Drain the pasta, and transfer it to a bowl. Top with the fresh tomato sauce. Toss it thoroughly, and serve at once.

ZUPPA DI PESCE
fish soup

Any kind of fish can be used in a fish soup. Variety will add flavor and taste. The principle of fish soup is to use low cost, small, but savory fish.

- ½ lb (225 gr) mussels
- ½ lb (225 gr) clams
- salt
- 5 tablespoons extra virgin-olive oil
- 2 garlic cloves, finely sliced
- crushed red pepper
- 1½ cups (450 gr) fresh ripe tomatoes, peeled and chopped
- 2-3 tablespoons Italian parsley, finely chopped
- 1 lb (450 gr) white fish (cod, orange roughy, seabass, or similar), cut in large dices
- 1 lb (450 gr) raw shrimps
- ½ lb (225 gr) squid, calamari, or small octopus
- 4 slices of country bread, toasted

- Rinse and drain the mussels and the clams.
- In a skillet put 1 cup (230 cc) of water, a pinch of salt, and the clams and mussels. Cover with lid.
- Bring to a boil. As soon as the shells begin opening, remove the mollusks from the skillet and place them, in their shells, in a bowl.
- When all the mollusks are removed filter the sand and residue, and keep the cooking water.

- In a skillet, place the extra-virgin olive oil, garlic, and red pepper.
- Turn heat to medium. As soon as the garlic becomes very light golden add the tomato, and 1 tablespoon of the parsley. Cook for few minutes.
- Add the clam water and approximately 2 cups (450 cc) water, and bring to a boil.
- Add the white fish, shrimps, and squid. Cook for about 10 minutes.
- Add the clams and mussels. Add salt if necessary.
- Stir in the remaining parsley, and cook for a few more minutes.
- Toast the bread slices. Place them in single serving bowls, and cover with the soup. Serve hot.

FILETTI DI SOGLIOLA AL POMODORO
sole fillets with tomatoes

- 4 sole fillets approximately 1½ lb (600 gr)
- ½ lb (225 gr) fresh ripe tomatoes, finely diced
- 2 tablespoons Italian parsley, chopped
- 2 garlic cloves, finely chopped
- 4 tablespoons extra-virgin olive oil
- salt and pepper

- Preheat oven to 350 F (175 C).
- Place the sole fillets on an oiled oven pan.
- In a bowl, combine the tomatoes, parsley, garlic, 1 tablespoon of the extra-virgin olive oil, and salt and pepper.
- Spray the tomato mix on top of the soles.
- Spread with the rest of the oil and place in the oven for about 15–20 minutes. Serve warm.

PESCE SPADA ALLA MARINARA
lemon sautéed swordfish

- 5 tablespoons extra-virgin olive oil
- 3 garlic cloves, finely chopped
- 1 lb (450 gr) sword-fish, cut in 4 slices
- salt and pepper
- 1 lemon, sliced
- 4 tablespoons Italian parsley, chopped

- In a skillet, pour the extra-virgin olive oil over medium heat, and add the chopped garlic.
- Add the fish before the garlic begins coloring. Season with salt and pepper.
- Top the fish with the lemon slices and the parsley, and sauté for about 5 minutes.
- Cover and cook for 5 more minutes.
- Remove the lemon, turn the fish over, and put the lemon slices back on the fish.
- Cook for 5 additional minutes. Serve warm.

The Big Night

Few will remember this 1996 movie with Stanley Tucci, Tony Shalhoub, and Isabella Rossellini. In the 1950s, two brothers—Primo (the chef) and Secondo (the maitre d')—came from southern Italy to open a small restaurant called the Paradise, but with little success. Here's the scene: The food is excellent, but they have no live music and no free side orders; and, although the food is "religiously" prepared, it takes too long to reach the tables. Across the street, Pascal's draws crowds: the food is mediocre but cheap and abundant; and the ambience is stereotypical.

Predictably, the Paradise has economic problems, and foreclosure is approaching. Secondo wants to try to change the menu to reverse the restaurant's fate, but Primo is inflexible. He will never surrender to the "rape of cuisine" perpetuated every night by Pascal. "To eat good food is to be close to God," he says, and "If you give people time, they will learn." But time is up for them.

Pascal, aware of the situation, pretends to help. He offers to bring to the Paradise the famous singer Louis Prima: The event will bring recognition to the restaurant, and the situation might turn around. In reality, he plans to sabotage the two brothers, hoping they will come to work for him.

Primo and Secondo prepare a great banquet, a "big night," well aware that if the event fails, the costs will put them out of business.

The focus of the movie is on the preparation, the serving, and the atmosphere of the great dinner. It will be an evening to remember for everybody: the celebrity will not show up, and the two brothers will be left to face themselves and their expectations in life.

Big Night is an allegory for the struggle of the quality shops against the large industries, the small "independents" against the establishment. It takes us back to the "Pizza Wars" of the 1980s, when the introduction of the free-delivery pizza chains put the small local pizzerias into a big crisis. People did not care about quality; they preferred to eat tasteless, cardboard-like pizza for the convenience of having it delivered, while smaller shops went out of business despite how good their product was.

At the end, the movie tells us to look not for trivial and flashy food, but for the excellence that may be found at the less pretentious shops across the street. It tells us that good food is love and a universal form of communication.

The centerpiece of the dinner was a mysterious *timpano,* a lavish pasta preparation and secret recipe, revered and venerated by the brothers all night—from its inception to the final point of cooking. Everything counts, from the right time to the right serving temperature. As a tribute to this great movie, we include here our recipe for the classic Neapolitan *timpano* ❖

RAGU' ALLA NAPOLETANA
tomato sauce neapolitan style

Ragu' tomato sauce was traditionally made in Naples using only tomato concentrate and paste, cooking it for up to 5–6 hours. We suggest a simpler recipe that uses canned tomatoes and will be ready in half the time.

serves 6

- 4 tablespoons extra-virgin olive oil
- 1 medium onion, finely chopped
- 2 lb (approximately 1 kg) pork for roasting
- 1 cup (230 cc) dry red wine
- 1½ lb (650 gr) tomatoes, puréed in a blender
- 1 garlic clove, finely chopped
- salt and pepper
- 9 oz (250 gr) tomato paste concentrate

- In a saucepan put the olive oil and onion. Turn heat to medium and sauté until onion becomes soft and translucent.
- Add the meat. Cook, turning the meat over to brown on all sides, for about 5-6 minutes.
- Pour the wine, and before the wine is completely evaporated add tomatoes.
- Cover the pan, and simmer for about 1 hour stirring occasionally.
- Add the garlic, salt, pepper, and tomato paste, stirring to combine.
- There should be enough liquid in the pan for the sauce to cook without adding any water. Add hot boiling water only if is necessary to prevent the sauce from sticking to the pan.
- If there is too much fat, skim it with a spoon while it surfaces.
- Cook covered slowly on medium-low heat, slowly until the meat is very tender, and the *ragu'* is very thick.

This dish can become a full lunch by itself. The sauce can be used to dress a large dish of *fusilli* pasta, while the meat can be sliced very thin and served as second course.

TIMPANO DI MACCHERONI
macaroni timbale

prepare the ragu' alla Napoletana according to the previous recipe

for the pasta
- salt
- 1 lb (450 gr) *rigatoni* pasta
- 2 oz (60 gr) parmigiano reggiano cheese

for the dough
- 1 lb (450 gr) flour
- 6 oz (180 gr) butter, lukewarm
- 2 eggs
- 1 oz (30 gr) sugar
- 2 tablespoons salt

for the filling
- 2 tablespoons extra-virgin olive oil
- 1 onion, finely chopped
- ½ lb (225 gr) shelled peas
- salt and pepper
- 2 oz (60 gr) butter
- 6 oz (180 gr) *provola* cheese or *pecorino romano* cheese, finely sliced.
- 4 eggs, hard boiled and sliced
- 6 oz (180 gr) *salame*, finely diced
- 2 oz (60 gr) parmigiano reggiano cheese, grated

preparing the pasta

- Cook the *rigatoni* pasta in abundant salted water for half of the time indicated on manufacturer's instructions.
- Drain and dress with half of the *ragu'*, and the parmigiano cheese. Reserve the rest of the *ragu'*.
- Slice the meat of the *ragu'* very thin, then cut the slices in squares about 2 inch (5 cm) and reserve.

preparing the dough

- Pour the flour on a work surface in a mound shape with a hole in the center.
- Put the butter, eggs, sugar, and salt in the hole. Add ½ cup (120 cc) water. Knead for several minutes until dough is smooth, and reserve.

assembling the timpano

- In a skillet, pour the olive oil and add the onion. Sauté until onion is soft. Add the peas, salt, and pepper. Cook until the peas are tender.
- Preheat oven to 500 F (260 C). Butter an oven pan about 10 inches (25 cm) in diameter and 3–4 inches (8–10 cm) deep.
- Divide the dough in 3 parts. Using a rolling pin flatten 2 of the dough pieces until each one is about ¼ inch (5 mm) thick.
- Line the bottom and sides of the pan with one of the flattened dough pieces. Lay the second dough on top of the first. Pinch the dough around the edges of the pan to stick the two layers to each other.
- In a bowl, mix the sliced meat with the reserved *ragu'*.
- Make one layer inside the pan with half of the *rigatoni* pasta.

- Add in layers the *ragu'* meat, peas, cheese, eggs, and *salame*.
- Complete with one layer of the remaining *rigatoni* pasta, *ragu'* sauce, and the grated parmigiano cheese.
- Flatten the reserved dough to about ¼-inch (6 mm) thick.
- Cover the pan with the dough, and pinch the dough all around the edge to seal. Make a large hole in the center of the dough.
- Bake for about 10 minutes, checking frequently, until small bubbles will appear around the edges of the pan.
- Lower the temperature to 425 F (220 C), and bake for about 30 more minutes.
- Remove from the oven, and cool at room temperature. Slide a knife along the edges of the pan to detach the dough. Remove from the pan, inverting upside down on a serving plate. Serve lukewarm.

GATTO' DI PATATE
potato mold

serves 6

- 2 lb (900 gr) potatoes
- 1 egg
- 2 tablespoons (30 gr) butter, diced
- 2 oz (60 gr) parmigiano reggiano cheese, grated
- 2 oz (60 gr) mozzarella cheese, diced
- 2 oz (60 gr) cooked ham, diced
- 2 tablespoons Italian parsley, chopped
- grated rind of 1 lemon
- pinch of nutmeg
- ½ cup (120 cc) milk, or heavy cream
- salt and pepper
- 2 tablespoons bread crumbs

- Boil potatoes, peel, and mash them in a food mill while still hot.
- Preheat oven to 350 F (175 C).
- In a bowl, combine the mashed potatoes, the egg, 1 tablespoon of the butter, the parmigiano, mozzarella, ham, parsley, lemon rind, nutmeg, milk, salt, and pepper together.
- Brush the bottom of a round oven pan, approximately 8 inches (20 cm) in diameter.
- Pour the potato mixture in the pan; level it with a spatula. Top with the bread crumbs and the remaining 1 tablespoon diced butter.
- Bake for about 30 minutes, until the surface is golden. Serve hot.

Mozzarella

Mozzarella is a soft cheese made in the Campania region using buffalo milk. The buffalos we know today, with their black cloak and sharp horns, were introduced in Italy in the seventh century by the Lombards.

Buffalos like water, and they adapted very well in the swamps of the Pontina area between Rome and Naples.

Buffalo Mozzarella has a distinctive flavor and is produced and delivered fresh daily, kept in the whey in which it is produced. Mozzarella cheese is extremely appreciated, and is part of many traditional preparations all over Italy, especially pizza in Naples.

Pizza

Pizza is a derivation from *focaccia,* flat bread that has been prepared since antiquity in different forms and garnished with herbs, olives, fat, raisin, honey, and nuts. In fact, the word *pizza* in Italian identifies any type of flat bread or pie—fried or baked.

Naples has many records of pizza since around the year 1000; the first mentions call these flat breads *laganae,* and later they are referred to as *picea.* In those times, pizzas were dressed with garlic and olive oil, or cheese and anchovies, or small local fish. They were baked on the open fire and sometimes were closed in two, as a book, to form a calzone.

Although you'd find many types of pitas or pizzas around the Mediterranean, it is in Naples that pizza in the form we know it today first emerged, after the tomato appeared on the table in the 1700s. That is also where, in 1830, the first pizzeria opened up, with a brick wood-burning oven, covered with lava stones from the Vesuvius.

Pizza became very popular, earning its place in Neapolitan folklore. Simple and economical, it turned into the food for all people, even sold on the streets, as shown in many illustrations of the time.

A famous episode extended the popularity of pizza beyond the limits of the city of Naples. It was 1889, and Queen Margherita was visiting the city. She was told about pizza and wanted to taste it. A

Pizza seller in the streets of Naples, engraving, early 1800s. The tradition of preparing and selling all kinds of pizzas in the streets remains well alive today in the small lanes of downtown Naples. Pizza and *calzoni, panzerotti,* and *pizzelle fritte* are delicious when eaten warm—prepared right on the spot—in the hundreds of small shops. As with fast foods, they can be either a snack or a full meal.

famous cook by the name of Don Raffaele, helped by his wife Donna Rosa, was invited to cook pizza at the royal palace. They prepared three pizzas, typical of that time: one with cheese and basil; one with garlic, oil, and tomato; and one with mozzarella, basil, and tomato. The queen, impressed by the colors of the last pizza, which resembled the national flag, preferred that one. Since then this pizza is known as *Pizza Margherita,* and Don Raffaele is credited with its invention, even if we know that it already existed for a long time.

In the beginning of the last century, with Italian immigrants, the first pizzerias appeared also in the United States, where pizza has become a mass phenomenon.

Yet, even today the best pizza is found in Naples, where it is rigorously made with buffalo mozzarella. Superior pizzas are considered those obtained by moderate variations of the simplest and most popular: Pizza *Napoletana* with tomato, garlic, oil, and oregano; Pizza *Margherita;* Pizza *Marinara* with tomato, anchovies, capers, and olives; and Pizza Four Seasons, divided in four quadrants, each dressed in a different way. Pizza with hot salami, the American pepperoni, is instead found in the Calabria region south of Naples, where this type of hot sausage is produced ❖

PASTA PER PIZZA
basic pizza dough

makes 4
12-inch (30 cm) pizzas

- 1 tablespoon active dry yeast, or 1 oz (25 gr) brewer's yeast
- 1½ cups (350 cc) warm water
- 3½ cups (500 gr) flour
- 1 tablespoon extra-virgin olive oil
- pinch of salt

- The temperature in the room should be around 68–75 F (20–24 C), for the dough to rise properly.
- In a small bowl, sprinkle the yeast on the warm water, and stir to dissolve it. Let stand until the yeast starts forming bubbles in about 5 minutes
- Pour the flour on a work surface or into a large bowl. Mold the flour in a mound shape with a hole, and pour the yeast mix, olive oil, and a pinch of salt in the center. Mix very well together to form dough.
- Sprinkle some flour on the work surface. Place the dough on the floured surface.
- Knead the dough very briefly with your hands: just long enough for the dough to take in a little more flour, and until it no longer sticks to your hands.
- With your hand, spread a little olive oil inside a bowl.

- Form a ball with the dough, and place it in the oiled bowl. On the top, make two incisions that cross, and spread the top with a very small amount of olive oil. This last step will prevent the surface of the dough from breaking too much while rising.
- Cover the bowl with a kitchen cloth, and set the bowl aside for approximately 1½–2 hours until the dough doubles in volume. The time required for rising will depend on the strength of the yeast and the temperature of the room.
- When the dough is double its original size, punch it down to eliminate the air bubbles.
- Cut the dough into four equal pieces.
- On the work surface, shape one piece of dough into a thinner round layer.
- Make a pizza about 12 inches in diameter, using your hands and a rolling pin.
- Repeat this step with the other 3 dough pieces to obtain 4 pizzas.
- Home made pizza can be cooked in different ways:
  - Regular metal pizza pan (needs to be oiled before receiving the pizza).
  - Non-stick pizza pan.
  - Perforated pizza pan (cooks very uniformly on the bottom).
  - Pizza stone. Place the stone in the oven about 10 minutes in advance to bring it to the right temperature. Excellent for uniform cooking. The pizza bottom needs to be kept floury to prevent it from sticking to the stone.
- Place the pizza in the pan. Using your fingertips, push from the center to the sides to cover the entire surface of the pan with a thin layer of pasta. At this point the pizza is ready to receive its topping.
- Add onto the pizza your preferred topping. Sprinkle with a pinch of salt and pepper if indicated by the recipe.
- Pizza should stay in the oven the shortest possible time, to prevent it from drying out too much. Pizza in restaurants is cooked in wood-burning ovens at very high temperature for about 10 minutes. The smoke of wood also gives pizza a distinctive flavor. It is impossible to reproduce perfectly the same conditions at home.
- Cook the pizza in a regular oven at 500 F (260 C) for about 20–25 minutes.
- The cheese for a home made pizza, if present in the recipe, should be added 5–10 minutes before removing the pizza from the oven.
- To check for readiness, lift one side of the pizza. The pizza is ready when the bottom surface is light brown.

Classic Pizza Toppings

all toppings are for one pizza

AGLIO E OLIO
oil and garlic

- 2 garlic cloves
- 2 tablespoons fresh oregano leaves, chopped
- 2 tablespoons extra-virgin olive oil

AGLIO, OLIO E POMODORO
oil, garlic, and tomato

- 12 oz (340 gr) fresh tomato, peeled, seeded, and diced
- 2 garlic cloves
- 2 tablespoons fresh oregano leaves, chopped
- 2 tablespoons extra-virgin olive oil

MARGHERITA BIANCA
mozzarella and parmigiano

- ½ lb (225 gr) fresh mozzarella
- 3 tablespoons grated parmigiano
- 2 tablespoons extra-virgin olive oil
- 1 tablespoons basil

MARINARA
tomato, capers, olives

- 12 oz (340 gr) fresh tomato, peeled, seeded, and diced
- 1 oz (30 gr) capers in salt, rinsed and drained
- 2 anchovy fillets
- 2 oz. (60 gr) black olives
- 2 tablespoons extra-virgin olive oil

ACCIUGHE
anchovies

- 1 garlic cloves
- 5 anchovy fillets
- 1 tablespoon italian parsley
- 2 tablespoons extra-virgin olive oil

COZZE
mussels

- 1½ lb (675 gr) mussels, shelled in a skillet over medium heat
- 12 oz (340 gr) fresh tomato, peeled, seeded, and diced
- 1 garlic cloves
- 2 tablespoons extra-virgin olive oil
- 1 tablespoon fresh oregano or Italian parsley, finely chopped

BIANCA CON I FUNGHI
mushrooms

- ½ lb (225 gr) white mushrooms, finely sliced
- 3–4 tablespoons extra-virgin olive oil
- 3 tablespoons Italian parsley, finely chopped
- 1 garlic clove, diced
- salt and pepper
- 2 oz (60 gr) mozzarella cheese, shredded or sliced

RUCOLA E BRESAOLA
arugula and beef prosciutto

- 1 bunch of arugula
- 2 oz (60 gr) *bresaola* (beef prosciutto) or prosciutto
- 1 oz (30 gr) parmigiano, in shavings
- 2 tablespoons extra-virgin olive oil

QUATTRO STAGIONI
four seasons

- 4 oz (115 gr) pound white mushrooms, finely sliced
- 2 oz (60 gr) black olives
- 2 oz (60 gr) small artichokes, canned in olive oil
- 2 oz (60 gr) clams, shelled in a skillet on medium heat.
- 6 oz (180 gr) fresh tomato, peeled, seeded, and diced
- 1 tablespoon fresh basil leaves
- 2 tablespoons extra-virgin olive oil

QUATTRO FORMAGGI
four cheeses

- 2 oz (60 gr) swiss cheese, finely diced
- 2 oz (60 gr) gorgonzola (Italian blue cheese), crumbled
- 2 oz (60 gr) ricotta cheese, crumbled
- 2 oz (60 gr) mozzarella cheese, finely diced
- 2 tablespoons parmigiano reggiano cheese, freshly grated
- 2 tablespoons fresh tomato, peeled, seeded, and diced
- 2–3 basil leaves
- 2 tablespoons extra-virgin olive oil

PATATE
potatoes

- ½ lb (225 gr) potatoes, sliced very thin
- 3–4 tablespoons extra-virgin olive oil
- 2 tablespoons fresh rosemary leaves
- 2 oz (60 gr) mozzarella cheese
- 2 tablespoons extra-virgin olive oil
- salt and crushed red pepper

PIZZA MARGHERITA
pizza with mozzarella cheese and basil

topping for one pizza

prepare the basic pizza dough according to the recipe on page 96

- 1 cup (250 gr) tomatoes, puréed in a blender
- 3–4 tablespoons extra-virgin olive oil
- salt and pepper
- 4–5 fresh basil leaves
- 2 oz (60 gr) mozzarella cheese, shredded or sliced

- Preheat oven to 500 F (260 C).
- In a bowl place the tomatoes. Stir in 1 tablespoon of the olive oil, salt, and pepper.
- Spread the tomatoes evenly over the pizza.
- With your hands, break the basil leaves into small pieces. Distribute the basil uniformly over the pizza. Spread the rest of the olive oil on the pizza.
- Bake the pizza for approximately 10 minutes; then add the mozzarella.
- Cook for 10 more minutes approximately. Lift one side with a fork to check for readiness. Pizza is ready when the bottom surface is light brown.

PIZZELLE FRITTE
fried pizza

prepare the basic pizza dough according to the recipe on page 96

prepare marinara sauce according to the recipe on page 114

- frying oil

- After the dough has risen, divide it into small pieces, each about 2 inches (5 cm) wide.
- Flatten each piece to make round disks about 3/8-inch (1 cm) thick.
- In a skillet, bring the oil to frying temperature. When the oil is hot, fry the *pizzelle* 3 or 4 at a time, until they are fluffy and light golden.
- With a spoon, pour hot oil over the *pizzelle* while they are frying. Do not pierce them with a fork—otherwise they will absorb too much oil.
- Place the *pizzelle* on paper towels on a large plate and let the oil drain briefly.
- Place an abundant spoonful of tomato sauce on each pizza and serve hot.

CALZONE
folded stuffed pizza

prepare the basic pizza dough according to the recipe on page 96

- ½ lb (225 gr) mozzarella cheese, drained, and cut in small pieces
- 9 oz (250 gr) ricotta cheese, thoroughly drained
- 4 oz (115 gr) *salame*, finely chopped
- 1 oz (30 gr) parmigiano reggiano cheese, freshly grated
- 2 tablespoons extra-virgin olive oil
- salt and pepper

- Preheat oven to 400 F (200 C).
- Shape the dough into a round, approximately 12-inch (30 cm) diameter, as though making a pizza.
- In the center, place the mozzarella cheese, ricotta, and *salame*.
- Sprinkle with the grated parmigiano, olive oil, salt, and pepper.
- Fold the pizza in half, and press well to close the edges.
- Bake the *calzone* for about 20 minutes, or until the surface is light brown.

Make sure the cheeses are well drained. Too much liquid could create steam during baking, which could cause the calzone to break.

As an alternative, the *salame* can be substituted with cooked ham or prosciutto.

PANZAROTTI
fried stuffed pizza

prepare the basic pizza dough according to the recipe on page 96

- 5 oz (140 gr) ricotta cheese, drained
- 2 eggs
- 1 oz (30 gr) parmigiano reggiano cheese, freshly grated
- 4 oz (115 gr) mozzarella cheese, drained, and finely diced
- 4 oz (115 gr) prosciutto, finely diced
- 2 oz (60 gr) *salame*, finely diced
- salt and pepper
- frying oil

- In a bowl, combine the ricotta cheese, eggs, grated parmigiano, mozzarella, prosciutto, *salame*, salt, and pepper.
- Flatten the dough, and shape it into small rounds, each approximately 4 inches (10 cm) in diameter.
- In the center of each disk, place approximately 2 tablespoons of the filling.
- Fold the rounds in two. Press well to close the edges, using a fork if needed.
- In a skillet, bring the oil to frying temperature. Fry the *panzarotti* 2 or 3 at a time, until they are light golden.
- Serve at once very hot.

MOZZARELLA IN CARROZZA
fried mozzarella sandwich

- 1 lb (450 gr) soft bread
- 1 lb (450 gr) mozzarella cheese, in one piece
- 2 eggs
- salt
- 3 tablespoons milk
- 1 cup (140 gr) flour
- frying oil

- Cut the bread in 16 slices approximately 4 inches (10 cm) square.
- Cut the mozzarella cheese in 8 slices approximately ¼-inch (5 mm) thick
- Beat the eggs and pinch of salt. Pour the milk in a shallow plate.
- Place the mozzarella slice between 2 bread slices to form a little sandwich.
- Dredge the sandwiches in the milk, then in the flour, shaking away the excess.
- Dredge in the eggs, on all sides until fully covered.
- In a skillet bring the oil to frying temperature.
- Fry the sandwiches 2 or 3 at a time until they are light golden. The heat of the oil will melt the mozzarella cheese while frying the eggs.
- Place the sandwiches on paper towels on a large plate and let the oil drain briefly.
- Serve at once very hot.

CAPRESE
mozzarella and tomato salad

- 1 lb (450 gr) mozzarella cheese, whole
- 4 medium size fresh ripe whole tomatoes
- 4–5 tablespoons extra-virgin olive oil
- salt and pepper
- 8 basil leaves

- Cut the mozzarella in slices about ¼ inch (5 mm) thick.
- Cut the tomatoes in slices about ¼ inch (5 mm) thick, keeping the slices together.
- Place each tomato on a serving plate.
- Place the mozzarella slices alternately among the tomato slices.
- Sprinkle with the extra-virgin olive oil, salt, and pepper freshly grated from the mill.
- Break the basil leaves with your fingers and place atop the tomatoes.

99

Frying and Eating

Every visit to Naples should begin not at the museums, the monuments, or the churches, but from the *vicoli* (the small streets) of the old city. The narrow alleyways are full of the cheerful noise and colorful language of the crowds busy all day in innumerable activities. Dramas and humorous scenes unfold continuously: The Neapolitans' compassion and funniness is the main attraction.

In these ancient streets—decked with clothes hung to dry, and where votive candles glimmer before countless religious images—the citizens of Naples argue, chat, gossip, work, rest, do business, and especially eat. The air is scented with the strong flavors of the grocery stores, the oregano from the omnipresent *pizzerie,* and the oil from the frying shops.

Standing in front of the display of the frying shop, you will be served by the owner, ready to fry on demand whatever food you would like. Almost any time of day or night, you can eat fried seafood, tiny *pizzelle, calzoni, crocchette,* and small fritters of vegetables. It may be difficult to refrain from seconds or from perhaps following with a sweet *graf* or *zeppola* (sweet fritters).

Everything is consumed standing up. Neapolitan street food is served hot and goes directly from the pan into the mouth in no time, or as Neapolitans say, *frijenno e magnanno,* (frying and eating) ❖

Venditore di paste dette Zeppole in Napoli (seller of fritters called *zeppole* in Naples), engraving by B. Pinelli, circa 1830. Bartolomeo Pinelli was a famous engraver in Rome. During a trip to Naples, he was fascinated by the rich street life, and he left a vivid documentation of the public life in those times.

ZEPPOLE
fritters with custard and jam

Like many other sweets, these fritters are linked to a religious celebration. Typically they are prepared on the occasion of the St. Joseph festivity, when a street fair takes place and is especially dedicated to children. Small toys and live birds are sold in endless rows of improvised street benches.

Fritter recipes come in many versions. The simplest is merely plain fried doughnuts topped with a little sugar. The richest like the recipe we present here, add custard and cherry preserves.

for the dough
- 2¼ cups (500 cc) water
- 2 oz (60 gr) butter
- pinch of salt
- 11 oz (300 gr) flour
- 4 eggs + 2 egg whites

for the custard
- 4 oz (115 gr) sugar
- 2 egg yolks
- 2¼ cups (500 cc) milk
- 3 oz (85 gr) flour
- 2 slices of lemon rind

for finishing
- frying oil
- 2 oz (60 gr) sugar
- 4 oz (115 gr) cherry jam

100

preparing the dough

- In a saucepan over medium heat place the water, butter, and pinch of salt.
- As soon as the water starts heating and forming little steam bubbles, add the flour, all at the same time.
- Stir vigorously until the dough is hard enough to come out from the walls of the pan.
- Remove from the heat, and stir in the eggs and egg whites.

preparing the custard

- In a small saucepan, beat together sugar and yolks until they are fluffy and a light mixture is obtained.
- Sift and stir in the flour a little at a time. Add milk. Add the slices of lemon rind.
- Place the saucepan over medium heat and stir constantly without it reaching boiling temperature, until custard is thicker.
- Remove the lemon rind.
- Cool at room temperature, stirring occasionally to prevent the formation of a thick layer on the surface.

preparing the zeppole

- Place abundant frying oil in a skillet with high edges. Bring the oil to frying temperature.
- Take one large tablespoonful of the dough at a time and place in the hot oil. Fry until fluffy and golden.

- Thansfer the *zeppole* on paper towels on a large plate and let the oil drain briefly.
- When the fritters are lukewarm, sprinkle them with sugar.
- Place the fritters on serving dishes. In the center of each fritter, place 1 tablespoon of custard and 1 teaspoon of cherry jam.

STRUFFOLI
honey neapolitan fritters

During the "Kingdom of the Two Sicilies," Naples and Sicily were very close in customs, laws, and also in cooking styles. Known in Sicily as *Pinocchiata,* this dessert is a Neapolitan tradition. Colorful and funny, it is an ideal preparation for a children's party.

- 2 cups (280 gr) flour
- 4 eggs
- 1 tablespoon (15 gr) sugar
- 1 oz (30 gr) butter, diced
- pinch of salt
- frying oil
- 10 oz (285 gr) honey
- 4 oz (115 gr) candied fruit, finely diced
- 3 oz (85 gr) multicolored non-pareils

- Pour the flour onto a work surface to form a mound shape with a hole in the center.

- In the well, add the eggs, sugar, butter, and pinch of salt. Knead to form smooth dough.
- Using a rolling pin, flatten the dough to about 3/8 inch (10 mm) thick.
- Cut into strips about 3/8-inch (10 mm) wide.
- Cut the strips into small pieces about 3/8-inch (10 mm) long. You will now have many small pieces of dough about 3/8-inch (10 mm) in size.
- Roll the dough pieces in the palm of your hands to form small balls. Keep hands and work surface well floured to prevent sticking.
- In a frying pan, bring the oil to frying temperature. Drop the little dough pieces into the pan a little at a time.
- Stir the frying *struffoli,* removing them from the pan before they begin coloring.
- Transfer the *struffoli* on paper-towels on a large plate and let the oil drain briefly.
- Place the honey in a large skillet over medium heat. When the honey is fluid, transfer the *struffoli* pieces to the skillet.
- Add the candied fruit. Stir for a couple of minutes until the *struffoli* are evenly covered with the honey.
- Transfer to a serving dish, giving the *struffoli* a cone shape.
- Sprinkle with the nonpareils. Serve when lukewarm, or the day after the preparation.

SFOGLIATELLE RICCE

flaky pastry with ricotta cheese filling

Sfogliatelle are the most amazing Neapolitan pastries. Made out of crisp puff pastry on the outside and filled with ricotta cheese, they are eaten warm when the pastry feels light and crispy.

Another type of *sfogliatelle* is the tender type similar to small ravioli, filled with ricotta cheese. Making *sfogliatelle* at home is a challenging and time-consuming process, recommended only for more-experienced bakers.

for the dough
- 3 cups (420 gr) flour
- 1 teaspoon salt
- ¾ cup (180 cc) warm water

for the filling
- 1 cup (230 cc) water
- ½ cup (100 gr) sugar
- ⅔ cup (90 gr) semolina flour
- 1½ cups ricotta cheese
- 2 egg yolks
- 2 teaspoons vanilla extract
- ¼ teaspoon cinnamon powder
- ⅓ cup (60 gr) candied orange, finely diced
- 4 + 4 oz (115 + 115 gr) butter

preparing the dough
- In a mixing bowl, combine flour and salt. Stir in the water.
- Transfer the dough to a work surface, and knead to make it smoother. The dough will be very dry.
- Reduce the dough to about ³/₈-inch (1 cm) thick with a rolling pin.
- Pass the dough through a hand pasta machine.
- Fold the dough on itself before inserting it through the machine again.
- Repeat the step of folding the dough and passing it through the pasta machine several times, until the dough becomes very smooth.
- Shape the dough into a ball, cover with plastic wrap, and place it in the refrigerator for about 2 hours.

preparing the filling
- Combine water and sugar in a saucepan. Bring the water to a boil.
- Sift the semolina into the boiling sugar-water, stirring continuously to blend the mixture and avoid lumps.
- Lower the heat to a constant simmer, and cook for a few minutes until thick.
- Place the ricotta in a food processor, and run the blade until the ricotta is reduced to a smooth paste.
- Add the ricotta to the semolina mixture. Turn heat to medium-low; stir in the egg yolks, vanilla, cinnamon, and candied orange.
- Transfer the filling to a bowl, and refrigerate it.

preparing the shells
- Beat 4 oz (115 gr) of the butter in a small bowl until fluffy.
- Remove the dough from the refrigerator, and cut it into four pieces.
- Lightly flour the dough, and pass it repeatedly through a hand pasta machine. Make sure the dough has a shape of a narrow strip about 8 inches (20 cm) wide. Keep passing the dough through the machine until the thinnest setting is reached. Four strips of the same width, about 8 inches (20 cm), are obtained.
- Place the strips of dough on a floured work surface.
- Brush the dough strips with the butter.
- Roll the first strip into a cylinder, starting very tight. Make sure the roll has uniform width of about 8 inches (20 cm) and is compact.
- At the end of the first roll, insert the next strip, brushed with butter and continue forming the cylinder.
- Continue with the rest of the strips until a roll about 8 inches (20 cm) long and 2½ inches (6 cm) in diameter is obtained.
- Wrap the cylinder in plastic, and place it in the refrigerator for a few hours.

assembling the sfogliatelle
- Preheat oven to 400 F (200 C). Line 2 cookie sheets with oven paper. Remove the filling from the refrigerator and fill a pastry bag with it.
- Remove the roll of dough from the refrigerator, and evenly cut out the two ends with a sharp knife.

- Cut the roll in slices about ½-inch (1 cm) thick.

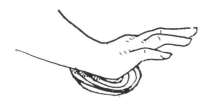

- With the palm of your hand, lightly press the center of a roll of dough outward in all directions.

- Lifting the roll, press it in the center to slide the layers on themselves to form a sort of cone shape.

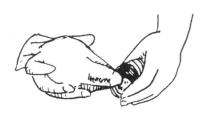

- Hold the cone in one hand and the pastry bag in the other. Fill the pastry with the cheese fill-ing; then close the pastry cone by pressing the edges together.
- Place on the cookie sheet. Repeat the operation until all the slices are filled.
- Soften the remaining butter, and brush it on top of all the pastries.
- Bake for about 25 minutes, or until the *sfogliatelle* are golden.
- Serve warm.

PASTIERA NAPOLETANA
wheat and ricotta easter pie

Pastiera is perhaps the most famous cake from Naples. Loved in Rome as well as in all southern Italy, it is traditionally served for the Easter festivity. The procedure to assemble the cake is not very difficult, but the cake does end up quite long.

for the wheat filling
- 4 oz (115 gr) hulled wheat kernels (or pearl barley)
- 1 oz (30 gr) butter
- 2 tablespoons milk

for the dough
- ½ teaspoon baking powder
- ¼ cup milk
- 3 cups (420 gr) flour
- 6 oz (180 gr) butter diced, at room temperature
- 2/3 cup (120 gr) sugar
- 1 whole egg and 1 yolk, at room temperature
- pinch of salt

for the cream
- 3 egg yolks, at room temperature
- ¼ cup (50 gr) sugar
- ¼ cup (35 gr) flour
- 2 cups (460 cc) warm milk
- 1 teaspoon vanilla

for the filling
- 1 lb (450 gr) ricotta cheese, drained
- 3 eggs
- ¾ cup (150 gr) sugar
- grated rind of 1 lemon
- ¾ cup (100 gr) candied fruit (preferably orange), diced
- 1 tablespoon orange flower water

for the egg wash
- 1 egg yolk
- 1 tablespoon milk

step 1 - preparing the wheat
- The day before the preparation, place the wheat kernels or barley in a bowl, and cover them with water. Let them soak overnight.
- The next day, when you are ready to prepare the cake, drain and rinse the wheat or barley.
- In a saucepan filled with water, pour the grains, and bring them to a boil, cooking until tender. This could take quite long.
- Drain the grain, and place it in a bowl. Add the butter and milk.
- Stir until the ingredients are well blended. Cool to room temperature.

step 2 - preparing the dough
- Dissolve the baking powder in the milk.
- Pour the flour onto a work surface, to form a mound shape with a hole in the center.
- In the well, add the butter, sugar, milk mixture, whole egg, egg yolk, and pinch of salt.

103

- Mix quickly together and form dough. Avoid warming the dough too much; otherwise it will fall apart.
- Place the dough in a bowl, cover with plastic wrap, and refrigerate while preparing the other ingredients.

step 3 - preparing the cream
- Place the egg yolks in a medium-size saucepan.
- Add the sugar, and beat the mixture vigorously until fluffy.
- Stir in the flour a little at a time.
- Add milk a little at a time, stirring continuously.
- Place the saucepan over low heat, and stir slowly but constantly.
- When the cream thickens and starts boiling, remove from the stove and stir in the vanilla. Transfer to a bowl.

step 4 - preparing the filling
- Separate 3 egg yolks and reserve the whites.
- Place the ricotta cheese in a large bowl. Add the yolks and the sugar, and mix together.
- Add the grated lemon rind, candied fruit, orange-flower water, grain from step 1, and the cream from step 3. Mix to combine well all the ingredients.
- Beat the 3 reserved egg whites until they form peaks. Add the ricotta-cream mixture combining gently with a wooden spoon, using a top-to-bottom motion.

step 5 - assembling the cake
- Preheat oven to 350 F (175 C). Butter a springform pan 10 inches (25 cm) in diameter x 2 inches (5 cm) deep. Sprinkle evenly with a small amount of flour.
- Cut one third of the dough and reserve it. Flatten the larger portion of the dough. Cover the bottom and walls of the pan with the dough.
- Pour the filling from step 4 into the pan.
- Flatten the reserved dough with a rolling pin, and form ¾-inch (2 cm) strips.
- Place the strips on the cake, crossing them in a diamond shape.
- One last strip is to be placed as closure all around the border of the pan.

step 6 - baking
- In a small bowl, beat together the egg yolk and milk. Brush the egg wash over the dough strips.
- Bake for about 45 minutes or until golden. The cake will be ready if a toothpick inserted into the paste comes out dry.
- Turn oven off. Don't remove the cake, but cool it slowly in the oven. Serve at room temperature or the day after the preparation.

MUDDRICA
ricotta honey cake

This cake is a preparation that goes all the way back to Greek and Roman times. During classical times, honey was the only sweetener available, and cheese was common. A similar cake called *savillum* is described by Cato, the famous Roman politician (± 180 B.C.), who left a very detailed recipe.

The preparation has survived for centuries in southern Italy, where it is made with locally produced honey and ricotta cheese.

The cake can also be enriched with walnuts, almonds, or pine nuts, and decorated on the surface with candied fruit, accompanied by whipped cream.

- 1¼ lb (approximately 550 gr) ricotta cheese, thoroughly drained
- 2 whole eggs + 3 yolks
- ½ cup (100 cc) honey
- ½ teaspoon cinnamon powder
- ⅓ cup (150 gr) chopped candied orange
- 2 tablespoons Marsala wine
- 1 tablespoon grated lemon rind
- 3 egg whites

- Preheat oven to 350 F (180 C). Butter a 9-inch (22 cm) cake pan.
- Place the ricotta in a food processor fitted with the metal blade. Run the blade until the ricotta is smooth.
- Transfer the ricotta to a bowl; add the eggs, egg yolks, honey,

cinnamon, candied orange, Marsala wine, and grated lemon rind.

- Beat the egg whites until they form peaks. Fold the egg whites gently into the cheese mixture, with a top-to-bottom motion.
- Transfer the mixture to the pan, and smooth the surface with a spatula.
- Bake for about 30 minutes or until surface is golden.

TORTA CAPRESE
chocolate almond tart

The Capri Island has always been a celebrated tourist destination. Called *Insula Sirenussae* (Island of the Sirens) or *Apragopolis* (Land of Leisure) in Roman times, it remains a destination of stunning beauty.

Many celebrated dishes were born in internationally acclaimed restaurants of Capri. *Insalata Caprese* (tomato, mozzarella, and basil salad), *Ravioli Capresi* (filled with soft fresh cheese), *Gnocchi Capresi* (topped with mozzarella and tomatoes), and the famous *Torta Caprese*. A very rich cake, at the same time it is extremely light and soft. It is a flourless cake and therefore the softness comes from the beaten egg whites.

- 4 oz (115 gr) semi-sweet chocolate, chopped
- ½ cup (110 gr) butter, lukewarm
- 7 tablespoons (90 gr) sugar
- 4 eggs, separated
- 1¹/₃ cups (110 gr) almonds, finely ground
- pinch of salt
- powdered sugar, for finishing

for the icing (optional)
- ½ cup (115 cc) heavy cream
- 4 oz (110 gr) semi-sweet chocolate, chopped

- Preheat oven to 400 F (200 C). Butter and flour a 9-inch (22 cm) round pan.
- Melt the chocolate in a double boiler over hot (but not boiling) water. Stir until the chocolate is fluid and smooth. Remove from the heat, and cool to room temperature.
- Using an electric mixer, or a bowl and a wooden spoon, cream the butter until soft.
- Add the sugar, and beat the mixture until fluffy. Add the egg yolks one at a time, beating for a while after adding each one.
- Beat in the cooled chocolate, and then fold in the almonds.
- In a bowl, beat the egg whites with a pinch of salt, until they form peaks.
- Fold the beaten egg whites, in several batches, into the chocolate mixture; use a large spoon and mix with a gentle top-to-bottom motion.

- Pour the mixture into the pan, and level the top with a flat spatula.
- Bake for about 15 minutes; then reduce the temperature to 350 F (175 C). Bake the cake for about 10 minutes longer, until cooked in the center. Test readiness by inserting a toothpick in the center. When the cake is ready, the toothpick will come out perfectly dry. Don't overcook the cake; otherwise it will lose its moisture and softness.
- Run a knife blade along the edge of the pan to detach the cake, but do not remove it. Place a lightly damp towel (wet but wrung out) over the cake to cool it and keep it moist. Unmould when lukewarm.
- Serve at room temperature, sprinkled with powdered sugar.

As an alternative, *Torta Caprese* can be served with a chocolate icing as follows:

- Place the cream in a saucepan over medium heat until hot but not boiling.
- Remove it from the stove, and add the chocolate. Stir until the chocolate is fluid and smooth.
- When the chocolate icing is cooler, spread it on the top and the sides of the cake.
- Do not refrigerate, but cool it to lukewarm; otherwise the chocolate icing will harden.

BABA'
rum soaked sponge cakes

Apparently *"babkas"* were "invented" in Poland. The King of Poland, Stanislav Leszczynsky, was in exile in France, and his cook served these small cakes at his receptions. Shortly thereafter, *babas* became quite popular in France and traveled to Naples with Napoleon's army, where they became a fully Neapolitan dessert.

Neapolitan *babas* have a peculiar shape: They are baked in small round-conical metal molds, about 2 inches (5 cm) round x 2 inches (5 cm) deep. After being unmoulded, they are saturated in rum liquor. In the absence of appropriate molds, muffin-baking pans can be used.

for the sponge
- 1 envelope active dry yeast
- ½ cup (120 cc) milk, warm
- ¾ cup (110 gr) flour

for the dough
- 8 tablespoons (110 gr) butter
- 3 eggs
- ½ teaspoons salt
- 2 tablespoons sugar
- 1½ cups (210 gr) flour

for the rum syrup
- 2 cups sugar
- ½ cup (120 cc) dark rum

for the glaze
- 1½ cups (200 gr) powdered sugar

preparing the sponge
- Sprinkle the yeast on the warm milk. Set aside for 4–5 minutes.
- Add the flour, and mix to form a smooth batter. Set aside covered for about 30 minutes.

preparing the dough
- Melt the butter, and cool it at room temperature.
- In a bowl, beat the eggs. Add the salt, sugar, and flour.
- Beat the sponge batter into the dough, and then beat in the melted butter. The dough will be quite fluid.
- Fill approximately half depth 30 *baba'* or small muffin molds with the dough.
- Let the dough rise until reaching the edge of the mold.
- Preheat oven to 400 F (200 C).
- Bake for about 15 minutes or until golden brown.
- Transfer the *babas* onto pastry racks to cool.

preparing the syrup
- In a small saucepan, pour 3 cups (700 cc) water. Stir in the sugar.
- Bring to a boil over medium heat, and then add the rum.
- Soak the *babas* in the rum syrup a little at a time, until they absorb the maximum quantity of liquid. Make sure the syrup is hot to facilitate absorption. Transfer to a plate to release the excess liquid.

preparing the glaze
- In a small saucepan, pour ½ cup (120 cc) water and add the sugar; place over medium heat.
- Stir while mixture simmers but without it reaching boiling temperature.
- Brush the syrup on the *babas*. Cool to room temperature, and serve lukewarm.

Babas will keep for a long time, but are best if served shortly after they are soaked.

CHAPTER *6*

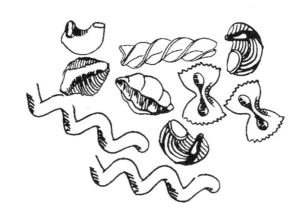

Macaroni Addiction

Dry Pasta

When talking about the origin of pasta, a distinction needs to be made between fresh and dry pasta. Fresh pasta is dough made of flour and water and is present in most cultures and on all continents. Dry pasta began in Italy and embarked from there to conquer the world. People have attributed Marco Polo with having introduced spaghetti to Italy from China, but that is incorrect. Mediterranean people even before the Romans knew fresh pasta, and dry pasta was unknown to the Chinese.

A Brief History of Pasta

Dried pasta was familiar in the Mediterranean area in the thirteenth and fourteenth centuries, and also was mentioned in Genovese documents. The first traces of dry pasta in Europe came from Sicily, where documents of the twelfth century tell of something like a factory of dry pasta, localized in the area of Palermo. From this site the pasta (called *itrjia*) was then exported to other regions of southern Italy.

Genovese sailors were among the most active traders within the Mediterranean. It is not surprising that in the thirteenth century Genova became trader, and then fabricator, of dry pasta, spreading it to many other countries—which led to this pasta gaining the name *Genovese*.

The oldest macaroni recipes found are from Sicily: macaroni with eggplant (eggplant was introduced by the Arabs in Sicily around the year 1000 from India) and macaroni with sardines. Both these delicious dishes are still present today in Sicilian cooking.

Other establishments appeared through southern Italy, and the pasta that today is called spaghetti (meaning "strings") or vermicelli (meaning "little worms"), by the threadlike shape, was at that time

Venditore di Maccaroni **(macaroni seller)** Engraving by B. Pinelli, circa 1830. Extremely popular in Naples, in the past the macaroni were cooked, sold in the streets, and eaten with bare hands.

called *tria*. And, by then, dried pasta from Italy was known in Provence and in England. The short pasta with the tube shape would be named macaroni, apparently from the Latin word *maccare*, meaning "to mash."

In those times, fresh and stuffed pasta—dressed with cheeses, spices, or sweets—was an aristocratic type of food, while dry pasta was considered a popular food, while. Macaroni, while well known, was not an important food in the diet of Italians, outside the places where it was produced.

The turning point was in Naples in the 1600s. Imports of meat and fresh produce became difficult and expensive due to an economic crisis. Flour was available instead, and pasta had become more affordable especially after the invention of the mechanical press. Dry pasta quickly became the people's food, to the point that Neapolitans were commonly called *mangiamaccheroni* (macaroni eaters).

Durum wheat semolina was produced in large quantity in southern Italy. Macaroni is a filling food for poor people, and pasta with cheese contains good nourishment. As a result, the poor of southern Italy did not suffer pellagra and famine as much as the northerners, who had maize as their only staple.

In 1785, Naples had 280 pasta shops. In the 1800s, pasta was sold by street vendors, who cooked it over charcoal fire; and it was eaten on the spot with bare hands. The pasta was sold with no dressing, or with merely a bit of grated sheep cheese, until the early 1800s, when the first tomato sauces appeared.

Southern Italy had hundreds of artisan pasta makers, but it was in 1824 in northern Italy, close to Genova, that the first industrial pasta factory was established by the Agnese family; a few years later the Buitoni family founded another pasta factory.

After the Italian unification in 1862, pasta spread all over the country, and traveled with Italian immigrants to the United States. Before long, pasta was eaten all around the world, and the rest "is history"!

How to Cook Pasta

The expression *al dente* in Italian refers to the correct cooking point of pasta. Literally it means, "when it is right for the tooth," that is, soft but firm, and never overcooked. General directions are given here on how to cook *al dente*.

Pasta must always be cooked in abundant salted water. The proportion should be 1½ quart (approximately 1½ liters) of water for 3–4 oz (100 gm) of dry pasta.

Only if cooking fresh homemade pasta (fettuccine, *pappardelle)*, add some olive oil to the water: one tablespoon is enough. The olive oil should prevent the pasta strips from sticking together.

Use a large, tall stockpot. Bring to a boil the water necessary to cook the desired amount of pasta. Add the salt only after the water begins boiling. Salty water boils at a higher temperature, therefore taking a longer time. Add to the water about 1 teaspoon of salt per quart. The amount may vary depending on personal taste.

Drop the pasta into the pot and mix with a long fork in order to keep the pasta pieces separate from each other.

Read the manufacturer's instructions printed on the envelope for cooking time, but the best thing to do is taste a little piece from time to time to test for readiness.

When the pasta is *al dente,* add some cold tap water to the pot to stop the cooking process. In fact, pasta keeps cooking even after you drain it. Also, this way the pasta will not be too hot when served.

Drain the pasta thoroughly, unless the recipe indicates otherwise. If you are using a "dry" type of dressing, reserve some of the cooking water. You may want to add some of the water back into the mixing bowl.

Pour the pasta into a bowl of adequate size. Add the dressing or sauce, toss it well, add cheese if indicated by the recipe, and serve immediately.

Matching Pasta with Sauce

The varied shapes of pasta and types of sauces create innumerable combinations. It is important to know the principles that draw pasta and dressing together. Even if you have done everything right—cooked and drained dry pasta exactly *al dente*, or handmade your pasta perfectly—you will not be completely successful unless you match the pasta type and shape with a congenial sauce.

Dry Pasta Cooking Times

Capellini	3-4 min.
Spaghettini	5 min.
Spaghetti, Linguine	7 min.
Bucatini, Zite	10 min.
Farfalle, Conchiglie	10 min.
Penne, Rigatoni	15 min.
Ravioli, Tortellini fresh	10 min.
	dry 20 min.

Fresh homemade pasta has a very brief cooking time, especially if it was just made. Depending on the thickness of the cut, it cooks approximately in 5 minutes.

When using factory-made pasta, the choice of sauce is affected by the shape and size of pasta you use. *Spaghettini* pasta are very light and thin: therefore they go well with oily, lighter, or fish sauces, as spaghetti does. You would not use a butter-based sauce with *spaghettini* or *capellini* (angel hair), because the pasta would not be strong enough to hold the sauce and would become sticky and unpleasant to eat and look at.

Spaghetti, as well as *bucatini*, also works with buttery sauces, white sauces (without tomato), and with light tomato sauces. Generally speaking, spaghetti is very versatile and matches well with any type of sauce.

Shaped pasta, such as *rigatoni, penne,* or *conchiglie,* generally work better with thicker, chunkier sauces; while *fusilli* is perfect with creamy, dense sauces.

Also, give consideration to the amount of pasta to be served. When making a small quantity, you can use any type of pasta. But if you are cooking for a large number of guests, short pastas (*rigatoni, penne, fusilli*) are easier to dress, toss, and distribute to the serving plates.

While factory-made pasta carries the sauce, homemade pasta absorbs it. Also, homemade pasta has a very light, delicate taste that merits being enhanced rather than covered. Therefore, with homemade pasta you would not use sauces with strong tastes because they would cover the light taste of the pasta itself, and you would not use oily sauces because they would make fresh pasta too slick. The taste of fresh pasta is generally enhanced by consistent tomato sauces or by butter-based sauces.

Traditionally established combinations, such as *Trenette al Pesto* or *Bucatini all' Amatriciana,* should never be changed, because they represent the result of centuries of trial and error ❖

Dry Pasta Types

Capellini	Angel hair
Spaghettini, Vermicellini	Thin spaghetti
Spaghetti, Vermicelli	Long solid strings
Bucatini, Perciatelli	Hollow spaghetti
Zite, Mezze Zite	Long hollow tubes
Linguine, Trenette	Flat spaghetti
Tagliatelle, Fettuccine	Dry egg noodles
Pappardelle	Wider egg noodles
Lasagne	Flat pasta sheets
Penne	Diagonal cut tubes
Tubetti, Cannolicchi	Small tubes
Tufali, Cannelloni	Large tubes for stuffing
Rigatoni	Tubes with ridges
Tortiglioni, Fusilli	Spiral shapes
Lumache	Hollow snails
Conchiglie	Shells
Gnocchetti, Cavatelli	Small shell shapes
Orecchiette	Ear shapes (Apulia)
Farfalle	Butterflies
Rotelle	Wheels
Peperini, Avemarie, Stelline	Very small pasta shapes for soups

Factory-made dry fettuccine eggs noodles can be an excellent substitute for fresh handmade pasta. They have a high yield: Only 2 oz (60 gr) makes one serving.

Macaroni and Vermicelli

Our journey in search of Italian pasta dishes begins in southern Italy, where the oldest recipes are found. It is from Sicily, in the Middle Ages, that macaroni pasta began its journey around the world. From a culinary standpoint, Sicily is in a league all by itself. Located in the middle of the Mediterranean, Sicily amazes us with some extraordinary pasta dishes that have sweet-and-sour accents.

Apulia is where *orecchiette*, ear-shaped pasta was born. Typically they are dressed with vegetables, such as rapini, broccoli, or arugula.

In Naples, we find extraordinary vermicelli (as spaghetti is called there) dishes with seafood—and the first tomato sauce, the world-renowned *marinara* ❖

PASTA ALLA NORMA
pasta with eggplant

This dish was named after the homonymous opera written by Vincenzo Bellini. The famous composer, who was born in the Sicilian city of Catania, gained great popularity; and, *Norma,* his most acclaimed opera, became synonymous with everything that was excellent. One day during a dinner

Macaroni seller in a street of Naples. Macaroni was a staple for Neapolitan people in the seventeenth and eighteenth centuries. A French traveler around 1850 wrote: "A man of the people goes to a macaroni merchant; he gets a dish full of this boiling pasta and throws on it a handful of grated cheese; he takes these macaronis with the hands and twists them in a way that a foreigner could rarely imitate".

among artists, the guests were served a dish of spaghetti dressed with eggplant, tomato sauce, grated salty ricotta cheese, and basil. One of the participants, inspired by the taste and flavors of the dish, exclaimed: "This is a Norma!" meaning it was as wonderful as the music of the opera. Since then, the dish has gone by this name, and many variations have become popular throughout Sicily.

- 1 lb (450 gr) eggplant, ripe but firm
- frying oil
- 4 tablespoons extra-virgin olive oil
- 1 clove of garlic, sliced
- crushed red pepper
- 5–6 basil leaves
- 2 cups (500 gr) tomatoes, puréed in a blender
- salt
- 2 oz (60 gr) black olives
- 1 tablespoon capers in salt, rinsed and drained
- 1 lb (450 gr) pasta (*fusilli* or *penne*)
- 4 oz (115 gr) *ricotta salata* cheese (see description below), freshly grated

- Cut the eggplants in ½ inch (1 cm) dice. In a skillet, bring the oil to frying temperature. Fry the eggplant until golden. Remove the eggplants and clean the skillet with a paper towel.
- Add to the skillet the extra-virgin olive oil, garlic, and red pepper. Sauté for 2–3 minutes without browning the garlic.
- Add the basil leaves, tomatoes, and salt. Cook for about 10 minutes.
- Add the fried eggplant, olives, and capers, and cook for 2–3 minutes. Adjust salt if necessary.

- Cook pasta in abundant salt water following manufacturer's instructions. Taste for readiness from time to time, until *al dente* (firm but not too soft or overcooked). Drain and transfer to a bowl.
- Dress with the eggplant sauce, mix well, top with the cheese, and serve at once.

The original Sicilian recipe calls for *ricotta salata* cheese, typical of the region. This cheese is a salted, oven-dried ricotta with a strong, pungent taste. It can be substituted by grated *pecorino* (romano) cheese. For those who prefer a milder taste we suggest using half parmigiano and half *pecorino* (romano) cheese, grated and mixed.

FUSILLI CON I BROCCOLI ARRIMINATI
fusilli with cauliflower sauce

The flavor of this sauce is a combination of sweet and sour in the tradition of many Sicilian dishes. Sicilian green cauliflower has a particular taste, and it can be found only locally, but this dish is a mouthwatering experience of Sicilian cooking and is enjoyable even if another type of cauliflower is used. The best pasta for this dish is *fusilli*, a spiral-shaped dry pasta. Serve this dish lukewarm at least two hours after the preparation, giving it time to set and blend all the flavors.

- 2 lb (900 gr) green cauliflower
- salt
- 6 tablespoons extra-virgin olive oil
- 1 medium onion, finely diced
- crushed red pepper
- 4 anchovy fillets, chopped
- 2 oz (60 gr) pine nuts
- 2 oz (60 gr) raisins
- 1 bag saffron powder
- 1 lb (450 gr) *fusilli* pasta

- Fill a large stockpot with water and bring to a boil; add cauliflower and salt. Cook for about 5 minutes, until cauliflower is half-cooked and not yet fully tender.
- Drain the cauliflower with the help of a large slotted spoon. Reserve the cooking water.
- Dissolve the saffron in 1–2 tablespoons of the cooking water.
- In a medium-size saucepan, pour the olive oil, and turn heat to medium. Add the onion, generous red pepper, and sauté gently until the onion becomes soft and translucent.
- Remove the saucepan from the stove, add the anchovy fillets, and quickly stir with a wooden spoon to dissolve them. When adding the anchovies, don't let them cook otherwise they will burn, giving the dish a very strong tang.
- Return the saucepan to the stove, add pine nuts, raisins, saffron, and cauliflower. Mix to combine and sauté briefly.
- Anchovies can be very salty, therefore adjust salt at this point if necessary.

- If sauce is too thick, add 1 or 2 tablespoons of the cauliflower cooking water.
- Bring the stockpot with the cauliflower cooking water to a boil.
- Cook the *fusilli* in the cauliflower cooking water following manufacturer's instructions. Taste for readiness from time to time, until *al dente* (firm but not too soft or overcooked). Drain and transfer to a bowl.
- Top with the sauce, toss, and set aside until lukewarm.

This dish can be served warm, but it will be tastier if eaten lukewarm, after a few hours, or even the day after it is prepared.

ORECCHIETTE CON LA RUCOLA
orecchiette with arugula

In Apulia the *orecchiette* are made by hand from a simple dough of water and flour. The dough is cut into small pieces the size of a bean, and then they are pressed with the thumb to create "ear" shapes. This pasta is traditionally dressed with vegetables such as rapini, broccoli, or turnips.

- 4–5 tablespoons extra-virgin olive oil
- 2 garlic cloves, diced
- 4 oz (115 gr) bread crumbs
- salt
- 1 lb (450 gr) *orecchiette* pasta
- 1 lb (450 gr) arugula
- pepper
- 4 oz (115 gr) *pecorino* (romano) cheese

- In a skillet, pour the extra-virgin olive oil and add the garlic. Sauté the garlic until it is very pale light brown.
- Remove the garlic from the skillet. Add the bread crumbs, and fry them until browned and crispy.
- Fill a stockpot with water, and bring to a boil. Add salt, the *orecchiette*, and arugula. Cook the pasta following manufacturer's instructions. Taste for readiness from time to time, until *al dente* (firm but not too soft or overcooked).
- Drain the pasta and arugula in a colander. Transfer it to a bowl, top with the breadcrumbs, pepper, and cheese; toss it and serve at once.

VERMICELLI ALLE VONGOLE
spaghetti with clams

- 3 lb (1500 gr) clams
- 5–6 tablespoons extra-virgin olive oil
- 2 garlic cloves, sliced
- crushed red pepper
- 3 tablespoons Italian parsley, chopped
- salt
- 1 lb (450 gr) spaghetti

- Wash the clams. In a skillet over medium heat, place the clams and ½ cup (120 cc) of water.
- Cover and simmer for a short time until the clams begin opening. Remove the clams from the skillet as soon as they open.
- Turn heat off. Filter the cooking water to remove sand and impurities, and reserve it.
- In a skillet over medium heat, pour the extra-virgin olive oil. Add the garlic and red pepper.
- Before the garlic begins coloring, add the clams and 2–3 tablespoons of the clam cooking water. Sauté briefly for about 1 minute, and then add half of the parsley and salt if necessary.
- Cook the spaghetti in abundant salt water following manufacturer's instructions. Taste for readiness from time to time, until *al dente* (firm but not too soft or overcooked). Drain and transfer to a bowl.
- Top with the clams and their sauce, and sprinkle with the rest of the parsley. Toss and serve at once.

VERMICELLI ALLA PUTTANESCA
spaghetti with olives, capers, and tomato sauce

A famous Italian painter often improvised dinner parties for his friends in his small rustic house on the picturesque Ischia Island, outside Naples. Fresh and light local wine was offered together with this dish of spaghetti.

- 5–6 tablespoons extra-virgin olive oil
- 2 garlic cloves, sliced
- 1 lb (450 gr) tomatoes, puréed in a blender
- 2 oz (60 gr) capers in salt, rinsed and drained
- 4 oz (115 gr) black olives
- 2 tablespoons fresh oregano leaves, chopped
- crushed red pepper
- 2 oz (60 gr) anchovies, chopped
- 3 tablespoons Italian parsley, finely chopped
- salt
- 1 lb (450 gr) spaghetti

- In a skillet over medium heat, pour olive oil, and add garlic.
- As soon as the garlic becomes very pale brown, add the tomato, capers, olives, oregano, and crushed red pepper.
- Cook over medium heat, until the tomato sauce is thicker.
- Add the anchovies, and sauté for 1 more minute until the anchovies are dissolved.
- Stir in the parsley, add salt if necessary, and turn heat off.
- Cook the spaghetti in abundant salt water following manufacturer's instructions. Taste for readiness from time to time, until *al dente* (firm but not too soft or overcooked).
- Drain and transfer to a bowl. Top with the sauce, toss, and serve at once.

VERMICELLI ALLA MARINARA

spaghetti with oregano and tomato sauce

This is the basic meatless tomato sauce, probably considered the precursor of all *ragu'* and tomato sauces of Italy. In spite of the name (the word "marinara" refers to seafood), the sauce has no fish in it.

- 5–6 tablespoons extra-virgin olive oil
- 2 garlic cloves, sliced
- 1 lb (450 gr) tomatoes, puréed in a blender
- salt and pepper
- 3 tablespoons Italian parsley, chopped
- 2 tablespoons fresh oregano leaves, chopped
- 1 lb (450 gr) spaghetti

- In a skillet over medium heat, pour olive oil and add garlic. Before the garlic begins coloring, add the tomatoes, salt, and pepper.
- Cook over medium heat for about 20–25 minutes, until the tomato sauce thickens. Stir in the parsley and oregano, and turn heat off.
- Cook the spaghetti in abundant salt water following manufacturer's instructions, checking for readiness from time to time, until *al dente* (firm but not too soft or overcooked).
- Drain the pasta, and transfer it to a bowl. Top with the tomato sauce, toss, and serve at once.

SPAGHETTI CON LA BOTTARGA

spaghetti with fish roe

Tuna fish roe, dry or fresh, is available in Italy and makes a delicious dressing for a simple pasta dish. In the United States, many different types of fish roe are available fresh in Asian food stores.

- 1 lb (450 gr) spaghetti
- salt
- 5 tablespoons extra-virgin olive oil
- 2 garlic cloves, sliced
- crushed red pepper
- 3 oz (85 gr) fish roe
- 1 tablespoon Italian parsley, chopped

- Cook the spaghetti in abundant salt water following manufacturer's instructions, checking for readiness from time to time.
- While pasta is cooking, pour the oil in a skillet and add the garlic and red pepper. Turn heat to medium, and sauté briefly.
- Before the garlic begins coloring, turn heat off, and stir in the fish roe.
- Drain the spaghetti when *al dente* (firm but not too soft or overcooked).
- Transfer to a bowl, top with the sauce and parsley. Toss and serve immediately.

SPAGHETTI AL NERO DI SEPPIA

spaghetti with squid-ink sauce

- 1¼ lb (500 gr) squid
- 4 tablespoons extra-virgin olive oil
- crushed red pepper
- 2–3 garlic cloves, finely diced
- salt
- 3 tablespoons Italian parsley, finely chopped
- 1/3 cup (80 cc) dry white wine
- 5 oz (150gr) tomato, puréed in a blender
- 1 lb (450 gr) spaghetti

- Cut the squid open and clean them. Remove and reserve the ink sacs. Wash the squid, dry, them and cut into very small dice.
- In a skillet, pour the olive oil, and add red pepper and garlic. Before garlic begins coloring, add the squid. Add salt, half of the parsley, and sauté for a few minutes.
- Add the wine, and let the wine evaporate. Stir in the reserved squid ink. Add the tomatoes. Cook on low heat for 20–25 minutes until the sauce is thicker.
- Cook the pasta in abundant salt water following manufacturer's instructions. Taste for readiness from time to time, until *al dente* (firm but not too soft or overcooked).
- Drain pasta very well, pour into the skillet over the sauce, turn heat to medium high, and sauté for a few seconds. Transfer the pasta to a bowl, top with the rest of the parsley, and serve immediately.

114

Spaghetti Roman Style

Dry pasta has been around since the Middle Ages. At the end of the nineteenth century, mechanization and industrialization made it affordable, largely available, and macaroni became a popular food.

Before the arrival of the tomato, macaroni was dressed simply and almost exclusively with cheese—either parmigiano in the north or pecorino sheep cheese in the south. Fried pork fat, maybe "reinforced" by garlic, onion, or herbs would give pasta condiment more flavor. In Italian cooking we still find that love for simplicity.

The recipes that follow—typical of Roman cooking, and in general of central Italy— seem to come directly from a medieval cookbook. These same dishes, or their close direct descendants, have been used for centuries ❖

AIO E OIO
olive oil and garlic

Aio e Oio is the dialectal way of saying garlic and oil. It is generally prepared very spicy, therefore don't be shy with the quantity of red pepper.

Street musicians at the Osteria. Engraving by B. Pinelli, circa 1830. It is still very popular in Rome to go to the *Castelli* (the Castles), which is the term used for the small towns in the countryside over the hills south of Rome. In the local *trattorie,* often *al fresco* (in the open air) under a vine pergola, it is possible to enjoy the simple food and wine of the Roman countryside.

- 1 lb (450 gr) spaghetti
- salt
- 5 tablespoons extra-virgin olive oil
- 2 garlic cloves, sliced
- 2–3 small hot red chili peppers
- 1 tablespoon Italian parsley, chopped (optional)

- Cook the spaghetti in abundant salt water following manufacturer's instructions, tasting for readiness from time to time.
- While the pasta is cooking, pour the olive oil in a skillet and add the garlic and red pepper; turn the heat to medium.
- Turn heat off as soon as the garlic begins coloring to a very pale brown.
- When pasta is *al dente* (firm but not too soft or overcooked), drain and transfer to a bowl.
- Top with the oil-garlic mixture. Spread the chopped parsley on top (if desired). Serve at once.

Do not overcook or burn the garlic! Browned garlic is considered a big mistake in Italian cooking. Use fresh hot peppers when available and slice them before adding them to the skillet. If fresh red peppers are unavailable, use whole dry red peppers, chopped coarsely, or a generous quantity of crushed red pepper.

115

CACIO E PEPE
romano cheese and black pepper

This is an extremely simple Roman dish, but there are a couple of precautions to take: The pasta should not be drained too much, and must be served very hot. The heat of the pasta melts the cheese and enhances the flavor of the black pepper. As soon as the pasta begins cooling down, it will no longer taste as good.

- ½ cup *pecorino romano* cheese, freshly grated
- black pepper, freshly grated from the mill
- 1 lb (450 gr) spaghetti
- salt

- In a bowl, mix the grated *pecorino romano* cheese and a very generous quantity of black pepper directly grated from the mill together.
- Cook the spaghetti in abundant salted water following manufacturer's instructions, tasting for readiness from time to time. Before draining, reserve about ½ cup of the pasta boiling water.
- When the spaghetti is *al dente* (firm but not too soft or overcooked), drain in a colander without shaking it too much, to maintain the moistness of the pasta.
- Pour the pasta into a bowl, top with the cheese, and toss.
- Add 1 or more tablespoon of the reserved cooking water if the pasta appears too dry. Toss thoroughly. Serve at once.

ARRABBIATA
tomato and red pepper

The shape of pasta traditionally used for this dish is *penne rigate,* small-ridged tubes cut diagonally at the ends. The name of this dish literally means "angry pasta," because it is dressed with abundant hot red pepper.

- 3 tablespoons extra-virgin olive oil
- 2 garlic cloves sliced
- 3–4 fresh hot red chili peppers
- 6 fresh basil leaves
- 2 cups (500 gr) tomatoes, puréed in a blender
- 1 lb (450 gr) *penne rigate* pasta
- salt

- In a frying pan, pour the olive oil, and add garlic and red peppers. Stir and sauté for a few seconds.
- Add half of the basil leaves and sauté until garlic is very pale brown. Don't overcook the garlic.
- Add the tomatoes and cook for about 10 minutes.
- Add the rest of the basil leaves and turn heat off.
- Cook the pasta in abundant salt water following manufacturer's instructions. Taste for readiness from time to time, until *al dente* (firm but not too soft or overcooked). Drain and transfer to a bowl.
- Top with the sauce. Toss thoroughly. Serve at once.

CARBONARA
eggs and bacon

The name of this dish means "in the style of the charcoal men," referring to the shops in past times that sold charcoal used for cooking. The pasta used in this preparation must be very hot when dropped into the bowl. The eggs are raw and they will cook instantaneously with the heat of the pasta, forming a tasty cream.

- 4 tablespoons extra-virgin olive oil
- 4 oz (115 gr) *pancetta,* diced (or substitute with bacon)
- crushed red pepper
- 2 eggs
- salt
- 1 lb (450 gr) spaghetti
- 2 oz (60 gr) *pecorino romano* cheese, freshly grated

- In a large stockpot, bring the water for the pasta to a boil.
- While waiting for the water to boil, pour the olive oil in a frying pan, and add the bacon and generous red pepper. Fry until the bacon is light brown.
- In a pasta bowl, beat the eggs with a pinch of salt.
- When the water comes to a boil, add salt and cook the pasta following manufacturer's instructions, testing for readiness from time to time, until *al dente* (firm but not too soft or overcooked).
- Drain the pasta and drop it immediately into the bowl over the beaten eggs.

- Mix vigorously. The heat of the boiling pasta will cook the eggs, making them resemble a light cream.
- Add the bacon with its frying fat, and the grated cheese. Toss thoroughly. Serve at once.

If the *pecorino romano* cheese is too strong or salty for your taste, substitute with a mix of half *pecorino romano* and half parmigiano reggiano cheese, freshly grated

AMATRICIANA
bacon and tomatoes

This dish originated in a town named Amatrice, located in the Appennini Mountains, near Rome. This area is famous throughout Italy for its production of wonderful pork meats, and for this dish.

There is a Roman recipe called *Gricia,* a dish of pasta dressed only with bacon and *pecorino* cheese (see following recipe). For centuries, it has been made not only in Rome, but all over central Italy. About fifty years ago apparently, a cook from Amatrice, in an effort to give a personal touch to the dish, added tomato, creating what we today call *Amatriciana.*

There is an ongoing dispute about how the "true" *Amatriciana* should be cooked. Some use onion, or garlic, or both in the preparation, others don't. Everybody agrees that absolutely no cream should be used.

- 4-5 tablespoons extra-virgin olive oil
- 4 oz (115 gr) *pancetta,* diced (or substitute with unsmoked bacon)
- ½ medium onion, diced
- crushed red pepper
- 2 cups (500 gr) tomato, finely diced
- salt
- 1 lb (450 gr) pasta *(bucatini, ziti,* spaghetti, or *rigatoni)*
- ¼ cup (50 gr) *pecorino romano* cheese, freshly grated

- In a frying pan, pour the olive oil, and add the bacon, onion, and generous red pepper.
- Sauté over low heat until onion becomes soft and translucent.
- Add tomatoes, and cook for approximately 10 minutes, until sauce is thicker.
- Cook the pasta in abundant salt water following manufacturer's instructions. Taste for readiness from time to time, until *al dente* (firm but not too soft or overcooked). Drain and transfer to a bowl.
- Top with the sauce, add freshly grated cheese, and toss thoroughly. Serve at once.

Use Italian *pancetta,* or substitute with seasoned and cured unsmoked bacon. The best pasta for this dish is *bucatini,* very long tubes that come in different sizes. If you are not too skilled in rolling pasta with a fork, cut the *bucatini* in pieces 2–4 inch (5–10 cm) long: If *bucatini* is not short enough, during eating they will begin winding and will splash the sauce.

GRICIA
bacon and cheese

- 5 tablespoons extra-virgin olive oil
- 4 oz (115 gr) *pancetta,* diced (or substitute with unsmoked bacon)
- crushed red pepper
- 1 lb (450 gr) pasta *(bucatini, ziti,* spaghetti, or *rigatoni)*
- salt
- ¼ cup (50 gr) *pecorino romano* cheese, freshly grated

- In a frying pan, pour the olive oil, and add the bacon and generous red pepper.
- Fry over medium heat until the bacon is browned.
- Cook the pasta in abundant salt water following manufacturer's instructions. Taste for readiness from time to time, until *al dente* (firm but not too soft or overcooked).
- Reserve 2 tablespoons of the cooking water. Drain and transfer pasta to a bowl.
- Add the 2 tablespoons of the cooking water to the bowl; top the pasta with the sauce and the freshly grated cheese. Toss vigorously. Serve hot at once.

Pesto Passion

Dried pasta—such as spaghetti and the tubular varieties—is more common in southern Italy and abroad. In the northern regions of Italy, pasta is more likely to be the fresh handmade type. And often the first course is not pasta at all, but risotto or polenta.

All the same, it is here in central and northern Italy that we find some of the most celebrated pasta preparations, including the pasta with mushrooms of Tuscany, or the *Trenette al Pesto* of Liguria ❖

PASTA AL SUGO DI FUNGHI PORCINI
pasta with porcini mushroom sauce

Porcini (Boletus edulis), one of greatest gifts of nature, is a rich, meaty mushroom. "Every year when September comes, the price of mushrooms goes down, and I buy plenty of *Porcini,*" wrote the famous cook Pellegrino Artusi a century ago. He was referring to the custom of buying many mushrooms when they are in season, in order to dry them and use them in the winter.

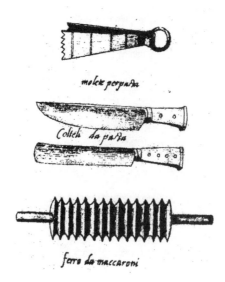

Ferro da maccheroni (rolling pin for macaroni), from Bartolomeo Scappi, *Opera dell'arte del Cucinare,* 1570. A similar tool is used today in the Apulia region to cut pasta into long strings named *troccoli* or *strascenat.*

If you go out for a drive after a fall thunderstorm in central Italy, you will find long lines of cars parked along the sides of the roads: Mushrooms have sprouted, and pickers are searching the woods. Although authorities require a licence and regulate the number of bags and places where picking is permitted, mushroom hunting continues to be a wonderful way to spend a day in the woods. It's easy—all you need are good shoes, a basket, and a knife. The reward can be *porcini*: a mushroom that is very versatile, delicate enough to give grace to an elegant dish, and yet has an extremely strong flavor.

Porcini

Porcini are very prized and appreciated mushrooms. They have a smooth, meaty texture and a strong woodsy flavor.

They can weigh from an ounce to more than a pound, and their caps can range from one to twelve inches in diameter. You will seldom find them fresh in the United States, but you might try looking for them in specialty produce markets in late spring or in the fall.

The dried form of this mushroom is readily available, however. *Porcini* mushrooms also come preserved in oil.

Drying is an age-old method of preserving wild mushrooms to enjoy them year-round. Dried mushrooms will keep for months without refrigeration.

Choose mushrooms that are a tan to pale brown in color; avoid those that are crumbly. Dried *porcini* must be softened in hot water for at least 20 minutes before using.

As a rule of thumb, one ounce of dried mushrooms will reconstitute to six to eight ounces. Once softened, the mushrooms may be sliced, chopped, or left whole, according to the recipe.

Add reconstituted mushrooms at the beginning of cooking. This allows their highly concentrated flavors to permeate the entire dish. Also, generally, cooks add the soaking water to the preparation for more flavor

But *never* eat wild mushrooms unless an expert has identified them. Toxic mushrooms may look a lot like other desirable species, and some of them, such as *Amanita muscaria,* contain a deadly neurotoxin.

Because fresh *porcini* are rarely found in the United States, we are substituting them with a combination of dry *porcini* and more common fresh mushrooms, such as chanterelle.

- ½ oz (15 gr) dry *porcini* mushrooms
- 4 tablespoons extra-virgin olive oil
- 2 cloves garlic, finely sliced
- crushed red pepper
- 1 lb (450 gr) fresh mushrooms, sliced
- 2½ cups (600 gr) tomatoes, diced
- 3 tablespoons Italian parsley, finely chopped
- salt
- 1 lb (450 gr) spaghetti

- Soak the dry *porcini* mushrooms in about 1 cup (230 cc) of warm water for about 1 hour. Drain the water, filter to remove impurities, and set aside. Chop the mushrooms.
- In a medium-size frying pan, pour the olive oil, and add garlic and crushed red pepper; sauté over medium heat, until the garlic starts becoming very light brown. Do not overcook the garlic.
- Add the fresh mushrooms and the soaked dry mushrooms. Turn the heat to high, and stir for about 1 minute.

- Add the tomatoes, 1 tablespoon of the parsley, and salt.
- Cook for about 10–15 minutes on medium heat, or until the sauce thickens.
- Turn heat off and adjust salt if necessary.
- Cook the pasta in abundant salt water following manufacturer's instructions. Taste for readiness from time to time, until *al dente* (firm but not too soft or overcooked). Drain and transfer to a bowl.
- Top with the sauce, toss thoroughly, garnish with the rest of the fresh parley, and serve at once.

TRENETTE AL PESTO
linguini with pesto sauce

- 4 oz (120 gr) small basil leaves
- 1 garlic clove, chopped
- 1 oz (30 gr) pine nuts
- ¼ cup (60 cc) extra-virgin olive oil from Liguria
- 2 tablespoons parmigiano reggiano cheese, freshly grated
- salt
- 1 lb small tender green beans
- 1 lb (450 gr) new potatoes, peeled and cut into large dices
- 1 lb (450 gr) *linguine* pasta
- 4 oz (115 gr) parmigiano reggiano cheese, freshly grated for topping

- Wash basil leaves and dry them with a towel. If the basil leaves are large, remove the center stems with a sharp knife.
- Place the garlic, basil, pine nuts, and one third of the extra-virgin olive oil in a food processor or blender.
- Run the blade, and stop occasionally to push the paste down. Add some more extra-virgin olive oil.
- Process the pesto until it is reduced to a fine paste and all the oil has been added. Stir in the grated parmigiano cheese and salt.
- Transfer to a nonmetallic bowl or jar. Cover with a drizzle of olive oil and reserve.
- In a stockpot, boil the beans and potatoes in salted water, until tender.
- Remove the vegetables from the pot; and in the same water, cook the linguini, following manufacturer's instruction, testing for readiness from time to time.
- Just before the pasta is *al dente* (firm but not too soft or overcooked) return the vegetables to the pot, and finish cooking.
- Drain the pasta and vegetables, transfer to a bowl, top with the pesto sauce and the grated parmigiano cheese. Toss, and serve immediately.

If you want to store pesto for a longer time, do not add the cheese; it will ferment and become rancid in a short time, dramatically changing the flavor of the pesto.

119

Store the pesto in a glass jar tightly sealed. Make sure the sauce is fully covered with olive oil to prevent darkening of the pesto. Use only nonmetallic containers and tools. Store the jar in the refrigerator for several weeks. Stir freshly grated parmigiano reggiano cheese and salt into the sauce just before serving. Pesto can be used in many preparations, including lasagne, soups, and gnocchi.

How to Peel Tomatoes

- Bring water to a boil in a pot.
- Core the tomatoes with a sharp knife.
- Turn tomatoes upside down and cut the base in an X-shape.
- Drop the tomatoes into the boiling water for a few seconds.
- Transfer the tomatoes into a bowl with cold water.
- Remove the tomatoes from the cold water.
- Using a knife, peel the skin away, beginning from the cuts made in the base.
- Cut the tomatoes in half.
- Remove the seeds and liquid if indicated by the recipe.
- Chop, mash, or purée the tomatoes as required.

PASTA AL BURRO E POMODORO
pasta with butter and tomato sauce

The comparison between this dish and the marinara sauce from Naples (see page 114) immediately shows the difference between southern and northern Italian cooking styles.

Where southern Italian cooking proposes a tomato sauce rich in the taste of garlic and oregano, the northern cooking offers the rich and smooth taste of butter and onion.

Always use fresh ripe tomatoes in this dish. No canned tomato or tomato paste compares with it.

- 3 tablespoons butter
- 3–4 tablespoons extra-virgin olive oil
- 1 medium onion, finely chopped
- salt and pepper
- 2 lb (approximately 1 kg) very ripe fresh tomatoes, peeled and puréed
- 4–5 fresh basil leaves
- 1 lb (450 gr) pasta (penne, spaghetti, or rigatoni)
- ½ cup (75 gr) parmigiano reggiano cheese, freshly grated

- In a medium-size saucepan, place the butter and olive oil. Turn the heat to medium.
- As soon as the butter starts foaming, add the onion, salt, and pepper.
- Sauté until the onion becomes soft and translucent.
- Add the tomatoes and basil leaves.
- Cook uncovered over medium heat for about 20–25 minutes, stirring frequently.
- Cooking time may vary depending on the type and ripeness of the tomatoes.
- Cook the pasta in abundant salt water following manufacturer's instructions. Taste for readiness from time to time, until al dente (firm but not too soft or overcooked). Drain and transfer to a bowl.
- Top with the sauce and the cheese, toss, and serve immediately.

120

Pasta Forever

Dry pasta is the most adaptable food ever invented. It is inexpensive, can be easily transported, and can be stored almost indefinitely. Pasta is nutritious, satisfying, and digestible. And it tastes good: Everyone likes a good dish of pasta.

Pasta can be dressed with almost any kind of condiment or vegetable, and can adapt itself to every cooking style—conforming to a new fashion or an ethnic cuisine. The imagination is the limit. Everything can go on pasta, and a cook's fantasy can be unleashed for the best-tasting dishes. Every day new shapes, colors, and textures hit the market, and new "classic" preparations are proposed ❖

PASTA MARI E MONTI
pasta with mushroom and shrimp sauce

Mari e monti means "seas and mountains." This pasta sauce owes its name to the unusual combination of ingredients: shrimps (from the sea) and mushrooms (from the mountains). For the best results, fresh *porcini* mushrooms should be used. Dried *porcini* soaked in warm water are a good substitute. If *porcini* are unavailable, any kind of fresh mushrooms can be used.

- 3 tablespoons extra-virgin olive oil
- 3 tablespoons butter
- 1 garlic clove, very finely chopped
- 5 oz (140 gr) fresh *cremini* mushrooms, sliced
- 2 tablespoons Italian parsley, chopped
- salt and pepper
- ½ lb (225 gr) raw shrimps, shelled and deveined
- ½ cup (120 cc) heavy cream
- 1 box or ½ lb (225 gr) dry fettuccine noodles

- In a skillet, pour the oil, and add 2 tablespoons of the butter and the garlic. Turn heat to medium.
- Before the garlic begins coloring a very pale brown, add the mushrooms and half of the parsley.
- Stir and cook for about 2–3 minutes. Add salt and pepper.
- Stir in the shrimps and cook for about 3 minutes. Add the cream, and turn the heat off.
- Cook the pasta in abundant salt water following manufacturer's instructions. Taste for readiness from time to time, until *al dente* (firm but not too soft or overcooked).
- Drain the pasta very well, pour it into the skillet over the sauce, turn heat to medium-high, and sauté for about 2 minutes.
- Remove the skillet from the heat before the sauce becomes too thick on the pasta.
- Transfer to a bowl, top with the rest of the parsley, toss, and serve immediately.

PASTA CON I CARCIOFI
pasta with artichokes

- 4 artichokes
- 1 lemon
- 3 tablespoons extra-virgin olive oil
- 2 tablespoons butter
- 1 clove of garlic, finely sliced
- 2 tablespoons Italian parsley, finely chopped
- 2 cups (500 gr) tomatoes, puréed in a blender
- salt and pepper
- 1 lb (450 gr) short pasta (*penne, maccheroncini, or rigatoni*)
- 2 oz (60 gr) parmigiano reggiano cheese, freshly grated

- Cut the lemon in half and squeeze it into a large bowl filled with fresh water.
- Clean the artichokes, removing the hard outer leaves, the skin, and the inside chokes. (See page 19).
- Slice each artichoke into thin wedges, and place in the bowl filled with water and lemon to prevent discoloration.
- Lightly rinse the artichokes in fresh water to remove the lemon flavor and drain.
- In a skillet, pour oil and add the butter; turn heat to medium.
- When the butter starts foaming, add garlic and parsley.
- Sauté until the garlic is very light golden. Add artichokes and sauté for 2–3 minutes.
- Add the tomatoes, salt, and pepper. Bring the sauce to a boil and cook over low heat for approximately 30 minutes.

- Cook the pasta in abundant salt water following manufacturer's instructions. Taste for readiness from time to time, until *al dente* (firm but not too soft or over-cooked). Drain and transfer to a bowl.
- Top with the artichoke sauce and the cheese. Toss and serve at once.

PASTA CON SPECK E PISELLI

pasta with speck and peas sauce

Speck is a special kind of smoked ham from the Alto Adige region of Italy. If speck is unavailable, smoked bacon can be used.

- ◆ 3 tablespoons extra-virgin olive oil
- ◆ 3 tablespoons butter
- ◆ 2 garlic cloves, finely diced
- ◆ 3½ oz (100 gr) *speck* (or substitute with smoked bacon)
- ◆ 5 oz (150 gr) frozen peas
- ◆ 1½ cup (400 gr) tomatoes, puréed in a blender
- ◆ salt and pepper
- ◆ 1 lb (450 gr) spaghetti
- ◆ 2 oz (60 gr) parmigiano reggiano cheese, freshly grated

- In a skillet, pour the olive oil and add the butter; turn heat to medium.
- As soon as the butter starts foaming, add the garlic and *speck*.
- Before the garlic begins coloring, add the peas, tomatoes, salt, and pepper.
- Cook for about 15 minutes, stirring occasionally.
- Cook the pasta in abundant salt water following manufacturer's instructions. Taste for readiness from time to time, until *al dente* (firm but not too soft or over-cooked). Drain and transfer to a bowl.
- Top with the sauce and the cheese, toss, and serve immediately.

PASTA CON BROCCOLI E GAMBERETTI

pasta with broccoli and shrimps

- ◆ 1 lb (450 gr) broccoli
- ◆ salt
- ◆ 4 tablespoons extra-virgin olive oil
- ◆ 2 garlic cloves, finely chopped
- ◆ crushed red pepper
- ◆ 1 lb (450 gr) raw shrimps, shelled and deveined
- ◆ 12 oz (340 gr) fresh ripe tomatoes, peeled and seeded
- ◆ 1 lb (450 gr) pasta, (spaghetti or *penne*)

- Clean the broccoli, keeping the tips and discarding the harder stems.
- Boil the broccoli in lightly salted water, until tender.
- In a skillet, pour the olive oil and turn heat to medium. Add the garlic and red pepper.
- As soon as the garlic becomes very pale golden, add the shrimps; stir for 1–2 minutes, until the shrimps become red.
- Add the tomatoes and cook while stirring for about 2 minutes.
- Add broccoli, cook for 2 minutes more. Add salt if necessary.
- Cook the pasta in abundant salt water following manufacturer's instructions. Taste for readiness from time to time, until *al dente* (firm but not too soft or over-cooked).
- Drain and transfer to a bowl. Top with the shrimp-broccoli sauce, toss, and serve hot.

SPAGHETTI AL TONNO
spaghetti with tuna sauce

- 4 tablespoons extra-virgin olive oil
- 2 garlic cloves
- crushed red pepper
- 2 cups tomatoes, diced
- ½ lb (225 gr) tuna fish, canned in olive oil, drained
- 3 tablespoons Italian parsley, finely chopped
- salt
- 1 lb (450 gr) spaghetti

- In a frying pan, pour the olive oil, and add the garlic and red pepper. Sauté until the garlic becomes very pale golden.
- Add the tomatoes, tuna fish drained of the oil, and half of the parsley.
- Using a wooden spoon, stir and crush the tuna into smaller pieces.
- Cook for about 10 minutes. Adjust salt, and cook for 5 more minutes.
- Cook the pasta in abundant salt water following manufacture's instructions. Taste for readiness from time to time, until *al dente* (firm but not too soft or overcooked). Drain and transfer to a bowl.
- Top with the sauce, toss, and spread with the rest of the parsley. Serve hot.

PASTA AFFUMICATA
pasta with smoked sauce

- 4–5 tablespoons extra-virgin olive oil
- 4 oz (115 gr) *speck* or smoked bacon, diced
- 2 cups tomatoes, diced
- ½ cup heavy cream
- salt and pepper
- 1 lb (450 gr) pasta *(penne or rigatoni)*
- 2 oz (60 gr) parmigiano cheese, freshly grated
- 2 oz (60 gr) *scamorza affumicata* cheese or smoked gouda (or other smoked cheese), freshly grated

- In a frying pan, pour the olive oil, and add the smoked bacon.
- Fry over medium heat until lightly browned.
- Add tomatoes and cook for approximately 5 minutes.
- Stir in the heavy cream, salt, and pepper, and cook until sauce thickens.
- Cook the pasta in abundant salt water following manufacturer's instructions. Taste for readiness from time to time, until *al dente* (firm but not too soft or overcooked). Drain and transfer to a bowl.
- Top with the sauce and toss thoroughly.
- Add the grated parmigiano and smoked cheese. Serve at once.

PASTA CON LE ZUCCHINE
pasta with zucchini

- 4 tablespoons butter
- 2 tablespoons extra-virgin olive oil
- 1 medium onion, finely diced
- 4 zucchini, sliced
- salt and pepper
- 4–5 tablespoons parmigiano reggiano cheese, freshly grated
- 1 lb (450 gr) spaghetti

- In a skillet, place 3 tablespoons of the butter, and pour the olive oil. Turn the heat to medium.
- When the butter starts foaming, add the onion, and sauté until the onion is soft.
- Add the zucchini, salt, and pepper.
- Cook for about 10 minutes or until zucchini are tender. Zucchini tend to quickly overcook, so check often for readiness.
- Place the remaining butter in a pasta bowl.
- Cook the pasta in abundant salt water following manufacturer's instructions. Taste for readiness from time to time, until *al dente* (firm but not too soft or overcooked).
- Drain and transfer to the bowl. Top with the zucchini sauce and the parmigiano cheese. Toss thoroughly, and serve at once.

PENNETTE AL MASCARPONE
pasta with mascarpone cheese

- 1 lb (450 gr) *pennette* (small *penne*) pasta
- salt
- 1 oz (30 gr.) butter
- ½ lb (225 gr) smoked bacon
- ½ lb (225 gr) *mascarpone* cheese
- 1 tablespoon Italian parsley, finely chopped
- crushed red pepper

- Cook the pasta in abundant salt water following manufacturer's instructions.
- While the pasta is cooking, place butter in a frying pan over medium heat.
- When the butter starts foaming, add bacon. Sauté the bacon for about 2–3 minutes, until golden.
- Place the *mascarpone* cheese in a pasta bowl. Add 2–3 tablespoons of the pasta cooking water.
- With a wooden spoon, mix the cheese with the water to obtain a creamy blend. Add the bacon to the bowl.
- Taste the pasta for readiness from time to time, until *al dente* (firm but not too soft or overcooked). Drain and transfer to the bowl.
- Toss vigorously, and top with the parsley and red pepper. Serve immediately.

PASTA CON GLI ASPARAGI
pasta with asparagus

- salt
- 1 lb (450 gr) asparagus
- 1 garlic clove, finely diced
- 5 tablespoons extra-virgin olive oil
- 12 oz (300 gr) fresh ripe tomatoes, peeled and diced
- 1 lb (450 gr) pasta (*penne*, *fusilli*, or spaghetti)
- 2 oz (60 gr) parmigiano reggiano cheese, freshly grated (optional)
- pepper

- Bring to a boil lightly salted water in a stockpot large enough to cook the pasta.
- Clean the asparagus with a vegetable peeler, removing the hard part of the stem and separating the tips from the bottoms. Reserve the tips, keeping them in fresh water.
- Briefly drop the asparagus bottoms in the boiling water until tender. Remove the asparagus with a slotted spoon, and reserve the water. Cut the asparagus in 1 inch (2.5 cm) long pieces.
- In a skillet large enough to contain the pasta, briefly sauté the diced garlic in the olive oil, until the garlic is very pale golden.
- Add the asparagus tips, and sauté for about 4 minutes.
- Add the boiled asparagus bottoms, and sauté for about 2 more minutes.
- Add tomatoes, salt, and pepper. Cook over low heat for about 5 more minutes.
- Cook the pasta in the same water where the asparagus were boiled in, following manufacturer's instructions.
- Taste for readiness from time to time, until *al dente* (firm but not too soft or overcooked). Drain the pasta and add it to the skillet.
- Toss it on high heat for about 1 minute, together with the asparagus-tomato sauce.
- Top with the grated parmigiano cheese (optional), serve immediately.

FETTUCCINE AL LIMONE
fettuccine in lemon sauce

- rind of 3 organic grown lemons, grated
- 2 oz (60 gr.) butter
- 1 cup heavy cream
- pinch of nutmeg
- ¼ cup vodka
- salt and pepper
- 1 box or ½ lb (225 gr) dry fettuccine noodles
- 2 oz (60 gr) parmigiano reggiano cheese, freshly grated

- Thoroughly clean the skin of the lemons with a small brush. Remove stains and dark spots.
- Using a vegetable peeler, remove the yellow portion of the lemon rind and cut in a fine julienne, or grate the rind.
- Avoid the white part of the lemon skin, which is bitter in taste.

- In a skillet large enough to receive the cooked pasta, place the butter and the cream. Turn heat to low.
- As soon as the butter starts foaming, add the lemon rind, vodka, salt, and pepper.
- Stir for about 1 minute, then turn heat off.
- Cook the pasta in abundant salt water. Taste for readiness from time to time, until *al dente* (firm but not too soft or overcooked).
- Drain the pasta very well. Pour it into the skillet containing the cream, and turn heat to medium-high.
- Sauté briefly. Remove the skillet from the heat before the sauce becomes too thick on the pasta.
- Pour into a large salad bowl, top with the cheese, and serve immediately.

PASTA AL GORGONZOLA
pasta with gorgonzola cheese

Italian blue cheese takes its name from a town located near Milan. The best gorgonzola cheese still is made in small factories, where it is fermented without the addition of any chemicals, and aged for long time. While the taste of gorgonzola can be very strong, the final taste of the sauce in this dish is mild from being combined with parmigiano cheese and cream.

- 2 oz (60 gr) gorgonzola cheese
- 1/3 cup milk
- 2 tablespoons butter
- ½ cup heavy cream
- 1 box or ½ lb (225 gr) dry fettuccine noodles
- salt
- 4–5 tablespoons parmigiano reggiano cheese, freshly grated

- In a skillet large enough to contain the pasta, place the gorgonzola cheese, milk, and butter.
- Turn the heat to medium and sauté for about 1 minute, until the butter begins foaming.
- Stir to dissolve the gorgonzola cheese, and add the cream.
- Cook the pasta in abundant salt water. Taste for readiness from time to time, until *al dente* (firm but not too soft or overcooked).
- Drain and pour into the skillet containing the cheese.
- Turn the heat to medium and toss until the pasta is fully covered by the sauce.
- Add the grated parmigiano cheese, and mix briefly.
- Serve immediately, with additional fresh grated parmigiano cheese on the side.

PASTA AL SALMONE
pasta with salmon sauce

This is a delicate and light dish, perfect for an elegant dinner. It is suitable as a dressing for many different kinds of pasta, but would be best appreciated on fresh handmade fettuccine.

- 6 oz (180 gr) smoked salmon
- 2 tablespoons butter, at room temperature
- ½ cup (120 cc) heavy cream
- salt and pepper
- 1 box or ½ lb (225 gr) dry fettuccine noodles
- 3–4 tablespoons parmigiano reggiano cheese, freshly grated

- In a food processor, reduce the salmon to a fine paste.
- In a skillet large enough to receive the cooked pasta, place the butter, salmon, heavy cream, salt, and pepper—but do not turn on the heat.
- Cook the pasta in abundant salt water. Reserve a few tablespoons of the cooking water. Taste for readiness from time to time, and drain the pasta about 2 minutes before *al dente* (firm but not too soft or overcooked).
- Pour the pasta over the salmon in the skillet, turn heat to medium-high, and sauté for about 2 minutes.
- Remove from the heat before the sauce becomes too thick on the pasta. Add 2 tablespoons of the cooking water if necessary.
- Transfer to a bowl, top with the cheese, and serve immediately.

PENNETTE POMODORO E MOZZARELLA

pasta with fresh tomato and mozzarella cheese

- ½ lb (225 gr) fresh soft mozzarella cheese, cubed
- ½ lb (225 gr) fresh ripe tomatoes, peeled, seeded, and diced
- 4 tablespoons extra-virgin olive oil
- 1 spring of fresh oregano
- salt and crushed red pepper
- 1 lb (450 gr) *pennette* (small *penne*) pasta

- In a bowl, combine the mozzarella cheese and tomatoes.
- Add extra-virgin olive oil and oregano. Season with salt and red pepper.
- Cook the pasta in abundant salt water following manufacturer's instructions. Taste for readiness from time to time, until *al dente* (firm but not too soft or overcooked).
- Lightly drain the pasta, leaving it very moist.
- Drop the pasta back into the cooking pot, add the mozzarella-tomato mixture, and mix to combine. The heat of the pot will melt the mozzarella cheese. Serve immediately.

SPAGHETTI CON LE POLPETTE

spaghetti with meatballs

This dish is so familiar in the United States that most children can describe it. It is one of those preparations most American believe is Italian--such as macaroni and cheese, pasta primavera, pizza with pepperoni, and veal parmigiana. Many think they are classic Italian recipes originated in southern Italy. In reality, these are inventions of Italian cooks at restaurants in the United States who modified authentic dishes to appeal to the taste of Americans at large.

- 2 oz (60 gr) soft bread
- ¼ cup milk
- 1 lb (450 gr) ground beef
- 1 egg, beaten
- 2–3 tablespoons parmigiano reggiano, freshly grated
- 1 tablespoon Italian parsley, finely chopped
- 1 garlic clove, finely diced
- pinch of nutmeg
- 2–3 basil leaves, finely chopped
- salt and pepper
- 2 oz (60 gr) flour
- 3 tablespoons frying oil
- 1 tablespoon butter
- ¼ cup dry white wine
- 2 cups (500 gr) tomatoes, puréed in a blender
- 1 lb (450 gr) spaghetti
- 4 oz (115 gr) parmigiano reggiano cheese, freshly grated

- Soak the bread in the milk for a few minutes. When the bread is very soft, drain the milk, and squeeze the bread to remove most of the liquid.
- In a large bowl, mix together the ground meat, bread, egg, grated parmigiano, parsley, garlic, nutmeg, basil, salt, and pepper.
- Shape the meat into little balls about 1 inch (2.5 cm) wide. Smaller balls will cook faster and remain softer.
- Place the flour on a large plate, and dredge the meatballs in the flour until uniformly covered.
- In a nonstick frying pan, pour the frying oil and add the butter. Turn heat to medium.
- When the butter starts foaming, add the meatballs, and fry them for about 10 minutes, until uniformly brown.
- Add the wine, turn heat to high, and let the wine evaporate.
- Turn the heat to medium, add tomato, salt, and pepper.
- Stir for few minutes; reduce heat to low, cover the pan, and cook for about 25–30 minutes until the meatballs are ready.
- Cook the pasta in abundant salt water following manufacturer's instructions. Taste for readiness from time to time, until *al dente* (firm but not too soft or overcooked). Drain and transfer to a bowl.
- Top with the meatballs, sauce, and parmigiano cheese. Toss, and serve immediately.

CHAPTER 7

The Island of the Sun

The Food of Sicily

Sicilian cooking is undeniably the most complex and colorful in Italy. Like hues on a painter's palette, the dishes on a Sicilian table represent the various cuisines of the many civilizations that passed through the island. The longtime isolation of the island and the Sicilians' innate attachment to tradition have allowed for the preservation and evolution of an elaborate cuisine. In Sicily, new and old, East and West, thrive side by side, blending uniquely together as in no other place in the world.

Homer Was Here

Little is known of the ancient populations—the Siculi, the Sicani, and the Elymi—who inhabited the island in prehistoric times. Early Greek colonizers who settled on the seaside from 700 B.C. to 400 B.C. and founded most of the coastal cities we know today, absorbed or defeated them.

For the Greeks, Sicily was a land of legend. The famous Greek poet Homer made Sicily the background for his mythological stories; Mount Etna was home to the god of the underworld, and the island of Vulcano was home to Aeolus, the god in the *Odyssey* who gifted Ulysses with a sack containing contrary winds. Homer's "wandering islands" are the Lipari archipelagos, with their floating pumice rocks. He depicts the strong currents of the strait of Messina—which reverse direction every few hours—with monsters sinking the ships that dare to cross.

It was amidst magic and superstition—in this land populated with gods, cyclops, and nymphs— that Greek civilization prospered. The city of Syracuse was unrivaled in those times for its splendor as well as its power. Defeating Athens in a sea battle that defined Hellenic history, Syracuse imposed her rule on most of *Magna Grecia,* the colonies along the coast of southern Italy.

A goddess pours wine for Hercules, from a decoration on a Greek vase. An olive tree stands in the background. *Magna Grecia*, the colonies in Italian territory, were occupied by Greeks for several centuries. Greek diet was frugal for the wealthy as well as the poor. From the mainland, the Greeks brought with them wheat, olives, wine, and figs. Wheat and other grains were consumed as porridge or flat bread similar to the pita of present day.

The dominion of Dionysius, ruler of Syracuse in the fourth century B.C., was larger than any other in the Mediterranean until Alexander the Great came into power centuries later.

The city gave birth to Archimedes and Theocritus, and was celebrated by Plato, who described the wealth of its citizens and the abundance of agriculture, forests, game, and fish. The warm climate allowed outdoor dining, a custom (now called *al fresco*) that remains alive and well today. Greek language was spoken in Sicily for centuries and then faded away into the Sicilian dialect, contributing many words to

it. The Greeks brought with them to the island the foods they appreciated the most: olives, grapes, wheat, and figs.

The Romans occupied Sicily around 260 B.C. , but they did not contribute much to Sicilian progress. On the contrary, they imposed a regime of exploitation, creating *latifundia*, large estates run with slave labor, and made Sicily the granary of Rome. The island was oppressed by heavy taxes, and all the wheat harvest was sent to Rome, busy conquering the world and hungry for grains. It also became a vacation spot celebrated by

128

Roman patricians such as Cicero, Martial, Apicius, and Petronius.

The Romans' contribution to Sicilian cooking is limited to the introduction of bread in place of the flat Greek *pitas,* and to the *maccu,* a purée or soup made out of mashed fava beans.

As elsewhere in Italy, the collapse of Rome set off a chain of invasions, incursions, and transfers of power from one ruler to the next. Sicily was prey to more foreign rulers than any other region of Italy. A horde of Franks sacked Syracuse; and then the Goths arrived. Finally the Byzantines, who conquered the island and ruled for more than three centuries, were able to reestablish order. The Benedictine monasteries founded during their rule revived the economy and agriculture—introducing new spices, foods, and ways of cooking.

East Meets West

The seminal moment for Sicilian cooking occurred, however, under the Saracen domination. Conquered by the Arabs around 830 A.D., Sicily became one of the most splendid Islamic provinces. Palermo, the island's capital, was an Oriental metropolis, legendary for its luxurious gardens and buildings. The Arabs gave a new face to the gastronomy of the island: They increased agriculture by

Sicilian *cannoli*. These wonderful little pastries have been celebrated as one of the best creations of the bakers of Sicily for at least 400 years. Traditionally they are given as a present during Carnival. The pastry shops of Palermo also displayed large trays holding "turbans" made from the same dough as the *cannoli* shell. This pastry later became a recipe by itself.

tapping into underground water sources; they improved and perfected tuna fishing; and they brought in new produce such as peaches, apricots, melons, dates, rice, sugar cane, eggplant, raisins, pistachios, oranges, and lemons, as well as new spices like clove, cinnamon, and saffron.

Under the Arab tutelage, the local cuisine acquired the sophisticated flavors that still make it unique one thousand years later. Oriental taste is alive in the many sweet-and-sour dishes, and especially in the desserts—extremely sweet, and full of honey, almonds, figs, nuts, and pistachios. Many Arabic words transferred to international gastronomic vocabulary: sorbet, sugar, saffron, and couscous, to mention just a few. It is in Sicily that we have the first testimony of the manufacture of dry pasta, as well as marzipan and nougat. Almost all foods that we think of today as typically Sicilian are typically Saracen.

At the turn of the millennium, the Normans conquered Sicily for a short but illuminated reign that restored the authority of the Christian church but also respected Arab art and culture. The new northern colonizers were amazed by the refined habits of the population they conquered. They brought with them a particular love for hunting and roasting meat. In this way, new northern flavors became integrated into the spicy taste of the most sophisticated and advanced cuisine of the time.

After a period of civil disorder, the French Angevins took power in a reign that proved a complete disaster. The people of Sicily rebelled against the *malasignoria* ("the bad lordship") of the French: During the infamously bloody "Sicilian Vespers," they murdered every French man they could identify.

A Spanish Twist

The Spanish Aragonese briefly ruled the island, inspiring Spanish eating habits and dishes. From this period survives caponata, the use of wild fennel, 'mpanate (empanadillas), and sponge cakes. They were followed by the Bourbons (with ties to both French and Spanish royalty), who founded the Reign of Sicily that survived until 1860. The products of the new world appeared: cocoa, tomato, squash, peppers, and potato quickly became part of "traditional" Sicilian cooking.

The tables of the wealthy acquired the baroque taste and look common to the rest of Europe, and characterized by ornate aesthetic forms. Cooks became like architects, creating elaborate "trophies of the table," as though they wanted to exorcize the actual situation of the common people, who were plagued by pestilences, riots, hunger, bands of outlaws ravaging the countryside, and Saracen pirates infesting the sea.

In the early 1800s, when the island was under English protectorate for about a decade, an Englishman by the name of John Woodhouse "invented" Marsala wine. He recognized that Sicilian

The Church and Tower of Martorana in Palermo. Engraving from the 1800s. The monks of the convent produced the famous "Fruits of *Martorana*," fine almond paste, shaped and colored to closely resemble all different types of fruit. Figs and apples, oranges and pears, molded in almond paste, are then painted to perfection. The convents of Sicily played an important role in the gastronomy of the island. Within the walls of these establishments the sisters occupied their time preparing the most complicated and refined dessert. Sweet rice, candied fruit, *biancomangiare,* sponge cakes, *cassate;* every convent had a specialty for which it was famous.

climate and wines had similarities with those of Madeira and Port, which the English valued and enjoyed. He successfully produced, promoted, and made popular Marsala wine.

We must add to the list of dominating powers in Sicily the Inquisition, which operated actively in the island until the early 1800s, and also we must mention the mafia. Probably originating as a secret society to empower the Sicilians against foreigners, the mafia degenerated into a criminal association.

When the northern Italian leader Garibaldi landed in Marsala in 1860, finally Sicily was united with the rest of Italy, in its most congenial form, the one we know today.

Greeks, Romans, Byzantines, Saracens, Normans, French, Spaniards, English, and finally Northern Italians; our palette is now complete.

The Scent of Orange Flowers

Not only history has shaped the cooking style of Sicily. The southern Mediterranean climate has had its influence, favoring the use of olive oil and fish over that of beef and pork fat. Religious ceremony has also influenced the culinary traditions: Pagan festivities merged with Christian holidays, and people continue experiencing the occult significance of certain foods—mostly breads and sweets with ritual shapes.

Here more than anywhere, the poorer people's imitation of the cooking of the upper classes created new flavors. They substituted the expensive ingredients, meat and fish, with bread crumbs, eggplant, and squash. Also, as in many other Mediterranean countries, street cooking flourishes.

The Sicilian desserts—colorful, precious, and extremely sweet—made history many times: First created by the Byzantines; next they were elaborated by the Arabs; then handed down in the monasteries; and later enriched in the kitchens of the barons and the peasants. In the 1500s, Caterina de' Medici took a Sicilian baker to France with her. And in 1689, Procopio de' Coltelli, a Sicilian baker, opened his Café Procope in front of the theater *Comedie Francaise* in Paris, giving European stature to Sicilian ice creams. It is to Sicilian cuisine that we owe our thanks for ice cream, candied fruit, nougat, marzipan, and desserts like *cannoli* and *cassata*.

La Mattanza (the slaughter). Every spring, great packs of giant blue-fin tuna migrate from the Atlantic through the Strait of Gibraltar to reproduce in the Mediterranean Sea. For centuries they have provided food for coastal communities from Spain to Turkey and Sicily. From the Sicilian coast, the fishermen organize a complex system of nets and boats, the *tonnara*, shaped to entrap hundreds of fish. In a single bloody catch, the fishermen enact the ritual killing of the tuna: They harvest the tuna, lifting them by hand with harpoons from the "chamber of death," the last room of the elaborate trap. This dark and beautiful ritual may soon disappear because of competition from the modern fishing industry.

On this island punctuated by orange groves, inhabited by emirs and barons and philosophers and poets, a place made lavish and succulent by Arab alchemies, nonetheless survival was never easy for the Sicilians. Although the economy was improved by the growing industry of tuna fishing, the manufacture of ceramics, the export of citrus and wines, the benefits would reach only a few. For a long time, the *baronie* (the noble caste that owned the majority of the land and still survives today), as well as the mafia, prevented innovation and the modernization of Sicily.

The people of Sicily responded to poverty and indigence with emigration by the hundreds of thousands to the new world. Yet, the smell of the *zagara*—the blooming orange flowers—stays in their memory forever, and those who left took with them their culture of pride, passion, and attachment to their traditions, as well as their dishes and cooking habits ❖

131

CAPONATA
sweet-and-sour eggplant

This Sicilian dish probably originated in Spaini The name stems from the Catalan word *caponada,* which refers to a similar relish. Pino Correnti, in his book on Sicilian cuisine, says the word appeared for the first time in 1709.

Caponata is a magnificent dish made from many different vegetables cooked separately and then blended together. Several versions of this dish have emerged that add fish or cheese. It is best served lukewarm, as an appetizer or a side dish.

serves 6

- 1 lb (450 gr) celery
- frying oil
- 4 tablespoons extra-virgin olive oil
- 2 garlic cloves, diced
- ½ lb (225 gr) onion, diced
- crushed red pepper
- 1 cup (230 gr) tomatoes, puréed in a blender
- 4–5 basil leaves
- 6 oz (180 gr) sicilian green olives, pitted
- 4 tablespoons capers in salt, rinsed and drained
- pepper
- 2 lb (900 gr) eggplant
- 2 tablespoons sugar
- 3–4 tablespoons vinegar (quantity varies depending on the strength)
- salt

- In a small saucepan, boil the celery sticks for about 6–7 minutes to tenderize them. Cut into small dice.
- In a skillet, bring the oil to frying temperature. Fry the celery for about 2–3 minutes, until tender. Set them aside.
- In a medium-size saucepan, pour the extra-virgin olive oil, and add the garlic, onion, and a generous amount of red pepper.
- Sauté for about 5 minutes over medium heat, or until the onion is soft and translucent.
- Add the tomatoes, basil, olives, capers, and pepper. Cook for about 10 minutes and set it aside.
- Cut the eggplant into approximately ¾-inch (2–3 cm) dice.
- In a large frying pan, heat the oil to frying temperature. Fry the eggplant gently for about 8–10 minutes, until light brown.
- Add the tomato sauce and celery. Stir to blend the ingredients together.
- Stir in the sugar and vinegar. Cover the saucepan, and cook for about 5 minutes, or until the caponata thickens.
- Adjust salt and pepper. Capers can be very salty therefore taste the caponata and add salt only if necessary.
- Set it aside in a bowl for at least 1 day. Serve lukewarm.

Caponata can be kept in a sealed container in the refrigerator for several days.

ARANCINI DI RISO AL RAGU'
stuffed rice balls

Arancini (small oranges) is an extraordinary preparation, which incorporates many Sicilian cooking styles: the Saracen with the rice and saffron, the French with the *ragu',* and the Spanish with the tomato base. Traditionally, *arancini* are round, the size and the color of a small orange, as the name suggests.

makes about 18
for the ragu'
- 4–5 tablespoons extra-virgin olive oil
- 1 medium onion, chopped
- 1 small carrot, finely diced
- ½ stick celery, finely diced
- 1 garlic clove, finely chopped
- ½ lb (225 gr) ground meat
- ¼ cup (60 cc) dry white wine
- 1½ cups (400 gr) tomatoes, puréed in a blender
- pinch of nutmeg
- 2 tablespoons milk
- salt and pepper
- 6 oz (180 gr) small green peas, fresh or frozen

for the rice
- 1 lb (450 gr) *arborio* rice
- 2 eggs
- 2 oz (60 gr) *pecorino* (romano) cheese, freshly grated
- ½ envelope saffron powder, dissolved in 3–4 tablespoons of warm water

for the arancini

- 2 eggs
- salt
- 2 oz (60 gr) flour
- 6 oz (180 gr) bread crumbs
- 3½ oz (100 gr) fresh soft sheep cheese, cut in ½ inch (1 cm) dice
- frying oil

preparing the ragu'

- Pour the olive oil in a saucepan, and turn the heat to medium. When the oil is hot, add the onion, carrot, celery, and garlic. Sauté until the onion is soft and translucent.
- Add the ground meat, and stir until brown.
- Add the wine. Turn heat to high, and let the wine evaporate.
- Add the tomato, nutmeg, milk, salt, and pepper. Turn the heat to low as soon as the sauce starts boiling.
- Cover, and cook slowly for about 40 minutes; add some water if necessary and stir occasionally.
- Stir in the peas and cook for additional 10 minutes, or until the sauce is thick. Cool at room temperature.
- When the sauce is lukewarm, strain residual liquid so that it is reduced to a dense paste.

preparing the rice

- Boil the rice in salted water until *al dente* (firm but not too soft or overcooked).
- Drain in a colander, and transfer to a work surface. When the rice is still hot, shape it into a mound with a hole in the center.

- Beat the eggs. In the well add the eggs, *pecorino* cheese, and saffron.
- Mix all the ingredients well. The rice will become consistent and sticky.

preparing the arancini

- In a shallow bowl, beat the eggs with a pinch of salt.
- Place the flour and the bread crumbs in different bowls.
- Shape the rice into 10–12 small balls approximately 3 inches (7–8 cm) in diameter.
- Take the balls one at a time in the palm of your hand. With your finger, push in the center to create a little depression.
- Insert 1 teaspoon of tomato sauce and 1 dice of cheese, and then close it up to re-form it into a ball.
- Dredge the *arancini* in the flour, then in the egg, and finally in the bread crumbs, one at a time.
- Compress the bread crumbs with your hands so that they stick firmly to the rice.
- In a frying pan, bring the oil to frying temperature.
- Preheat oven to 375 F (190 C).
- Place the *arancini* in the hot oil, and fry them for about 2 minutes, until golden brown.
- Place the *arancini* on paper towels on a large plate while removing them from the frying pan and let the oil drain briefly.
- Transfer the *arancini* to an oven pan. Place in the oven for about 4–5 minutes, until they appear dry.
- Serve when still hot.

MELANZANE GRATINATE
stuffed grated eggplant

Sicilians have many recipes for eggplant. Each one varies from town to town and from family to family. This is our family's recipe.

- 3–4 tablespoons extra-virgin olive oil
- 3 tablespoons bread crumbs
- 4 eggplants
- 2 fresh ripe tomatoes approximately 5 oz (150 gr), diced
- 2–3 garlic cloves, finely diced
- 2 tablespoons Italian parsley, finely chopped
- 5–6 basil leaves, finely chopped
- salt and pepper (or crushed red pepper)

- Preheat oven to 380 F (190 C).
- Oil an oven pan and spread some of the bread crumbs over it.
- Cut the eggplants in half lengthwise.
- Remove from the center a small amount of the pulp to form longitudinal cavities.
- Chop the pulp finely, and transfer it to a bowl.
- Add the tomato, garlic, parsley, basil, salt, pepper, and 1 tablespoon of the olive oil.
- Distribute the mixture in the cavities of the eggplants.
- Place the eggplants in the pan open side up, cover with the bread crumbs, and sprinkle with the rest of the olive oil.

- Add to the bottom of the pan ½ cup (60 cc) water.
- Cover the eggplant with aluminum foil. Place the pan in the oven, and cook for about 10 minutes.
- Remove the aluminum foil. Cook for about 20–30 more minutes, or until the eggplant is golden and soft. Can be served hot or at room temperature.

INVOLTINI DI MELANZANE

eggplant rolls

serves 6

- frying oil
- 5 long eggplants, cut lengthwise in 4 slices each
- 4 oz (115 gr) bread crumbs
- 5 tablespoons extra-virgin olive oil
- 1 medium white onion, finely diced
- 3 oz (85 gr) *pecorino* (romano) cheese, freshly grated
- 1 teaspoon fresh oregano leaves, finely chopped
- salt and pepper
- 2 hard-boiled eggs, wedged
- ½ lb (225 gr) tomatoes, puréed in a blender

- In a skillet, bring the oil to frying temperature. Lightly fry the eggplant until golden on both sides. Set it aside.
- In a small skillet, fry half of the bread crumbs with 1 tablespoon of the extra-virgin olive oil, until golden.
- In a skillet over medium heat, pour 3 tablespoons extra-virgin olive oil. Add the onion. Sauté until the onion is soft and translucent.
- Stir in the fried bread crumbs. Turn heat off, and cool to lukewarm.
- When the onion is cold, combine the grated *pecorino* cheese, oregano, salt, and pepper.
- Preheat oven to 370 F (190 C).
- Spread over the bottom of an oven pan 1 tablespoon extra-virgin olive oil and a small quantity of the bread crumbs. This will prevent the eggplant rolls from sticking to the pan.

- Place the eggplant slices on a work board. On each slice, put 1 tablespoon of the onion mixture, 1 egg wedge, and 1 tablespoon of tomato purée; and roll them.
- Place the eggplant rolls in the oven pan, side by side in rows.
- Spread the remaining tomatoes and bread crumbs on the rolls.
- Bake for about 20 minutes. Serve warm.

Eggplant - Aubergine

The Italian name for eggplant is *melanzana*, from the Latin "Mela Insana" (Bad Apple). Believed to be poisonous, it took a long time for eggplant to be accepted in European kitchens.

The Chinese knew eggplant as early as 600 B.C. The plant originally came from India, and from there it spread to the Middle East, becoming a popular Arab food. When the Arabs conquered Spain and southern Italy, they brought the eggplant with them.

The most common type of eggplant—or *aubergine*, as it should properly be called—used in Italian preparations, is the glossy, smooth-skinned, elongated type, which has a deep purplish-black color.

Eggplant actually is a fruit. A good source of dietary fiber, it is fat-free and low in calories: only 28 calories per serving of 3½ ounces (110 grams).

Select only plump, heavy, unwrinkled eggplants that feel quite firm to the touch. Eggplant comes into season in summer, when it is harvested ripe; it is best eaten soon after purchase.

Eggplant becomes pithy and bitter as it becomes overripe. In that case, to reduce the bitterness, proceed as follows:

- Cut the eggplant as directed in the recipe.
- Place the cut-up eggplant in a colander.
- Lightly spread a small quantity of salt evenly over it.
- Set it aside for 15 minutes to ½ hour to drain.
- Lightly rinse the eggplant to remove the salt.
- Pat it lightly with kitchen paper to dry.

MELANZANE ALLA PARMIGIANA
eggplant parmesan

The name of this dish might plainly refer to the abundant use of parmigiano, quite uncommon in Sicilian cooking. Or, it might be a reference to the northern "style of Parma," because this preparation is a lasagna type of dish and lasagna is more frequently made in the northern and central regions of Italy, where the the pasta is substituted with eggplant.

serves 6

- 4 tablespoons extra-virgin olive oil
- 1 medium size onion, very finely chopped
- salt and pepper
- 2½ cups (550 gr) tomatoes, puréed in a blender
- 10 fresh basil leaves
- 1½ lb (700 gr) eggplant
- frying oil
- 4 oz (100 gr) mozzarella cheese, diced
- 4 oz (115 gr) parmigiano reggiano cheese, freshly grated

- In a medium-size saucepan, pour the olive oil, and turn heat to medium.
- Add onion, salt and pepper. Sauté until onion becomes soft and translucent.
- Add the tomatoes and 3–4 basil leaves. Reserve the remaining basil leaves for later in the preparation.
- Cook on medium heat for about 20–25 minutes, stirring frequently.
- Slice the eggplant lengthwise, approximately 1/4 inch (6 mm) thick.
- In a skillet, bring the oil to frying temperature. Fry the eggplant slices until golden.
- Place the slices on paper towels on a large plate and let the oil drain briefly.
- Preheat oven to 370 F (190 C).
- Spread 2 tablespoons of the tomato sauce over the bottom of an oven pan approximately 9 x 13 inch (22 x 33 cm).
- Add 1 layer of eggplant slices, cover with tomato sauce and diced mozzarella, and spread with grated parmigiano.
- Repeat the layers until all ingredients are used. Top with the reserved basil leaves.
- Bake for about 30 minutes. Serve warm.

PEPERONI ARROSTITI
roasted bell peppers

- 4 bell peppers of different color
- 4 tablespoons extra-virgin olive oil
- 1 garlic clove, diced
- 5–6 mint or basil leaves
- salt and pepper
- ½ lemon (optional)

- Preheat oven to 350 F (175 C).
- Wash and dry the peppers, place them in a flat pan, and place the pan in the oven.
- Turn the bell peppers several times. Remove pan from the oven when the transparent skin is burned in several places, and starts peeling off.
- Peel the peppers, cut in half lengthwise, and remove the seeds.
- Slice into long strips approximately 1 inch (2 cm) wide.
- Place the peppers on a serving dish. Top with the oil, garlic, mint, salt, and pepper. Squeeze a few drops of lemon (optional).

Bell peppers can be roasted in different ways: on the flame of the stove, on a barbecue grill, or in the oven. When roasted in the oven, they become softer and more uniformly cooked.

Place the peppers in a paper bag while they still are hot, and let them cool at room temperature. The skin will be much easier to peel off.

Roasted peppers can be prepared in large quantities and preserved, covered with olive oil, in a glass jar.

PEPERONI RIPIENI
stuffed bell peppers

- 4 bell peppers of different colors
- 4 + 2 tablespoons extra-virgin olive oil
- 1 medium onion, finely diced
- 2 garlic cloves, finely diced
- 1 tablespoon Italian parsley, finely chopped
- 4 anchovies, finely chopped
- 1 tablespoon raisins
- 1 tablespoon pine nuts
- 2 oz (60 gr) olives, pitted, drained, and finely ground
- 6 tablespoons bread crumbs
- salt and pepper

- Preheat oven to 350 F (175 C).
- Wash the bell peppers, cut them in half, and remove the seeds.
- In a skillet, pour 4 tablespoons of the extra-virgin olive oil and turn heat to medium.
- Sauté the onion and garlic, until onion is soft and translucent.
- Remove the skillet from the heat. Stir in the parsley, anchovies, raisins, pine nuts, ground olives, bread crumbs, salt, and pepper.
- Drizzle with 2 tablespoons of extra virgin olive oil. Mix all the ingredients thoroughly.
- Fill the bell peppers with the mixture.
- Place the filled bell peppers side by side in an oiled oven pan.
- Bake for about 40 minutes, or until the surface is golden.
- Remove pan from the oven and let the stuffed peppers cool at room temperature. Serve lukewarm.

MACCU
fava bean purée

The word *Maccu* is derived from the Latin word *maccare* (to mash).

It is a very simple purée of dry fava beans. Among the oldest and most celebrated Sicilian dishes this recipe can be traced back to Greek and Roman times.

Maccu also is used in soup, together with other legumes, such as beans, peas, chickpeas, and lentils.

- 2 lb (approximately 1 kg) dry fava beans
- salt
- 5 oz (150 gr) fresh wild fennel, if available
- 5–6 tablespoons extra-virgin olive oil
- pepper

- The night before, place the dry fava beans in a large bowl full of fresh water.
- Let the fava beans soak in the water overnight.
- The next day, when you are ready to cook, rinse the fava beans.
- Place the fava beans in a pot full of water.
- Add salt and fennel. Bring to a boil. Cook until the fava beans are very tender.
- Drain the beans.
- Using a fork, reduce to a purée.
- Top with the extra-virgin olive oil and freshly grated black pepper. Adjust salt if necessary.

PASTA CON ACCIUGHE E PANGRATTATO
pasta with anchovies and bread crumbs

This recipe undoubtedly survived from medieval times. It is fascinating how much the ancient ways of cooking are currently well alive at the Sicilian table.

- 5 oz (150 gr) bread crumbs
- 5 + 2 tablespoons extra-virgin olive oil
- 1 garlic clove, crushed whole
- 4 oz (115 gr) anchovies, chopped
- 1 oz (30 gr) pine nuts
- 1 oz (30 gr) raisins, soaked in warm water and drained
- 4 tablespoons Italian parsley, finely chopped
- 1 lb (450 gr) *linguine* pasta

- In a small skillet, briefly toast the bread crumbs until golden.
- In a larger skillet, pour 5 tablespoons of the olive oil, and add the garlic.
- Sauté briefly; discard the garlic before it begins coloring.
- Add the anchovies. Quickly smash them with a fork. Immediately add the pine nuts, raisins, and parsley.
- Turn heat off; transfer the anchovy sauce to a small bowl; and set it aside.
- Add 2 tablespoons of extra-virgin olive oil to the pan. Turn heat to medium, and add the toasted bread crumbs.

- Fry briefly, just long enough for the bread crumbs to absorb the anchovy condiment remaining in the pan.
- Cook pasta in abundant salt water following manufacturer's instructions. Taste for readiness from time to time, until *al dente* (firm but not too soft or overcooked). Drain and transfer to a bowl.
- Top with the anchovy sauce and the bread crumbs. Serve immediately.

PASTA 'NCASCIATA
baked pasta with cheese

The name of this dish suggests the way it is prepared: *'ncasciata*, that is, "with *cacio*", the dialectal word for "cheese."

serves 6
- 3 medium eggplants
- frying oil
- 4–5 tablespoons extra-virgin olive oil
- 1 garlic clove, crushed whole
- 1 medium onion, sliced
- 3½ oz (100 gr) ground meat
- 3½ oz (100 gr) chicken livers, finely diced
- 5 oz (180 gr) peas
- salt and pepper
- 2 lb (900 gr) tomatoes, finely diced
- 1 lb (450 gr) *rigatoni* pasta
- 2 oz (60 gr) *salame*, finely diced
- 4 oz (115 gr) fresh mozzarella cheese, diced
- 2 oz (60 gr) *caciocavallo* (or parmigiano cheese), freshly grated
- 2 hard–boiled eggs, shelled and sliced
- 4 tablespoons basil leaves, chopped

- Cut the eggplants in slices approximately ³/₈ inch (1 cm) thick.
- In a skillet, bring the oil to frying temperature. Fry the eggplant slices until tender, and set aside.
- In a pan, pour 3 tablespoons of the olive oil and add the garlic. Sauté briefly. Discard the garlic before it begins browning.
- Add the onion, ground meat, chicken livers, peas, salt, and pepper. Sauté for a few minutes.
- Add tomatoes, and cook for about 30 minutes.
- Preheat oven to 425 F (220 C).
- Cook pasta in abundant salt water following manufacturer's instructions. Taste for readiness from time to time, until *al dente* (firm but not too soft or overcooked). Drain and transfer to a bowl.
- Top the pasta with the tomato sauce, *salame*, mozzarella cheese, grated *caciocavallo* cheese, and basil.
- Line an oven pan with the fried eggplant slices and the egg slices in a pattern.
- Fill the pan with the pasta. Bake for about 15 minutes.
- Unmould the pasta by turning it upside down onto a large serving dish. Serve warm.

SCALOPPINE AL MARSALA
veal scaloppini with marsala

This dish might be of French origin. Although it doesn't have the characteristics of a "traditional" Sicilian recipe, the use of Marsala wine certainly gives it a Sicilian flavor.

- salt
- 2 oz (60 gr) flour
- 1 lb (450 gr) thin veal slices
- 2–3 tablespoons extra-virgin olive oil
- 1 oz (30 gr) butter
- pepper
- ½ cup (120 cc) dry Marsala wine

- Add a pinch of salt to the flour. Spread on a large flat plate.
- Dredge both sides of the veal slices in the flour. Shake away the excess flour.
- Pour oil and add butter in a frying pan, and turn the heat to medium.
- As soon as the butter starts foaming, turn the heat to low, place the veal in the pan, and fry gently on both sides for about 5 minutes or until tender. The veal will have a light golden color.
- Sprinkle with salt and pepper.
- Add the Marsala wine; let it simmer over medium heat, until the wine is partially evaporated and the sauce is thicker.
- Transfer to a warm plate, and serve immediately.

RAGU' DI TONNO
stewed tuna fish in tomato sauce

This recipe provides a great second course of tuna fish, and, additionally, a wonderfully tasty sauce to use as the dressing for a first course of pasta.

Choosing a large chunk of tuna, approximately 3–4 inches (8–10 cm) thick, will make it easier to slice the fish at the end of the preparation.

- 2 lb (approximately 1 kg) fresh tuna fish, in one piece
- 2 tablespoons fresh rosemary leaves, chopped
- 2 garlic cloves, chopped
- 3 cloves, finely chopped
- salt and pepper
- 3–4 tablespoons extra-virgin olive oil
- ½ cup (120 cc) dry white wine
- 1 medium onion, finely diced
- 2½ cups (600 gr) tomato, puréed in a blender

- Make a few incisions on the tuna fish.
- In a small bowl, mix the rosemary leaves, garlic, cloves, salt, and pepper.
- Stuff the incisions of the tuna with the spice mixture.
- Season the fish all around with salt and pepper.

- In a saucepan, pour oil, and turn heat to medium. When the oil is hot, brown the tuna uniformly on all sides.
- Add the wine and let it evaporate.
- Remove the fish from the pan and keep it warm.
- Add the onion to the pan, and sauté until soft and translucent.
- Place the fish back in the pan and cook for about 5 more minutes, turning one or two times.
- Add the tomato purée and ½ cup (120 cc) warm water. Adjust salt and pepper. Cover and cook over medium-low heat for about 20 minutes, or until the tuna fish is tender.
- Remove the fish from the pan, cut into slices, and keep it warm.
- If the *ragu'* is too watery, thicken over medium heat in the uncovered pan.
- Serve the fish with part of its sauce. Use the rest of the *ragu'* to dress a first course of pasta.

PESCE AL FORNO CON IL PANGRATTATO
broiled fish with bread crumbs

- 3½ oz (100 gr) bread crumbs
- 1 teaspoon oregano
- salt and pepper
- 1½ lbs (700 gr) fish fillets
- 5 tablespoons extra-virgin olive oil
- ½ onion, finely sliced
- 1 lemon, juiced
- 2 teaspoons capers in salt, rinsed and drained

- Preheat oven to 350 F (180 C).
- In a shallow bowl, mix the bread crumbs, oregano, salt, and pepper.
- Dredge both sides of the fish fillets in the bread crumbs.
- Spread 1 tablespoon of the olive oil over an oven pan.
- Place the breaded fish fillets in the pan; top with onion, lemon juice, capers, the rest of the bread crumbs, and the remaining extra-virgin olive oil.
- Cook in the oven for about 30 minutes. Serve warm.

SEPPIE RIPIENE
stuffed squids

This classic preparation has many variations in the way the filling is prepared. The anchovies can be substituted with finely diced fresh shrimps for a milder taste.

- 1½ lb (700 gr) small squid
- 2 anchovy fillets, finely chopped
- 2 garlic cloves, finely diced
- 3 fresh tomatoes (approximately 300 gr), peeled and finely diced
- 2 tablespoons Italian parsley, finely chopped
- ½ cup (100 gr) bread crumbs
- 1 egg
- salt and pepper
- 3 tablespoons extra-virgin olive oil
- ½ lemon

- Clean squid and separate the tentacles. Cut tentacles into small dice.
- Preheat oven to 350 F (175 C).
- In a bowl, combine the tentacle dice, anchovies, garlic, tomatoes, parsley, bread crumbs, egg, salt, and pepper.
- Fill the squid with the mixture. Close the opening of each squid with a toothpick.
- Place the squid in an oiled oven pan. Cook in the oven for about 40 minutes, or until the squid are tender.
- Serve warm, squeezing the half lemon on the squid.

Capers

This seasoning, so common in Italian cooking, comes from the eastern Mediterranean region. It is a small bush, adorned with nice pink-purple flowers, that mostly grows on rocky terrain and is common in central and southern Italy.

The edible part of the plant is the small unopened bud, which is harvested every year starting from May–June.

The best capers for cooking come from the small island of Pantelleria, south of Sicily, close to the African coast. The capers grow wild on the sunny hills of Pantelleria, and harvesting them is a tough job because of the difficult terrain and the summer heat.

When buying capers, choose those preserved in salt rather than vinegar. Vinegary taste in capers will intrude into the dish.

Keep the capers in a sealed jar that has an abundant amount of coarse salt in it, and the capers will last for years. To use capers, just rinse them under running water.

Here's an appetizer recipe from Tuscany Renaissance times: In a bowl, mix capers (washed and drained) and raisins (soaked and drained), add a small quantity of orange juice, and finely chopped orange peel.

AGGHIOTTA DI PESCE SPADA
sautéed sword fish in tomato and vegetables sauce

Agghiotta, in Sicilian dialect, means a person greedy for appetizing, juicy fish.

- 4 slices of swordfish approximately 1½ lbs (700 gr)
- 2 oz (60 gr) flour
- 4–5 tablespoons extra-virgin olive oil
- 1 medium onion, finely chopped
- 1 garlic clove, finely chopped
- 1 celery stick, finely chopped
- 2 tablespoons capers in salt, rinsed and drained
- 2 oz (60 gr) green olives, pitted
- 1 tablespoon raisins
- 1 cup fresh ripe tomato, peeled and chopped
- salt and pepper

- Dredge the fish in the flour.
- In a skillet, bring the olive oil to frying temperature. Fry the fish fillets until golden.
- Transfer the fish to a plate covered with paper towels to drain the excess oil.
- In the skillet containing the oil, place the onion, garlic, and celery. Sauté until the onion is soft and translucent.
- Add the capers, olives, raisins, tomato, salt, and pepper. Cook the sauce over medium heat for about 10 minutes.
- Add the fish back to the skillet, and cook for few minutes. Serve warm.

SALMORIGLIO
lemon sauce

The word *salmoriglio* comes from the Italian word that means "marinade." This sauce has a delicious, fresh flavor and is used on broiled fish

- ½ cup (120 cc) warm water
- 2 lemons, juiced
- 1 bunch of parsley leaves, very finely chopped
- 1 garlic clove, finely chopped
- 1 teaspoon fresh oregano leaves, finely chopped
- ½ cup (120 cc) extra-virgin olive oil
- salt and pepper

- Place a saucepan half filled with water over medium heat and bring to a boil.
- In a smaller saucepan, pour the warm water and lemon juice. Add the parsley, garlic, oregano, olive oil, salt, and freshly grated black pepper.
- Place the pan with the sauce into the hot water, and whisk vigorously, until a uniform mixture is obtained.

Salmoriglio rosso (red lemon sauce) can be obtained by adding tomato sauce to the water.

SARDE A BECCAFICO
stuffed sardines

Here is one more sweet-and-sour fish preparation, unique to the Sicilian island. Originally from Palermo, this dish has assumed many variations in different cities.

Beccafico is a Sicilian bird, whose name means "fig picker." The sardines are cooked with their tails up in a shape resembling small birds.

- 2 lb (approximately 1 kg) fresh sardines
- 1 orange
- 1 lemon
- 4–5 tablespoons extra-virgin olive oil
- 1 small onion, finely chopped
- 1 garlic clove, finely chopped
- 3½ oz (100 gr) bread crumbs
- 2 tablespoons raisin
- 2 tablespoons pine nuts
- 1 tablespoon Italian parsley, finely chopped
- salt and pepper
- 1 small bunch of bay leaves
- 1 tablespoon sugar

- Wash and clean the sardines eliminating the heads, bones, interiors, fins, and scales.
- Cut the orange and lemon in half, juice one half of each and cut the other half into thin slices.
- Preheat oven to 350 F (180 C).

- In a frying pan, pour 2 tablespoons of the olive oil, and add the onion.
- Sauté briefly, add garlic, and sauté until the onion is soft and translucent.
- Add bread crumbs and fry until golden. Remove from the heat.
- Combine the raisins, pine nuts, parsley, orange juice, lemon juice, salt, and pepper.
- Place the sardines flat on a work surface and place 1 teaspoon of the stuffing on top of the large part of each sardine.
- Roll the sardines and place them in rows side by side in the pan, touching each other, with the tails up.
- Place the bay leaves vertically between the sardines.
- Spread the remaining stuffing on top and also spread the 1 tablespoon of sugar.
- Decorate with the orange and lemon slices.
- Bake for about 30 minutes, or until golden.
- Serve this dish hot, or at room temperature.

SPIEDINI DI SEPPIE
squids skewers

Skewers are a common type of preparation among all the Mediterranean countries, where we find them composed of beef, veal, or mutton, accompanied with vegetables. The Sicilian recipe uses squid with an extraordinary result.

- 2 lb (approximately 1 kg) small squid
- 1 cup (50 gr) bread crumbs
- 1 tablespoon fresh oregano leaves, finely chopped
- 3 anchovies, finely chopped
- 2 tablespoons Italian parsley, finely chopped
- 2 garlic cloves, finely chopped
- salt and pepper
- 2 tablespoons extra-virgin olive oil
- 2 lemons, wedged

- Clean and skin the squid. Run the skewers through them one by one.
- In a bowl combine the bread crumbs, oregano, anchovies, parsley, garlic, salt, and pepper.
- Add in the extra-virgin olive oil to obtain a moist compound.
- Dredge the skewers in the bread crumb mixture.
- Cook on a grill, barbecue, or charcoal fire, for about 5 minutes on all sides.
- Serve immediately together with the lemon wedges. The skewers can also be cooked under the broiler for about 10–15 minutes.

Ricotta

Ricotta is a white, moist, fresh, soft cheese with a slightly sweet flavor.

The word *ricotta* means "cooked twice." In fact, this cheese is made by reheating the whey from another cheese, such as *pecorino* (romano sheep cheese): The whey, drained off while making other cheeses, is reheated, then skimmed and placed in wicker baskets to drain.

Technically, ricotta is not actually a cheese but rather a cheese by-product.

Italian ricotta generally is made from sheep's milk. Also cow's milk ricotta is widely popular: It is sweeter in taste than sheep's milk ricotta, and has a less-intrusive taste.

Ricotta is a popular ingredient in many Italian recipes and desserts.

Home Made Ricotta

makes 1 lb (400 gr)
- 2 quarts (2 liters approximately) whole milk
- 2/3 cup (160 cc) heavy cream
- 2/3 cup (160 cc) whole milk yogurt

- In a saucepan, pour the milk, the cream, and the yogurt.
- Place the saucepan over medium heat until temperature reaches about 175 F (80 C). Use a thermometer to check the temperature.
- Adjust the heat so that the milk is just below the boiling point, but never lower then 160 F (70 C).
- Line a colander with cheesecloth.
- When the cheese begins to form, by stirring the milk you can see the separation between the solid cheese lumps and the grayish liquid.
- Keep the saucepan on the heat 4–5 minutes longer from the moment the lumps begin forming to allow the full coagulation of the cheese.
- Remove the saucepan from the heat.
- Using a strainer, remove the cheese and place it in the colander.
- Lightly press the surface of the cheese to facilitate the elimination of liquid.
- Leave the ricotta to drain until no more liquid is coming out.

If the ricotta is too granular, before using it in a preparation, place it in a food processor and run the blade until it's smooth.

CANNOLI
sicilian cannoli

Cannoli—the Sicilian dessert par excellence. Typically part of the festivities for Carnival, *cannoli* are sent as a present to friends, no fewer than a dozen at a time.

makes about 26

for the cannoli
- 2 cups (280 gr) flour
- 1 oz (30 gr) sugar
- 1 teaspoon chocolate powder
- ½ teaspoon salt
- 1 oz (30 gr) butter, melted
- 1 cup (230 cc) dry Marsala wine
- 1 oz (30 gr) butter, for brushing
- 1 egg white
- frying oil

for the filling
- 1½ lbs (700 gr) ricotta cheese, drained
- 1 teaspoon vanilla powder
- ½ lb (225 gr) powdered sugar
- 4 oz (115 gr) candied fruit, finely diced
- 2 oz (60 gr) bittersweet chocolate, diced
- 2 oz (60 gr) powdered sugar, for dusting

To make *cannoli* you need the metal tubes sold for this purpose. Pieces of cane can also be used, approximately ¾ inch in diameter and 6 inches long (2 cm in diameter, 15 cm long).

preparing the cannoli shells
- In a bowl or food processor, mix together the flour, sugar, chocolate powder, salt, butter, and enough Marsala wine to obtain firm dough.
- Transfer to a lightly floured work surface and knead until smooth.
- Place the dough on a plate, cover with plastic wrap, and set aside for about 1 hour.
- Transfer the dough to a lightly floured work surface and knead again for few minutes.
- Place the dough back on the plate, cover with plastic wrap, and set aside for 1 more hour.
- Again transfer the dough to a lightly floured work surface and cut into 3 pieces.
- Pass each piece through the pasta machine, starting with the widest number. Repeat the step until number 5 on the dial is reached and thin smooth pasta sheets are obtained.
- Keep the pasta dough and sheets covered with plastic wrap at all times while working to prevent the dough from drying out too much.
- Cut the dough into squares 4 x 4 inch (10 x 10 cm).
- Lightly butter the metal tubes.
- Wrap the squares around the tubes or cane diagonally. Don't press the dough against the tubes too much; otherwise it will be difficult to remove them afterward.
- Wet the overlapping part with the egg white and press on the edges to stick them together.
- In a saucepan, bring the oil to frying temperature. Fry the *cannoli* until golden brown a few at a time.
- Remove from the pan and transfer on paper towels on a large plate to drain the excess oil briefly.
- Remove the *cannoli* shells from the tubes while they are still warm.
- Repeat the operation of forming the *cannoli* and frying until all the dough is used.

filling the cannoli
- In a bowl, combine the ricotta cheese, vanilla, and powdered sugar.
- Reserve 2 pieces of candied fruit per each *cannoli* for decoration.
- Combine the candied fruit and chocolate dice with the cheese filling.
- Using a pastry bag or a small spoon, fill the *cannoli* with the cheese mixture, and garnish the ends with pieces of candied fruit.
- Sprinkle with powdered sugar before serving.

CASSATA
sicilian layer cake

Cassata is the most famous Sicilian cake, traditionally prepared for Easter.

It combines the many cooking styles of the Island: the Saracen candied fruit, Spanish sponge, French glaze, and Roman cheese.

Cassata from the pastry shops is covered with a thick, sugar glaze. Homemade *cassata* is covered with whipped cream and decorated with candied fruit and pistachios.

for the sponge cake
- 5 eggs
- 1 teaspoon vanilla powder
- ¾ cup (150 gr) sugar
- ¾ cup (110 gr) flour
- 1/3 cup (50 gr) corn starch
- pinch of salt

for the filling
- 1 lb (450 gr) *ricotta* cheese, drained
- 3½ oz (100 gr) sugar
- ½ cup (120 cc) dark rum or other flavoring liquor
- ½ lb (225 gr) bitter chocolate squares, diced
- 3½ oz (100 gr) mixed candied fruit (e.g., citrus, orange, cherries), diced

for the decoration
- 1½ cups (360 cc) heavy cream
- 1 teaspoon vanilla
- 3 tablespoons powdered sugar
- 4 oz (115 gr) pistachios, finely chopped
- ½ lb (450 gr) candied fruit (e.g., citrus, orange, cherries), in large wedges

preparing the sponge cake
- Preheat oven to 350 F (175 C).
- Butter a round cake pan about 9 inches (22.5 cm) in diameter, 2 inches (5 cm) deep; or line it with a disk of parchment paper.
- In a bowl, mix the eggs, vanilla, and sugar.
- Beat vigorously with an electric mixer for 10–15 minutes, or until very soft and approximately doubled in volume.
- In a bowl, sift together the flour, cornstarch, and a pinch of salt.
- Sift the flour into the beaten eggs, folding the dough gently with a rubber spatula, 3–4 times.
- Mix smoothly with a round, top to bottom, motion.
- Pour the mixture into the pan; smooth the top with a spatula; and bake for about 30–45 minutes, until golden.

assembling the cassata
- Place the ricotta cheese in a bowl.
- Stir in the sugar and 1 tablespoon of the rum.
- Combine the chocolate and candied fruit, and set aside.
- Cut off the crust from the sponge cake.
- Cut the sponge into slices of approximately ½ inch (1 cm) thick.
- Butter a rectangular container and cover the bottom and walls with parchment paper.
- Pour rum into a bowl. Add ½ cup (120 cc) of water.
- Soak the cake slices in the watered liquor, and use them to cover the bottom and walls of the container.
- Pour the ricotta filling into the container, and level with a spatula.
- Cover with more slices of sponge cake soaked in rum, and press with your hand to compact the filling.
- Place in the refrigerator for a minimum of 2 hours.

decorating the cassata
- Unmould the cake, turning it upside down onto a serving plate.
- Mix the cream, vanilla, and powdered sugar. Whip until firm.
- Cover the *cassata* with the whipped cream.
- Press the chopped pistachios along the sides.
- Decorate the top geometrically with pistachios and large wedges of candied fruit.

BUCCELLATI
(cucciddati)
fig cookies

for the dough
- ♦ 4 cups (560 gr) flour
- ♦ 2/3 cup (150 gr) sugar
- ♦ 1 teaspoon baking powder
- ♦ 1 teaspoon salt
- ♦ 16 tablespoons (220 gr) butter
- ♦ 4 eggs

for the filling
- ♦ 12 oz (340 gr) dried figs, finely diced
- ♦ ½ cup (50 gr) raisins
- ♦ ½ cup (30 gr) candied orange, diced
- ♦ ½ cup (50 gr) almonds, finely chopped
- ♦ 3 oz (85 gr) semi-sweet chocolate, cut into small dice
- ♦ 1/3 cup (100 gr) apricot preserve
- ♦ 3 tablespoons dark rum
- ♦ 1 teaspoon cinnamon powder
- ♦ ¼ teaspoon cloves, ground

for the egg wash
- ♦ 2 eggs
- ♦ pinch of salt

preparing the dough
- Place the flour, sugar, baking powder, and salt in the bowl of a food processor fitted with a metal blade. Run the blade a few times to mix.
- Add the butter to the bowl and pulse to combine.
- Add the eggs, and run the blade until forming a consistent dough.
- Transfer the dough to a floured work surface, and wrap in a plastic foil.
- Place in the refrigerator.

preparing the filling
- Place the figs in a saucepan, cover with water, and bring to a boil. Drain thoroughly and cool to room temperature.
- In the bowl of a food processor fitted with a metal blade, combine the figs, raisins, candied orange, almonds, chocolate, apricot preserve, rum, cinnamon, and cloves. Pulse the blade until a smooth compound is obtained.

assembling the cookies
- Preheat oven to 350 F (180 C).
- Prepare the egg wash by beating the eggs with a pinch of salt.
- Remove the dough from the refrigerator, and unwrap it on a floured work surface.
- Add a small quantity of flour. Knead the dough to make it soft and smooth. Cut the dough into 10–12 pieces.
- Flatten each piece into a rectangle approximately 3 x 15 inch (7 x 35 cm).
- Brush the egg wash on the dough.

- Place approximately 1/3 cup of filling in the center of the rectangle lengthwise.

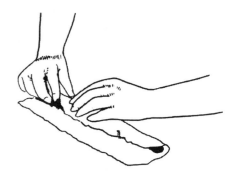

- Take one edge of the dough and bring it over the filling to form a roll.

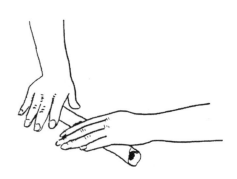

- With the palm of your hands roll the cylinder to make it even.

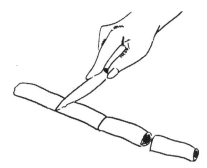

- Cut the roll into 4–5 pieces approximately 3–4 inch (8–10 cm) long. Set them aside. Continue forming the rolls until all the dough and the filling are used.

- Using a sharp knife, cut 4–5 incisions on the surface of the rolls.
- Transfer the rolls to 3 cookie pans lined with parchment paper. Brush the surface of the buccellati with the remaining egg wash.
- Bake for about 20 minutes or until golden. Transfer onto racks to cool.

BISCOTTI REGINA
sesame cookies

- 2 cups (300 gr) flour
- 7 oz (200 gr) butter, lukewarm
- 3½ oz (100 gr) sugar
- pinch of salt
- grated rind of 1 orange
- 1 teaspoon orange extract
- 1 egg
- ½ cup (120 cc) milk
- ½ lb (225 gr) sesame seed

- Pour the flour onto a work surface, to form a mound shape with a hole in the center.
- In the hole add the butter, sugar, pinch of salt, orange rind, orange extract, and egg.
- Use a fork to mix the ingredients; then combine the flour and knead the mixture to form smooth dough.
- Form a ball shape, cover with a plastic wrap, and set it aside for about 30 minutes.
- Preheat oven to 375 F (175 C). Butter a flat cookie pan.
- Cut the dough into 4-5 pieces. Shape each piece into cylinders about ¾ inch (2 cm) wide and 3/8 inch (1 cm) thick.
- Cut the cylinders into pieces approximately 1½ inch (4 cm) long and shape them in a rounded elongated form.
- Place the milk in a shallow bowl. Dredge the dough pieces first in the milk and then in the sesame seed, until completely covered.

- Place the cookies on the pan side by side.
- Bake for about 30–35 minutes or until golden. Place on racks to cool.

BIANCO MANGIARE ALLE MANDORLE
white almond pudding

The *biancomangiare* (*blanc-manger* in French, for "white eating") was important in medieval cooking. *Biancomangiare* was a general term for both sweet or savory dishes made predominantly of white ingredients.

Flour, almond paste, rice flour, sugar, chicken, milk, and cream were commonly used. The dishes made including a variety of these ingredients were appreciated because they were considered light, rich, and elegant—in opposition to dark dishes that were considered less healthy and of inferior quality. Because the *biancomangiare* normally contained limited spice, doctors suggested it to people in poor health.

In Sicily, the *biancomangiare* recipe that survives those remote times is a light, flavorful dessert made of almonds and full of the aromas of the island.

- 1¼ lbs (550 gr) almonds, peeled
- 3–4 drops of bitter almond extract
- 1 oz (30 gr) corn starch
- 3 oz (85 gr) sugar

for the decoration

- 1 oz (30 gr) mixed candied fruit, (orange, citron, lemon) in small dice
- 1 oz (30 gr) semi-sweet chocolate, finely diced
- 1 oz (30 gr) pistachios, shelled and finely diced
- 10 whole almonds, peeled
- 3–4 cinnamon sticks broken into small pieces

- Grind the almonds in a food processor.
- Add the almond extract and pulse until finely ground and fully combined.
- Place the almonds in a bowl with 1 quart (1 liter) water for a few hours. The water will assume a white milky color.
- Filter the almonds from the water.
- Reserve the water in a saucepan. Transfer the almonds to a cloth, and tie it to form a small sack.
- Squeeze the sack to expel as much water as possible into the bowl.
- Place the sack back into the almond water for few minutes, and again squeeze the water off.
- Repeat this step 3–4 times, so that as much of the almond flavor as possible is transferred to the water.

- In a small bowl, dissolve the cornstarch in a few tablespoons of water.
- Thoroughly stir the starch water into the almond water. Stir in the sugar.
- Place the almond mixture in a saucepan over medium heat.
- Slowly bring to a boil, stirring constantly with a wooden spoon.
- When the almond water starts boiling, stir for about 2 more minutes until thicker, and then remove from the heat.
- Transfer to a shallow serving dish, and cool at room temperature. Keep in the refrigerator until serving.
- Decorate the top with the candied fruit, chocolate, pistachios, whole almonds, cinnamon pieces, and jasmine flowers if available.

BUDINO DI COCOMERO
(gelo di mellone)
watermelon pudding

This recipe makes a superb dessert out of a relatively modest fruit. The watermelon must be ripe and dark red for the final preparation to be a bright color.

- 3 lb (1350 gr) watermelon pulp
- ½ cup (100 gr) sugar
- 2/3 cup (90 gr) corn starch
- 1 teaspoon vanilla
- 2 tablespoons pistachios, blanched and diced
- ½ oz (15 gr) semisweet chocolate, cut into small dice
- 3 tablespoons candied fruit
- cinnamon powder, for garnish
- 2 tablespoons shelled whole pistachios, for topping

- Skin and seed the watermelon, cut into small chunks, place in the food processor, and reduce to a liquid.
- In a saucepan, mix sugar and cornstarch. Add the watermelon liquid, a little at a time, stirring to avoid lumps.
- Place the pan over medium heat and bring to a boil.
- Simmer on low heat for about 5 minutes, stirring continuously, until thicker.
- Remove from heat and stir in the vanilla. Pour in a bowl, and cool at room temperature.
- When the compound is cold, add the pistachios, chocolate, and candied fruit
- Place in the refrigerator for a few hours.
- When cold, unmould and serve, sprinkled with cinnamon powder, and pistachios.

Bibliography

Agostini, Pino-Zorzi, Alvise. *A Tavola con i Dogi*, Arsenale Editrice, Verona, 1991

Artusi, Pellegrino. *La Scienza in Cucina e l'Arte di Mangiar Bene*, Gulliver, 1994

Barret, Judith-Wasserman, Norma. *Risotto*, Collier Books, 1989

Batini, Giorgio. *Buon Appetito Toscana*, Bonecchi, Firenze, 1998

Bellei, Sandro. *La Cucina Modenese*, Franco Muzzio, Padova, 1995

Bergonzini, Renato. *L'Aceto Balsamico*, Mundici & Zanetti, Vicenza,1990

Birri, Flavio-Coco, Carla. *Cade a Fagiolo*, Marsilio, Venezia, 2000

Boni, Ada. *Italian Regional Cooking*, Dutton & Co., New York, 1969

Boni, Ada. *La Cucina Romana*, Newton Compton, Roma, 1996

Boni, Ada. *The Talisman Italian Cook book*, Crown Publishers, New York, 1958

Bosi, Roberto. *La Cucina dei Pescatori*, Calderini, Bologna, 1996

Bugialli, Giuliano. *Bugialli on Pasta*, Simon and Schuster, New York, 1988

Capatti, A-Montanari, M. *La Cucina Italiana, Storia di una Cultura*, Laterza, Bari, 1999

Capnist, Giovanni. *I Dolci del Veneto*, Franco Muzzio, Padova, 1988

Castelli, A.C. *Cynara Erotica*, A.C. Castelli Assoc., New York, 1995

Cesari Sartoni, Monica-Molinari Pradelli, Alessandro. *La Cucina Bolognese*, Newton Compton, Roma, 1996

Chamberlain, Samuel. *Italian Bouquet, An Epicurean Tour of Italy*, Gourmet Books Inc., New York, 1968

Codacci, Leo. *Caterina De' Medici, Le ricette di una Regina*, Maria Pacini Fazzi Editore, Lucca 1995

Correnti, Pino. *Il Libro d'Oro della Cucina e dei Vini di Sicilia*, Mursia, Milano, 1976

Cowell, F.R. *Life in Ancient Rome*, Perigee Books, New York, 1980

Di Leo, Maria Adele. *I Dolci Siciliani*, Newton Compton, Roma, 1998

Dobbelin, Hans Joacim. *Panorama della Cucina Toscana*, Sigloch, Kunzelsau, 1988

Dommers Vehlig, Joseph. *Apicius, Cookery and Dining in Imperial Rome*, Dover Publications Inc, New York, 1977

Flandrin, Jean-Louis-Montanari, Massimo. *Food, A Culinary History*, Columbia University Press, New York, 1999

Francesconi, Jeanne Carola. *La Cucina Napoletana*, Newton Compton, Roma, 1997

Frijenno Magnanno, Prisma Libri, Napoli 1989.

Giorilli, Piergiorgio-Lauri, Simona. *Il Pane*, Zanichelli, Milano, 1996

Goldstein, Joice. *Cucina Ebraica*, Chronicle Books, San Francisco, 1998

Gosetti, Fernanda. *I Dolci*, Fabbri Editori, Milano, 1993

Gozzini Giacosa, Ilaria. *A Taste of Ancient Rome*, The University of Chicago Press, Chicago, 1992.

Hazan, Marcella. *Essentials of Classic Italian Cooking*, Alfred A. Knopf, New York, 1993

Imbriani, Luciano. *Cucina e Vini del Grande Nord*, Edizioni Acanthus, Milano, 1983

Jacob, H.E. *Six Thousand years of Bread*, Lyons & Burford, New York, 1997

Larousse Gastromique, Crown Publishers, New York 1981

Maffioli, Giuseppe. *Il Ghiottone Veneto*, Morganti Editore, Treviso

Malgieri, Nick. *Cookies Unlimited*, Harper Collins, New york, 2000

Malgieri, Nick. *Great Italian Desserts*, Little Brown & Co., Canada, 1990

Malgieri, Nick. *How to Bake*, Harper Collins, New york, 1995

Malgieri, Nick. *Perfect Pastry*, Macmillan, New york, 1998

Marchese, Salvatore. *Cucina e Vini della Val d'Aosta*, Muzzio, Padova, 1998

Marchesi, Gualtiero. *La Cucina Regionale Italiana*, Mondadori, Milano, 2000

Marenghi, Franco. *Tuttopasta*, Arnoldo Mondadori, Milano, 1997

Menesini, renzo. *Le Erbe Aromatiche in Cucina, Aromatic Culinary Herbs*, Maria Pacini Fazzi Editore, Lucca, 1992

Mistretta, Giorgio. *Sapori d'Italia*, DeAgostini, Novara, 1999

Molinari Pradelli, Alessandro. *La Cucina Ligure*, Newton Compton, Roma, 1996

Molinari Pradelli, Alessandro. *La Cucina Lombarda*, Newton Compton, Roma, 1997

Molinari Pradelli, Alessandro. *La Cucina Sarda*, Newton Compton, Roma, 1997

Montanari, Massimo. *La Fame e l'Abbondanza*, Laterza, Roma, 1997

Pepin, Jacques. *La Technique*, Simon and Schuster, New York, 1976

Race, Gianni. *La Cucina del Mondo Classico*, Edizioni Scientifiche Italiane, Napoli, 1999

Rama, Giuseppe. *Il Risotto come si fa a Isola della Scala*, Demetra, Verona, 1996

Rebora, Giovanni. *La Civilta' della Forchetta*, Laterza, Bari, 1998

Redon, O.-Sabban, F.-Serventi, S. *A Tavola nel Medioevo*, Edizioni Laterza, Bari, 1994

Righi Parenti, Giovanni. *La Cucina Toscana*, Newton Compton, Roma, 1995

Rinaldi, Mariangela-Vicini Mariangela. *La Storia E' Servita*, Publigold srl, Milano, 1996

Root, Waverley. *The Food of Italy*, Atheneum, New York, 1971

Sabban, F.-Serventi, S. *A tavola nel Rinascimento*, Edizioni Laterza, Bari, 1996

Sacchettoni, Dido. *Alle Radici della Buona Tavola*, Longanesi, Milano, 1990

Sada, Luigi. *La Cucina della Terra di Bari*, Franco Muzzio, Padova, 1991

Sada, Luigi. *La cucina Pugliese*, Newton Compton, Roma, 1994

Sandri, Amedeo. *La Polenta nella Cucina Veneta*, Franco Muzzio, Padova, 1985

Santini, Aldo. *La Cucina Fiorentina*, Franco Muzzio, Padova, 1992

Santini, Aldo. *Venerdi' Baccala' e Ceci*, Maria Pacini Fazzi Editore, Lucca, 1997

Saracco, C.-Garberoglio, M.-Zuccaro, E. *Vini e Piatti Tipici Regionali*, Calderini, Bologna, 2000

Saracco, Carlo-Garberoglio, Mauro. *Cucinare con il Vino*, Calderini, Bologna, 1996

Sernas, Maria Stella. *I Sapori del Sapere*, Passigli Editori, Firenze, 2000

Serventi, S.-Sabban, F. La Pasta, *Storia e Cultura di un Cibo Universale*, Laterza, Bari, 2000

Solci, Guglielmo-Comoli, Davide. *De Gustibus, La Roma Imperiale a Tavola*, Alexa Edizioni, Milano, 1999

Sorcinelli, Paolo. *Gli Italiani e il Cibo*, Mondadori, Milano, 1999

Stanziano, Angelina-Santoro, Laura. *Puglia-La Tradizione in Cucina*, Schena Editore, Bari, 1998

Tannahill, Reay. *Food in History*, Crown Trade Paperbacks, New York, 1989

Teti, Vito. *Il Colore del Cibo*, Meltemi, Roma, 1999

Toussant-Samat, Maguelonne. *History of Food*, Barnes & Noble Books, New York,1998

Tropea, Ivana. *La Cucina Romana*, Edizioni Del Riccio, Firenze, 1994

Truini Palomba, Maria Giuseppina. *La Cucina Sabina*, Franco Muzzio, Padova, 1991

Valli, Emilia. *La Cucina Siciliana*, Calderini, Bologa, 1997

Wright, Clifford A. *A Mediterranean Feast*, William Morrow and Co., 1999

Zanini De Vita, Orietta. *Il Lazio a Tavola*, Alphabyte Books, Perugia, 1994

General Index

Italian recipe names are indicated in italic characters

cont.

cont.

cont.

cont.

cont.

153

Conversion Tables

U.S. vs. Italian measures

There are several differences between the measuring system used in America versus the one used in Italy (and the rest of the world):

USA	Italy
Cups	Cubic centimeters
Gallons	Liters
Pound–Ounce	Grams
Feet–Inches	Meters
Fahrenheit	Celsius

In order to avoid confusion we indicated both measurements in all our recipes. The conversions indicated on this page are approximate equivalents.

Abbreviations

oz	ounce
lb	pound
gr	gram
kg	kilogram
mm	millimeter
cm	centimeter
cc	cubic centimeter
F	Fahrenheit
C	Celsius

Translation of Measures to Metric

Grams	Oz	Cups	Table Spoon
Butter			
30	1	1/8	2
55	2	1/4	4
110	4	1/2	8
220	8	1	16
454	16	2	32
Sugar (granulated)			
50	2	1/4	4
100	3½	1/2	8
200	7	1	16
300	11	1½	32
400	14	2	-
450	16	2½	-

Grams	Oz	Cups
Flour (all–purpose)		
35	1¼	1/4
45	1 2/3	1/3
70	2½	1/2
90	3 1/3	2/3
110	4	3/4
140	5	1
175	6¼	1¼
210	7½	1½
280	10	2
350	12½	2½
420	15	3
560	20	4

U.S. Weight to Metric

Pounds	Ounces	Grams
1/16	1	30
-	1½	45
1/8	2	60
-	2½	75
3/16	3	85
-	3½	100
1/4	4	115
-	4½	125
5/16	5	140
3/8	6	180
7/16	7	200
1/2	8	225
5/8	10	285
3/4	12	340
1	16	450
2	32	900

U.S. Lenghts to Metric

Inches	Metric
1/8	3 mm
1/4	6 mm
1/2	12 mm
1	25 mm
2	51 mm
3	76 mm
4	101 mm
5	127 mm
6	152 mm
8	203 mm
9	228 mm
10	254 mm
12 (1 foot)	305 mm
20	508 mm

Note: 1000 mm = 1 meter

U.S. Volumes to Metric

Table Spoon	Cups	Metric
1	1/16	15 cc
2	1/8	30 cc
4	1/4	60 cc
2 2/3	1/3	80 cc
8	1/2	120 cc
5 1/3	2/3	160 cc
12	3/4	180 cc
16	1	230 cc
	1½	360 cc
	2	460 cc
	2½	600 cc
	3	700 cc
	4 (1 quart)	950 cc
	1.06 quart	1 liter
	4 quart (1 gallon)	3.8 liter

Note: 1000 cc = 1 liter

Temperatures

F	C
200	95
220	105
245	120
275	135
300	150
325	165
345	175
370	190
400	205
425	220
445	230
470	245
500	260
525	275
550	290